DERBY

*From Regency
to Golden Jubilee*

DERBY

From Regency to Golden Jubilee

HARRY BUTTERTON

The Breedon Books
Publishing Company
Derby

First published in Great Britain by
The Breedon Books Publishing Company Limited
44 Friar Gate, Derby DE1 1DA
1993

ISBN 1 873626 18 5

Printed and bound by Hillman Printers (Frome).
Covers printed by BDC Printing Services Ltd of Derby.

Contents

Preface   6

Notable Changes to
Central Derby 1812-1887   7

Chronology of Events
in Derby 1812-1887   8

The Nineteenth-Century Set
Present into past,
Past into future   11

Expansion and Movement:
Streets and Transport   18

At Work — Or Not   32

Important Buildings
and Streets   46

Authority   61

Foundations   70

Home   79

Arboretum   84

In Pursuit of Leisure   92

Celebration   105

Index   111

Author's Preface

ANY less-than-all-embracing historical title requires a little explanation. Unpicking the seamless web of time results in more or less whimsical threads; why start here, why stop there? One generally recognisable historical period shades imperceptibly into another. However, it did seem that the span of a well-nourished individual's lifetime would provide, in the context of a sizeable provincial town like Derby, one exposed to the full force of the modern developments of the age, a significant amount of change and contrast as well as a measure of the other vital historical ingredient of continuity.

In fact, applied to the last century in the case of Derby, this latter element might have seemed at the time to be in danger of total submergence! Whilst Queen Victoria's Jubilee represented no sort of stop in a headlong spate of development, it is possible to see it as the crest of a wave which had been hardly gathering momentum in 'Regency Times'.

This latter, in contrast, was something of a 'moveable feast' in that the term 'Regency' covers at least a decade. But the concept when applied to the Prince Regent seemed to provide such a contrast, even foil, to the idea of Victoria's Jubilee, a progression from personal disrespect to reverence, that it might serve as a suitable human framework for the story of a whole community's headlong plunge into the modern age.

The pin-pointing of 1812 as the start of the saga would produce the Jubilee finishing point a convenient seventy-five years later. It was also a year with a considerable resonance on the wider European stage, above all with Napoleon Buonaparte's experience of Moscow, even though it is the national stage that provides the relevant setting for any significant local story.

One characteristic of the medium adopted in this book in covering a story with many aspects to it may need some prior indication. I have deliberately relied heavily on extracts from journals or newspapers of the time, especially the reports and editorials of the 'Derby Mercury' in order to flavour the narrative as far as possible with something of the way in which Derby people thought and felt about what was happening in and to their town. I am unable to regard any account of the past oblivious to this element as in any real sense 'history'.

H.E.BUTTERTON
Darley Abbey
February 1993

Acknowledgements

The most cursory glance through the notes on the sources for most sections of this book will reveal the author's great debt to Maxwell Craven's work on Derby's past as put before the public in his *Derby: An Illustrated History* (Breedon Books, 1988). Without it, the present offering simply could not have been written. Certain sections rely heavily for a foundation on Roy Christian's two studies of *The Development of a City*. A posthumous acknowledgement is also due to the editors and reporters, yes and the readers too, of the marvellous *Derby Mercury*, without whom it would be impossible to attempt to get inside the town of over a century ago. Finally, the author wishes to record his gratitude to the staff of the Local Studies Library in Derby for their inexhaustible patience accompanied with such cheerfulness and grace.

Dedication

To Mary, Alice and Andrew

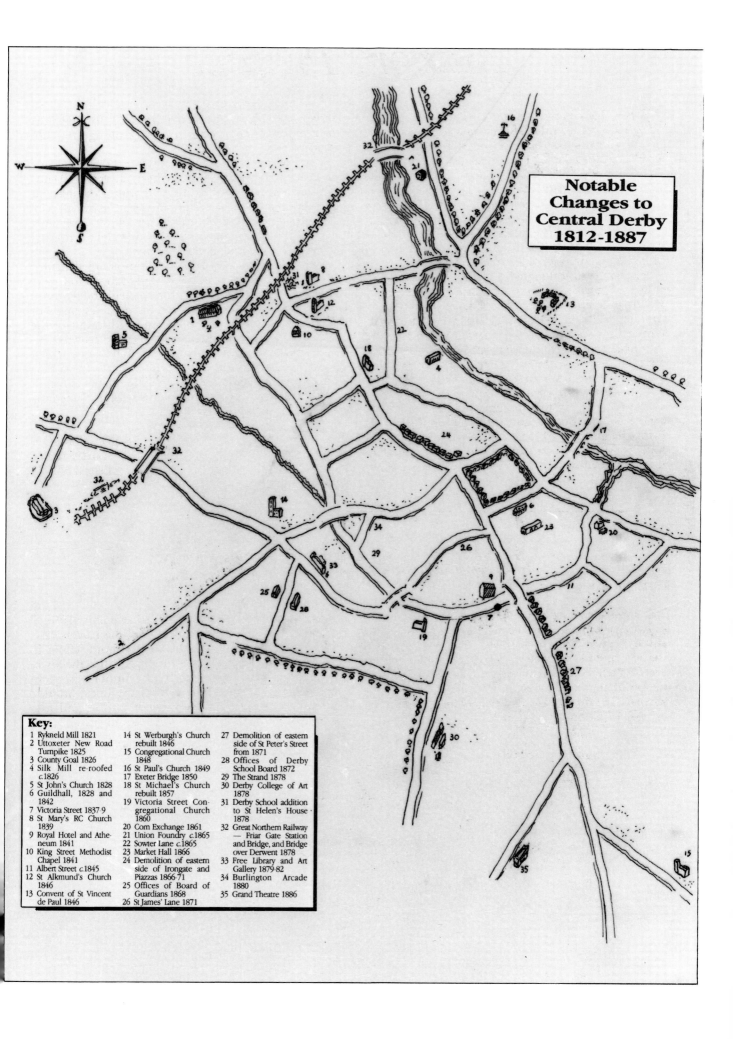

Notable Changes to Central Derby 1812-1887

Key:

1 Rykneld Mill 1821
2 Uttoxeter New Road Turnpike 1825
3 County Goal 1826
4 Silk Mill re-roofed c.1826
5 St John's Church 1828
6 Guildhall, 1828 and 1842
7 Victoria Street 1837-9
8 St Mary's RC Church 1839
9 Royal Hotel and Atheneum 1841
10 King Street Methodist Chapel 1841
11 Albert Street c.1845
12 St Alkmund's Church 1846
13 Convent of St Vincent de Paul 1846
14 St Werburgh's Church rebuilt 1846
15 Congregational Church 1848
16 St Paul's Church 1849
17 Exeter Bridge 1850
18 St Michael's Church rebuilt 1857
19 Victoria Street Congregational Church 1860
20 Corn Exchange 1861
21 Union Foundry c.1865
22 Sowter Lane c.1865
23 Market Hall 1866
24 Demolition of eastern side of Irongate and Piazzas 1866-71
25 Offices of Board of Guardians 1868
26 St James' Lane 1871
27 Demolition of eastern side of St Peter's Street from 1871
28 Offices of Derby School Board 1872
29 The Strand 1878
30 Derby College of Art 1878
31 Derby School addition to St Helen's House 1878
32 Great Northern Railway — Friar Gate Station and Bridge, and Bridge over Derwent 1878
33 Free Library and Art Gallery 1879-82
34 Burlington Arcade 1880
35 Grand Theatre 1886

1812-1887

1812 Lancasterian and National Day-Schools started.
1814 Celebration of Napoleon Bonaparte's capture.
1815 Society founded for *ameliorating the condition of infant chimney sweeps.*

1816 Visit of Grand Duke Nicholas to the Shot Tower.
1817 Foundation of Derby Choral Society; Trial and sentencing of Pentrich Revolution leaders.

vents in Derby

1818   Britannia Foundry began production.
1819   Public execution of Hannah Barking.
1820   First gaslight in the Market Place; Formation of Gas, Light and Coke Company.

1821   Rykneld Mills opened.
1824   Start of 'Derby and Chesterfield Reporter'.
1825   Boden & Morley's Lace Mills opened; Mechanics' Institute opened; Uttoxeter New Road Turnpike opened.
1826   Silk Mill fire, roof replaced; New County Gaol opened in Vernon Street.

Derby in 1852, from the newly-constructed Exeter Bridge. Familiar buildings include the churches of All Saints', St Alkmund's and St Mary's as well as the Silk Mill.

1827 Completion of street numbering.
1828 New Guildhall, architect Matthew Habershon; opening of St John's Church, Bridge Street.
1831 Main public buildings lit by gaslight; Reform Bill Riots.
1833 Concert by Paganini; Beginning of Silk Mill Lock-Out.
1834 Visit of Robert Owen; Sabbatarian petition to Parliament; Opening of Phoenix foundry.
1835 Demolition of Castlefields House; New Corporation for Borough.
1836 Establishment of Borough Constabulary; Holy Trinity Church, London Road built.
1837 Start of rearrangement of workhouses under new Poor Law.
1838 Concert by Johann Strauss at the Mechanics' Institute.
1839 First locomotive arrived (Midland Counties Railway); Rules for new workhouse on Osmaston Road approved; Birmingham and Derby Junction Railway opened; Opening of St Mary's RC Church; Mayor's Distress Fund started; Victoria Street completed.
1840 North Midland Railway completed; Derby Station opened; Opening of the Arboretum; Merger of Borough and County gaols; Committee of Enquiry into the working of the Factory Act in Derby; Christ Church, Normanton Road, built; Concert by Liszt.
1841 Fire destroyed the Guildhall; Completion of Royal Hotel and Atheneum scheme; Rebuilding of Wesleyan Methodist Church, King Street.
1842 Flooding of town centre; Visit of Feargus O'Connor, Chartist leader; Bath Street Silk Mill opened; Last Guildhall completed: architect Henry Duesbury; Uttoxeter New Road Cemetery opened.
1843 Death of Joseph Strutt; First visit of Royal Agricultural Show; Opening of Midland Hotel.
1844 Midland Railway Company formed.
1845 Extensions and Crystal Palace added to the Arboretum; Start of the 'Derbyshire Advertiser' weekly.
1846 Rebuilding of St Werburgh's Church; Opening of new St Alkmund's Church; Opening of Convent of St Vincent de Paul; Last 'appearance' of Shrovetide Football.
1848 First meeting at Derby Racecourse; Election of Michael Thomas Bass as MP; Congregational Church, London Road opened.
1849 St Paul's Church, Chester Green, opened; Report to the General Board of Health on conditions in Derby.
1850 First Co-operative Society in Derby; Opening of Exeter Bridge; Opening of Bishop Lonsdale Teacher Training College.
1851 Opening of Peel Foundry; Restoration of St Peter's Church; Opening of County Lunatic Asylum.
1852 Visit of Queen Victoria to Messrs Holmes' coach-building works.
1853 New grand entrance to the Arboretum built.
1854 Demolition of Exeter House.
1855 Opening of Nottingham Road Cemetery.
1857 Rebuilding of St Michael's Church; Start of Derwent Rowing Club.
1858 First Derby Regatta.

1860 Opening of Masson Foundry; Opening of Victoria Street Congregational Church.
1861 Strike of weavers; Opening of Corn Exchange; Opening of General Baptist Church, Osmaston Road; Opening of Wesleyan Methodist Church, London Road; Opening of New Cattle Market.
1862 Last public execution in Derby.
1863 Derby School moved to St Helen's House; Derby Town Cricket Club established on the Racecourse site.
1864 Foundation stone of Market Hall laid.
1866 Official opening of the new Market Hall.
1867 Opening of Congregational Church, Normanton Road; Opening of Bass Recreation Grounds.
1868 Completion of Poor Law Guardians' offices, Becket Street.
1870 Opening of Primitive Methodist Church; Foundation of Derby School Board; Opening of St Luke's Church; Opening of Co-operative store in Albert Street; Foundation of Derbyshire County Cricket Club.
1871 St James' Street built; Rebuilding of Irongate completed; Piazzas demolished; Start of widening of St Peter's Street.
1872 Opening of Offices of Derby School Board, Becket Street; Opening of St Anne's Church, Whitecross Street.
1874 Opening of Spa Lane Silk Mills; Opening of Ley's foundry.
1876 Start of Haslam's Union Foundry.
1877 Incorporation of Litchurch and Little Chester in the Borough; network of horse-bus routes established; Opening of Midland Railway Carriages and Wagon Works; New workhouse on Uttoxeter Road opened.
1878 Opening of Great Northern Railway line; Opening of Derby College of Art; The Strand built.
1879 Opening of Free Library and Museum; First issue of 'Derby Daily Telegraph'; Start of Derby Town Rowing Club.
1880 First horse-tram; Strand Arcade built; Municipal water supply established.
1881 Controversy over Sunday-running of tramcars; Visit of the Prince of Wales to the Royal Agricultural Show; Manufacture of refrigeration equipment for ships at Haslam's Union Foundry; Opening of St Thomas the Apostle Church; Opening of St Andrew's Church, Litchurch.
1882 Opening of Wesleyan Methodist Church, Normanton Road; Town refuse-disposal unit set up; Free entry to Arboretum.
1883 Opening of Children's Hospital; Borough Fire Service established.
1884 Foundation of Derby County Football Club; Start of Derby Photographic Society; First issue of 'Derby Daily Express'; Death of Michael Thomas Bass MP.
1886 FA Cup Final Replay at Derby's County Cricket Ground; Opening of St Barnabus' Church; Grand Theatre built and burnt down.
1887 Celebration of Queen Victoria's Golden Jubilee, 'Derby Mercury' editorial; Visit of Lord Salisbury, Tory Prime Minister; Death of Andrew Handyside.

The Nineteenth-Century Set
Present into past, Past to future

EVEN in the age of the video camera, it would be difficult to capture, in one enveloping sequence, a precise cameo of a town's transformation over 75 years of constant change. To focus on Derby in 1812, or Derby in 1887, in order to compare them visually, is impossible today. The trouble is that whatever angle we take, as Maxwell Craven in his recent comprehensive history of Derby has so rightly observed,[1] the intrusions of the present century are so gargantuan in scale as to distort the representation attempted in any particular broad camera shot.

There are, however, two glimpses of Derby that we might focus on to savour something of the change wrought on the face of an urban community by nineteenth-century, and in particular Victorian, development.

It is not the scene from further Chaddesden's St Andrew's View. True, that might convey a real sense of the sometimes raw, dynamic aspect of Victorian Derby with the slender panels and pinnacles of ancient All Saints' marooned as the still centre of a sea of dwellings and workplaces washing against the bristling heights of Littleover. But the twentieth-century estates are too much in the foreground to form a clear impression of the Victorian creation.

Nor is it that view from nearer Chaddesden, the green bank of Nottingham Road Cemetery. The all-pervading Cathedral tower may here appear more fulsome, and the neo-Gothic clock-towers on the middle horizon may strike an authentic chord of northern civic pride, but now it is the monolithic office blocks and spreading light ancillary roofs that are too insistent.

No, perhaps rather the views from Darley Park and the recreation ground near St Luke's Church may capture for us something of the contrast between Regency and late-Victorian Derby.

Today, if we study that lovely prospect from the former patio of Darley Hall, we may find the closest approximation yet to those early sylvan views of Derby that culminate in Joseph Farington's painting of 1808, although that was done from the opposite direction, in Cross Lane, now Macklin Street.

This is perhaps the nearest we can get to the town of Derby as it was before the Victorian wand transformed it. Of course, we have to discount the lesser of the two magnificently alert cats' ears of All Saints' and St Mary's, the more distant spire on the horizon, and the miniature Guildhall dome, each an anachronism to the Regency scene above the variegated huddle of mainly horizontal roof-lines stretching across the picture.

These also, admittedly, give less of the spikey-cubist effect of the proliferating gables which feature in Farington's and earlier views. Above all, we have to eliminate from our minds the two ugly if modest stumps of modern flats that puncture the scene for us today.

But there is still the rolling greensward before us and the pewter shine of the river amongst the broad stockade of trees, still the sylvan landscape of the westward ridge disguising for us, as for the Evanses as they looked south from their hall, the slow and gradual out-reach of suburban terrace and villa on this northern edge.

They might have garnered satisfaction from the short halt to the burgeoning of people and brick from the combined forces of nature and property on this side of Derby. Only the faintest inkling here of the teaming expansion southwards over the distant Normanton crest, and none at all of any to east and west behind those protective thickets. Except, that is, for the new and slender Shot Tower, from 1809 pointing ominously nearly 150 feet into the sky beyond the river to the left.

Now over to Stockbrook Street, near St Luke's, a church symbolic of Victorian striving to provide spirituality to the labouring masses, here settled around the mill just over the street with its grim rows of shallow-arched windows, square-paned in metal and set in mellow midshires brick, and the faded announcement of 'Thompson's Elastic Webbing' upon the gable.

St Luke's itself is redolent of Victorian aesthetics: trios of lancet windows with circles over, set in quintets of gables in grimed stone, apsidal end with stark turret. Over all, a tall tower with high triangle of roof recalling the ancient community of Saxons and sculptured figures crowding corner niches.

The more distant view of the town encapsulates

Victorian growth, despite the barrack-like exercises of inferior modern office megablocks. We have, below the distantly wooded fringes of Duffield Road and far Chaddesden, enough of the single peaks of nineteenth-century achievement set around that still ageless column of All Saints'. There are gothic towers ecclesiastic and civil, broached spire, giant bonded warehouse and far-reaching tentacles of villa and terrace spreading along and beneath the Burton Road.

These are the elements of individual and collective expression out of the smothering tide of growth which, in the course of almost two centuries, has gone far to obliterate the traces of earlier times.

If we now venture through our chosen portal of time, between Regency 1812 and Victoria's Golden Jubilee Year of 1887 — a 75-year span of change and development — perhaps we should try to get our bearings from the widest possible reference point.

What items of national intelligence would the Royal Mail coach from London, drawing up in King Street, or at the later time the electric telegraph, bring to the town that might concern the well-to-do readers of the Thursday weekly 'Derby Mercury' of 1812 or the 'Derby Evening Telegraph' of 1887?

Certainly, at the beginning of our period, they would read of unrest amongst the labouring classes at home. On 2 January 1812, the 'Derby Mercury' — 'Printed and published by John Dewry, in the Irongate, every Thursday' — had on its opening page:

A proclamation by His Royal Highness, The Prince Of Wales, Regent of the United Kingdom of Great Britain and Ireland, in the Name and on Behalf of His Majesty against 'Stockingers, or Persons employed in the Stocking Manufactories' in the counties of Nottingham, Derby and Leicester who were alleged to have committed acts of violence to coerce their employers into granting better conditions and wages, offering a reward of eight pounds per convicted person for information leading to that end.

Concerning who issued this proclamation and the broader context for its substance, readers would undoubtedly hear more during the coming twelve months. The bigamist Prince Regent, the future George IV, who had been in charge of government since the previous year, would be rocking London with further scandal, his father, 'farmer' George, sadly an intermittent violent maniac since November 1788.

Subscribers would soon hear, too, of what has proved to be the only assassination of a Prime Minister in British history, when another mad person disposed of Spencer Perceval. The new incumbent of 10 Downing Street, Lord Liverpool, was to last longer than any other holder of his office and would not leave that much-desired residence until 1827,[2] a record destined not to be matched even by Mrs Thatcher.

From beyond these shores, news would come of the latest-known war situation overshadowing Europe: of Napoleon Bonaparte and the Iron Duke; of the French *Grande Armee* to and from Moscow in unparalleled disaster, a long procession of famished ghosts struggling through the snow; and Wellington's army in Iberia, how they stormed Badajoz, a scoundrel minority tarnishing their hard-won reputation with 48 hours of drunken orgy, looting and rape; followed by Salamanca, the greatest British victory on land since Blenheim a hundred years earlier.[3]

Readers and those who could not afford the luxury of the 'Mercury' alike would hear of the blockade of English trade and consequent unemployment, falling wages, rising prices.

Seventy-five long years later came reports of the London celebrations of the Queen's Golden Jubilee. Her long reign since 1837 had obliterated the scandals of George IV, and had placed the Royal Seal upon the Victorian gospel of family values.

The description of Derby's own celebrations of this great event in July is more appropriate to the final section of this book. Here it may be sufficient to observe that the setting is transformed for the readers of the 'Mercury', although, in the daily struggle for mere existence of many of those who could not even think of subscribing to that journal, it could not have been an entirely happy state of affairs of which, as we shall also see later, the paper's editor was far from unconscious.

Otherwise, the politically aware citizens of the town might register the obsessive Parliamentary issue of the day, namely should Ireland be granted Home Rule? Charles Stewart Parnell was the man of the hour. In Europe, cunning Otto von Bismark was busy forging the first links in the complicated arrangement of treaties that, when allied to armed threat, would eventually lead to the outbreak of World War One and an entirely new world we are struggling with yet.

They might hear of the publication in London of the first English translation of Karl Marx's epoch-making book 'Das Kapital', basis of so much upheaval to the East in the succeeding century.[4] There might be hints of the preparations in Whitehall for the passing, the very next year, of the Act setting up our modern system of local government which led to the creation at home of the Derbyshire County Council.

The Prime Minister of the day, again Tory, was Lord Salisbury of Hatfield House. His opponent was the Grand Old Man of politics, Liberal William Ewart Gladstone.

Apart from a notice, one of an innumerable company, of Thomas Cook's New Year rail excursion to Scotland, the 'Derby Mercury' for Wednesday 28 December contains an account of Lord Salisbury's visit to Derby the previous week, when he delivered speeches at the Drill Hall and the new Grand Theatre.

After quoting numerous opinions of national and local papers from all parts of the country, the 'Mercury' concluded that *Lord Salisbury's speech at the Grand Theatre was one of the finest he ever delivered.*

There were no less than seventy reporters at the theatre, including twenty from London. The main theme was, of course, the Irish Question. Of far greater interest to us today, however, is surely another section of the report which reads: *Monday week was the busiest day ever known in the telegraphic department of the Derby Post Office.*

The staff there telegraphed Lord Salisbury's speeches to all parts of the realm, signalling no less than 157,000 words.

Some of the telegrams to London were despatched at the extraordinary rate of 300 words per minute. Shades of the exit from our Victorian space-capsule here, a vivid premonition of another frantic world.

What sort of Derby would receive the tidings of Moscow and Salamanca in 1812? Farrington's painting

This lithograph of 1830 shows St Mary's Bridge. Originally a wooden structure dating from the Danish occupation of Derby, it was replaced by a stone structure in the 14th century and rebuilt between 1788 and 1794. Apart from a wooden footbridge, at the beginning of our period it was still the only bridge over the River Derwent in Derby

of four years previously reflects for us a sideways impression of the thin nexus of streets off the ancient north-south thoroughfare known by a whole sequence of names — Queen Street, Irongate, Cornmarket, St Peter's Street — from the enclosing roofs to which rise the towers of ancient churches, All Saints' of course, Old St Alkmund's, Old St Werburgh's, St Michael's and, if we could brush aside the company of trees, St Peter's around the corner.[5]

Medieval St Mary's Bridge is still the only road river-crossing, in its handsome balustered new design by Thomas Harrison of Chester, barely over a dozen years old. The ancient Bridge Chapel at the town end is nearly five centuries old with a seventeenth-century house tacked on to it.

The 1698 'shorthand' description of Celia Fiennes, horseback tourist visiting friends from her Wiltshire manor-house, still holds good: *Derby town lies down in a bottom built all of brick or for the most part.*[6] The fact that the structures climbing up Green and Babington Lanes in 1992 are all of a later date, and the brick face of Blacksmith's Yard off Sadler Gate, are both clues to the integrity of her observation.

Right in the very bottom, the Markeaton Brook, open to the sky save for the sequence of stone bridges connecting streets on either side of it, still runs through the centre to join the broad Derwent.

But we must not be deceived by the static beauty of Farington's vision. Times were, always are, a-changing. The very next year, after he painted it before going down to the Assembly Rooms the same evening for appropriate entertainment, the Derby skyline was

punctured by the Shot Tower with crenellated topping, 149 feet high, to aid the processing of lead from the Peak into pipes and sheeting.

William Cox's works on the Derwent bank, near the Morledge, was neighbour to John Brookhouse's plaster mill which used Chellaston alabaster, both concerns originally dating from the 1780s.[7] There was an even bigger lead mill up on the Normanton Road, and many other signs of industry about the town besides the famous Old Silk Mills of wide reknown. Other notable concerns were Richard Brown's workshops for *monuments, gravestones and chimney pieces* near St Helen's House and James Fox's lathe manufactory across the river in City Road. There was also William Strutt's pioneering fire-proof silk mill of 1774 in the Morledge, on the site of present-day Albert Street.[8]

On the opposite river bank to this were even older *slitting, rolling and battering mills* apart from Duesbury's Crown China factory, in the process of migrating from the Nottingham Road.[9]

All this development was bringing to an end the blessed time characterised in a recent publication by Roy Christian when Derby 'for perhaps a generation' towards the end of the eighteenth century was 'equally balanced between being a town of gentry and one of trade'.[10]

By 1812, the effects of the improvement in road travel, notably the growth of fast coaching on toll-roads and better springing of stage coaches, meant that the gentry in the surrounding countryside would be looking to London for winter amusement rather than provincial Derby, where the attractions of the Assembly Rooms had helped leave a legacy of fine Georgian houses along Friar Gate in the west end of town, from which to carry on 'dancing, card playing and displaying marriageable daughters'.[11]

Now the town was beginning to grow apace. According to the author of the 1827 'Walk Through Derby': *The number of inhabited houses according to the census of 1811, was 2,644 and of inhabitants 13,043. The increase during the the preceeding years, appeared by this estimate to be about 500 houses, and above 2,200 inhabitants.*[12]

A decisive influence on this was the new waterway known as the Derby Canal and constructed during the previous century, which had been opened for business in 1796. It connected the town with the Trent and Mersey Canal and gave direct access by inland waterways to the London markets. It reached the town at the crucial point, explained by the writer of the 1827 walk:

Adjoining the town of Derby is a large weir, where the canal crosses the Derwent, which was navigable to this place for many years before this canal was undertaken . . .a little West of the Derwent, the canal crosses a brook in a cast-iron acqueduct.[13]

The crossing was known as the Long Bridge, constructed of wood; the aqueduct was at the edge of The Siddals, further out towards the south.[14] The result was a series of busy wharves, a hive of industry. Also, in earnest of a new century with problems of capitalist expansion, our 1827 recorder writes:

Five thousand tons of coal are annually to go free of all rates, for the use of the poor of the town of Derby; and three members of the Corporation, and the same number of proprietors, to be chosen annually to distribute them.[15]

In a north-running direction, an arm of the canal ran by Little Chester to Little Eaton. By means of a mineral railway operating with horse-drawn wagons from the terminus, it was able to tap the coal-bearing hill country beyond Denby.

So what should we have a look at in Regency Derby of 1812? The ancient churches, of course, at least three of which, All Saints', St Peter's and St Alkmund's, will be in a state of considerable disrepair to judge from the description in White's 'Directory of Derbyshire' for 1857.

This records All Saints' as having undergone *a thorough restoration about ten years ago,* St Alkmund's as having been completely rebuilt in the 1840s, and the chancel of St Peter's, *an ancient gothic structure nearly covered with ivy . . .a square tower embattled with lofty pinnacles, and a peal of five bells,* as being restored in 1851 with a new *handsome window filled with stained glass.* So there was plenty of work in 1812 for the next two generations or so to save our ecclesiastical heritage — or through over-zealousness to grievously tamper with it.

However, we will no doubt rejoice at the spectacle of All Saints' which White records as still called by some inhabitants by its original name of 'All Hallows'. Our 1827 guide enthuses thus:

The stranger, who wanders through Derby in quest of objects worthy of remark, will find some defects, and more beauties: but when he arrives at All Saints' he arrives at the chief excellence — the pride of the

place. It stands as a prince among subjects; a giant among dwarfs. Viewed at any distance, or in any attitude, the associated ideas of taste, grandeur, and beauty, fascinate the mind; the eye is captivated, and continually turns to its object, but never tires.[16]

Amen to that! White finds the 1725 interior *particularly light, elegant and spacious* (echoing the writer of 'The Walk)', the much older tower *crowned with rich battlements, crockets, high pinnacles and other decorations . . .considered one of the most splendid in the Kingdom.*[17]

For those not wishing to worship according to the Anglican tradition, we might notice two chapels of considerably less antiquity, namely the Unitarian Chapel in Friar Gate, described by Glover in 1849 as *a plain brick building . . .with a school and vestry-room and burying ground at the back,* built in 1697 and presently distinguished by the membership of the influential Strutt family, and the Independent Chapel near the brook in the middle of town, on what subsequently became Victoria Street, again a *plain brick building . . .lighted by twenty-two windows, to which is attached a convenient vestry* and just thirty years old in 1812.[18] This was to be *raised ten feet, new fronted, and remodelled internally in 1836.*[19]

The Unitarian Chapel in Friar Gate, the first non-conformist chapel to be erected in Derby.

However, we might also just notice a company of plain and not-so-plain new structures which must confirm an impression of optimism and energy in the Nonconformist community in an expanding town. Only four years old, on St Helen's Street, is the Friends' Meeting House, once again *a plain stone building;* eight years old on King Street is the Wesleyan Methodist Chapel lit by *semi-circular headed windows* and with triangle-topped frontage (to be rebuilt to seat 1,600, no less, in 1841); ten years old on Brook Street is the General Baptist Chapel, *a brick building*

The Friends' Meeting House in St Helen's Street, erected by subscription in 1808.

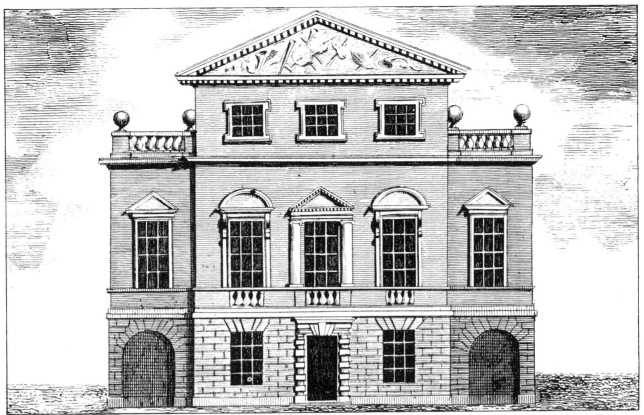

Pickford's relatively modest Assembly Rooms, built in the Market Place between 1763 and 1764 for the exclusive entertainment of the county's gentry.

with stone front (soon to be twice enlarged, in 1814 and 1819, to seat 700 people); and finally, on Agard Street, of a similar age the Particular Baptist Chapel, *a brick building with a portico . . .lighted by eleven windows.*[20]

We may perhaps pass building activity in progress in Chapel Street, where the Roman Catholics hope to complete their small chapel with trio of lancet windows the following year (it will last them, again considerably enlarged, for a quarter of a century before the new achievement of St Mary's).

But there are also some secular delights from earlier centuries that may catch the observant eye. The black and white trellis of the 'Mayor's Parlour', so-called, in Tenant Street, its bow and lattice windows and steep-pitched gables redolent of distant Tudor ancestry; from the succeeding century the fine stone jointing of the red-brick Jacobean House in the Wardwick; the balustered roof, tall half-wheel-topped windows and elaborate entrances of the 1660 Assize Courts — each is worth more than a passing side-glance from a hurried walk.[21]

For refreshment, there is the little Dolphin Inn, huddling beneath but contemporary with that wondrous All Saints' tower from Henry VIII's time; and further out to the north, the cuddly Seven Stars of 1680.

However, Regency Derby is graced, above all, by the legacy of the previous hundred years — the Georgians, the age of architect Joseph Pickford and his friend and artist, Joseph Wright.

The classical style is overwhelming. Quartets of pillars or pilasters above round-headed archings below triangular pediments and proud-standing urns, as at noble St Helen's House (1767, for the last nine years

the home of William Strutt), or Richard Jackson's Guildhall of 1731 (just four years before Pickford's birth), or the County Gaol in Friar Gate (1755).

Facing the Guildhall across the Market Place is Pickford's more modest Assembly Rooms, built for the exclusive entertainment of the owners of those manor houses out in the surrounding country, with its scaled-down pillars accompanying a central first-floor window. Just as they do the doorways and fanlights of his and his neighbours' new elegant homes, again in Friar Gate out west. He has also refronted what is still the biggest house in Derby, on the river around the corner from the Market Place — Exeter House where the Bonnie Prince stayed nearly seventy years ago.[22] The Market Place itself has its own more rustic hundred-year-old pillars in the form of the Piazzas, as elderly companions of Pickford's work (where the Assembly Rooms are in 1992):

'Ward and Co's Annual' of 1710 said: *On the west side is a handsome range of brick . . .This hall, for*

Exeter House, photographed by Richard Keene in 1854, the oldest known photograph of Derby.

*so it may be called, is built partly over the Shambles,
while in front it rests upon stone columns, forming
a covered and slightly elevated pavement, where the
country people sell eggs, butter and poultry.*[23]

Similarly, round-headed archings distinguish the
front of the 1773 Bold Lane Theatre, tastefully
converted from a former malthouse, possibly again
by Pickford.[24]

We will turn aside briefly near All Saints' and head
down to the river to glance at the most distinguished
industrial legacy of former times, the Old Silk Mills,
joint foundation, with the Canal, of Derby's contemporary if war-troubled prosperity. There is, in fact,
something of artistic value here too. The drawbridge-
like entrance is shielded by the lovely gates of Robert
Bakewell.

'The Derbyshire Red Book' of 1906 would say: *They
are inseparably associated with the English silk trade,
which originated in Derby. The gates, pilasters, and
arch top are of most elegant design and workmanship
and are a fine example of Old English wrought-iron
foliage and scroll-work, and were originally made for
Sir Thomas Lombe, whose history as the founder of
the first silk mill in this country is well known.*[25]

But it is the mill itself that is famous and has even
been visited by people from beyond these shores.
Because in this ponderous building, now ninety years
old (completed 1722), with its five regimented ranks
of windows set in brick on a foundation of stone arches
standing upon, according to William Hutton, *huge
piles of oak,*[26] we can say with hindsight that for the
very first time in history, a mass of workers were
brought together disciplined by a single source of
power.

This is an undershot waterwheel, set in the moat
from the River Derwent, over which the gates stand
proud, though it is the distinctive merry-go-round bell-
tower roof that catches the eye from a distance.

It was all in order to make fine silk and break a
centuries-old Italian monopoly; but industry based on
power will surely transform the appearance of this
still elegant town. The engineer-in-charge was George
Sorocold, who was also responsible for the other giant
waterwheel you see just along the river bank from
the mill, still pumping the town's water supply
through four miles of wooden pipes made of the bored-
out trunks of elm trees.[27]

Finally, a visit to the two-year-old wonder of the
town followed by two quick glances at a world we
have now, in this late twentieth-century state, all but
irretrievably lost of the town's surroundings nearly
two hundred years ago.

This will take us back to our earlier attempt to
comprehend the broad extent of change through
seventy-five years to a town of modest size and
considerable charm but within it, particularly from
its physical setting on a rather sharp river at the virtual
terminus of the dividing backbone of coal-proud
northern England, the thrusting seeds of industrial
growth.

The Derbyshire General Infirmary was opened in
1810, on a piece of ground to the south of the centre
which was part of the old Castlefields estate. The
Borough family significantly fled their old light-stone
manor house for rural Shropshire in 1803, before the
encroachments of industry and commerce, and sold

*The Derbyshire General Infirmary, opened in 1810 on part
of the old Castlefields estate.*

up. The hospital ground was bought by the Corporation largely under the influence of William Strutt
because, according to 'Walk Through Derby' *it is
elevated, airy and dry, abounding with excellent water,
and accessible by a good road.*[28]

Regarding the detail of the institution, our writer
of 1827 states, in the course of nearly six pages devoted
solely to it:

*The middle and principal story is a little elevated;
it is approached by steps and a Portico supported by
four Doric pillars, of the same stone as that of which
the walls are formed, which is a hard compact
millstone grit . . . The roof of the central part is drawn
into a conical form, terminating in a dome containing
six windows which completely illuminate the hall
from the floor of the principal storey upwards . . . One
considerable improvement, and which contributes
much to the health and comfort of the patients, is,
the construction of two light and spacious rooms, (one
for each sex) called Day (or convalescent) Rooms: in
which those patients, to whom it may be agreeable,
may eat their meals and pass their day, instead of being
confined to the same room day and night, as is the
usual practice.*[29]

Last, back into the fresh air, our excursion beyond
the town boundaries: North-west beyond graceful Friar
Gate, the walker of 1827 notes:

*The vicinity of Derby affords a number of pleasing
prospects and agreeable walks. On Windmill Hill, the
spectator is gratified by a beautiful and extensive view
of the adjacent country; and if viewed from the prospect
house erected there by S.Richardson Esq, the scene
is still more extensive. Two or three situations on the
way to Littleover, afford a very pleasing view of the
Town extended through the valley below.*[30]

South-east, describing the view from the new
Spondon Station, 'The Nottingham and Derby
Railway Companion of 1839' states:

*It stands on an eminence, and thus commands a
most beautiful view of the romantic vale of the
Derwent. The village of Spondon contains nearly two
hundred houses, and standing in an airy and pleasant
situation, is inhabited by several genteel families.*[31]

Two comments from the vantage point of our late-
twentieth century may be in order here. On the one
hand, Spondon-dwellers may savour the 'airy' bit; on
the other, the reference to 'genteel families' reflects

the sycophantic side of the Victorian view of the world as further evidenced in the amount of space in general devoted by the guide writers to the history of the wealthy families in the big houses around Derby. The land held by these families was another very significant factor in the story of the town's growth in the first half of the nineteenth century.

Notes

1. Maxwell Craven, *Derby, An Illustrated History*, 1988.
2. Asa Briggs, *The Age of Improvement 1783-1867*, 1979.
3. Arthur Bryant, *Age of Elegance 1812-1822*, 1950.
4. Donald Read, *England 1868-1914*, 1979.
5. Roy Christian, *Derby in the Making. The Devlopment of a City* 1990.
6. Celia Fiennes' Diary, quoted in Roy Christian, op.cit.
7. Maxwell Craven, op.cit.
8. Ibid, quoting the *Derby Mercury*.
9. Ibid, quoting Hutton (1791).
10. Roy Christian, op.cit.
11. Ibid.
12. *Walk Through Derby*, 1827, Derbyshire Heritage Reprint 1983.
13. Ibid.
14. Maxwell Craven, op.cit.
15. *Walk Through Derby*.
16. Ibid.
17. *White's Directory of Derbyshire*, 1857.
18. *Glover's Directory of Derby*, 1849.
19. Ibid.
20. Ibid.
21. *Walk through Derby*.
22. Maxwell Craven, op.cit.
23. *Ward & Co's Annual*, 1892, from description of Derby in 1710.
24. Maxwell Craven, op.cit.
25. *Derbyshire Red Book*, 1906, quoted in H.Butterton, *Silk Mill*, 1991.
26. Hutton (1791), quoted in H.Butterton, op.cit.
27. Brian Cooper, *Transformation of a Valley*, 1983.
28. *Walk Through Derby*.
29. Ibid.
30. Ibid.
31. *The Nottingham and Derby Railway Companion*, 1839, Derbyshire Record Society Occasional Paper No.3, 1979.

Expansion and Movement: Streets and Transport

*T*HE town of Derby is probably a mile in length, from the end of St Peter's Parish, in the south, to that of St Helen's in the north, and in breadth, upon an average, three-quarters of a mile.[1] So the 'Report to the General Board of Health' summarises Derby in 1849, in time-honoured terms of measurement almost exactly in the middle of our period of investigation.

In the previous century, P.P.Burdett had portrayed Derby as being slightly smaller, 1,400 yards by 800 yards according to his particular scale.[2] The intervening very modest expansion of 400 yards or so in either arm of the cross is detailed in the 'Board of Health Map' of 1852 as having taken place largely in three sectors: north-westwards between the Ashbourne and Kedleston Roads; south-eastwards over Castlefields with the coming of the railway; and south along the Osmaston Road.[3] By 1887, however, the description was well and truly out of date, as the following statistics may illustrate:

Population figures for Derby — rounded up.[4]
1811 15,000 **1831** 23,000 **1841** 37,000
1866 53,000 **1881** 81,000 **1891** 94,000

During the period we have chosen, Derby's population increased by nearly six-fold, more than doubling during the first thirty years of it and more than trebling during the last forty-five. The greatest expansion was in the south-eastern direction in the vicinity of the railway, where the separate parish of Litchurch (with only thirty people in 1801) brought a huge boost of 14,000 to the total when it was finally incorporated into the Borough of Derby in 1877.[5]

During the third decade of our period (1831-41) and then again during the final decade (1881-91) alone, there was an increase of 13,000 and 14,000 respectively, well over the entire population of the town at the beginning of the century. No less than 43 per cent of the adult population in 1851 originated from outside the county borders, a much higher proportion than in either Nottingham or Leicester and a tribute to the pulling power of both railway and general industrial development in Derby.[6] By the end of the century, the County Borough total was to reach 115,000.[7]

What enabled this surge of building to take place

and so respond to the vast expansion of employment opportunities in the town, especially after the coming of the railway in 1839, was the long-delayed sale of land from the tight circle of estates about the country houses all round the Borough.

The nearest in was Castlefields and we have already seen how the Infirmary came about, to be followed by the Railway Station nearly twenty years later: the manor house itself remained empty for thirty years until its demolition in 1835.[8] Maxwell Craven has detailed the process by which this and other estates, in particular that of Normanton House which paved the way for movement on the Osmaston and Normanton Roads, were sold and so opened up the prospects for expansion.

So the very garden of Castlefields House, which stood on a site between today's Main Centre and Traffic Street,[9] disappeared beneath brand-new Park Street. On the south-east corner of its park arose the graceful terraces of railwaymen's houses that are treasured at the present time. All this matched the in-filling of scarce urban space further in that had been the crisis response to population pressure up until then: Cross Lane, put across the park of Jacobean House; and Sacheverell Street, that of Babington House.

Out west-by-north, pieces of the Mickleover, Littleover and Strutt estates enabled the well-to-do to establish their Regency villas along the straight turnpike of Uttoxeter New Road and round in an arc by The Firs, Mill Hill, Parkfield Cedars, Parkfield House and Darley Grove.[10]

Yet the very first move had been on public land. The writer of 'Walk Through Derby' (1827) describes it thus:

Among modern improvements in Derby should also be mentioned the lighting and paving of the streets, and the removal of those obstructions that prevented a free passage. For accomplishing these beneficial purposes, by an act passed in 1792, Commissioners were empowered to levy a small rate on the inhabitants, and also to sell Nuns' Green, much of which is now covered with houses.

Around 1812, work was going ahead covering this ancient open space behind the stylish frontage of Friar Gate. By 1820, instead of a happy hunting ground for dog and child, raw textile mills overshadowed the western approaches of Markeaton Brook amongst a

Henry Burns' lithograph showing a view from the Meadows in 1846. Amongst the buildings on the skyline is the Guildhall, rebuilt after a fire five years earlier.

grid of workers' terraces. And more than keeping pace with these was the 'Little City', a series of even meaner rows about a silk-mill, set above Green Lane and Farington's idyllic viewpoint south of centre.[11] These raw, new streets would be unlit and undrained, outside the remit of the 1792 political deal.

In all, no fewer than forty new streets were built between 1800 and 1842.[12] The momentum was maintained. Whilst the Arboretum, latest and possibly greatest act of benevolence on the part of the Strutt dynasty to the town, was at its rural edge on its public opening in 1840, by 1860 it was in the middle of the new Rosehill district of terraces.

The Normanton estate had been blown open and streets named after local worthies, in particular Joseph Strutt himself and John Loudon, his designer. By the end of the 1880s, New Normanton was submerged, succumbing to two columns of advance before and after the Borough boundary extension of 1877.

Many streets were named after national rather than local worthies now. At first, off the town end of Lower Dale Road, these were of earlier vintage such as Cromwell, Fairfax and Byron; later, more contemporary notables such as Gladstone (although, curiously, not Disraeli, possibly reflecting the period's Liberal dominance of parliamentary representation). Palmerston and Livingstone came to resound over the area known as Normanton Common.

Reaching the far edge at this time, earlier military echoes as in Havelock and Balaclava were favoured. Further over, even more exotic 'California' was the post-'49 label for the area around the handsome form of St Luke's, built in 1870.

A close study of the Ordnance Survey Map of the 1880s, keeping in mind the 1852 'Board of Health Map', reveals the full extent of our period's residential development, also its limits taking the perspective of a hundred years on.

Always bearing in mind the time-gap between survey and final publication in a fast-changing world, with its opportunity for the laying out of streets by the day the map is available for its very first students, the first edition of the OS reveals a width of two open fields between Rosehill and Pear Tree. This is still a separate small community around Pear Tree House, as is Normanton beyond, around Normanton House. West of the Normanton Road, which featured two lead-works on either side of a silk-mill in 1855, Overdale, The Firs, St George's and Elmhurst on the Uttoxeter Road are now the limits of the terraced streets where the earlier map showed open fields.

This particular bulge has easily doubled the east-west stretch of the town. Yet another area of terraces now extends from Rowditch across the Ashbourne Road to the Markeaton Brook between two concentrations of various mills and workplaces half-a-mile beyond the County Gaol, which in 1855 with Vernon Street was at the edge of open fields.

If we circle further out starting from Duffield Road in the North, Strutt's Park beyond the relatively new Great Northern Railway line (responsible, as we shall see later in this chapter, for some street development in reverse) and Little Chester, astride it across the river (only since 1877, with Litchurch, inside the Borough), feature yet more terraces, of more substantial quality in general. These are aligned mostly north-south and east-west respectively. However, over half-a-mile of open parkland separates the imposing isolated villas,

A view of Derby looking from Nottingham Road c.1850. It shows the railway bridge across Derby Canal.

the retreats of the wealthier citizens, along the Duffield Road from the community of Darley Abbey.

Similarly, Chaddesden, beside its Hall, is separated by a mile-and-a-half of nondescript open field between industrial concerns from the Racecourse grandstand and Nottingham Road Cemetery; Spondon, over Cherry Tree Hill, by a further mile beyond Spondon Park; Alvaston and Boulton by an open mile beyond the railway land of Litchurch; and tiny curious Allenton, half a dozen short terraces named after its early 1880s greenfields-site builder, Allen,[13] yet again a mile beyond the Victoria Iron Works right on the southern edge of town past still lordly Osmaston Hall within its soon-to-be-troubled park.

Going north-west, Littleover still lies protected by a thinner half-mile of open field beyond Overdale, apart that is from the villas about Fairfield and Littleover House. Isolated Mickleover is further beyond that, set in a mile of fields. But while as yet Chain Lane connects the Burton and Uttoxeter Roads in truly rural style, the coming of the Great Northern Railway has exposed these desirable south-westerly sites to further commuter pressure, railway captains following on where wealthy Regency predecessors led much earlier in the century.

Having thus beaten the town bounds, we may turn to examine the successive media of movement which, in one way and another, both forced and enabled this expansion to take place: canal, coach, railway, carrier, tram.

The Derby Canal was pioneer, as we have seen, contributing to the earlier industrial development of the Regency period, the age of the Shot Tower and the busy Morledge wharvings. In the 1830s, its proprietors would resist and then succumb to the onset

of the railway age, when its superiority over road-use for the transportation of freight would be all but wiped out by the thrusting application of steam technology to locomotion.

It was condemned to a slow decline, reaching into the present century. But in 1858, Glover's 'Directory' could still advertise a fighting programme. From their office on the Cockpit Hill, the Grand Junction Canal Company scheduled daily boats to and from a range of distant places including London, Leamington, Leicester and Warwick. From the wharf of J.&W.Soresby, an east-west axial service on two days a week reached Hull and Wolverhampton in either direction. Carrier (goods) services were also advertised to places north, including Liverpool, Manchester and Staffordshire Potteries, as well as *Intermediate places* to Burton upon Trent and Rudgley *(sic)*.

At least one correspondent of the 'Derby Mercury' in the early 1830s attributed some success to the Canal proprietors in resisting the onset of the railway in the area. The celebrated meeting at the Sun Inn, Eastwood, on 16 August 1832, which eventually resulted in the formation of the Eastern Counties Railway and, seven years later, the arrival of the first tracks into Derby, would have more enthused the up-country coal-owners well beyond Denby than industrialists within a few minutes of the Morledge quayside.

The two-month old Leicester and Swannington Railway was taking a valuable market away from their North Midland hands. The following curious letter was published in the 'Mercury' on 26 February 1834, ten months before the first meeting for those interested in the railway enterprise in Derby town, at the Bell Inn, Sadler Gate, barely attracted double figures.[14]

Midland Counties' Railway

Disinterested Person, who has lately seen the 'Mercury' as a paper of Railway notoriety, and also he regrets to state witnessed the poor spirit manifested in Derby and the neighbourhood, towards so valuable an undertaking — a poor spirit, he says, because if he may judge from the number of subscribers who have entered their names in Derby, he would say, that there the movement in improvements of this kind, is with a retarding velocity.

The Public will surely be aware that the late writers in opposition to the Railway are interested persons, or if not so, they seem very like what they are not, for Canal Proprietors are seldom at a loss for a good stock of cold water to throw on works of this sort.

Shall I guess wrong if I guess that the late writers were more afraid of losing their own money, than anxious that the Public should be careful how they emptied their pockets? No, I think not. The writer of this, proposes the following short and easy method of finding what interest the shareholders will be most likely to receive from the profits of the Midland Counties' Railway. The sum made out by the Railway Engineers is twenty per cent, per annum, and the sum intended to be made out by the opposition is 0 per cent per annum. Here are two parties, the one for, the other against.

Rule: Divide the sum of the two numbers by the number two, as the parties are two, and the quotient will be the amount to pay the shareholders.

Example: 20 + 0 = 20 ÷ 2 = 10 per Cent.

Which the Proposer of this plan hopes will be adopted by the shareholders in making their calculations. He is satisfied that all whose interest has not rendered them incapable of judging, will agree with him in concluding, that this is the very best way to find the amount it will pay, and will be found nearer the truth than the calculations of Engineers, Canal Companies, or anybody else.

A.Farmer.

However, interest in the new form of transport grew to match the prospect of not one but three railway companies proposing to set their sights on Derby.

In the meantime, for passenger transport it was the golden age of the stage coach, which also ended around the middle of the century with the establishment of the railway. By then, its glory days had lasted over a century, as long a reign as its successor the steam locomotive. There were attempts, which obviously did not mature, to adapt to the new power source, as this report in the 'Mercury' just two months after our moderate-railway-enthusiast's letter demonstrates, together with the frantic coach activity of that time:

COACHES versus STEAM. There are now twenty coaches to and from Lichfield and Birmingham every day, and some of them perform the distance (16 miles) in one hour and five minutes. At Manchester on Thursday, a trial was made with a new steam carriage, built by Messrs Sharp, Roberts, & Co, of that place, carrying fifty to sixty persons. It went off in good style on the Oxford Road, and performed six miles in twenty minutes.[15]

Just as the railway expresses did later on their tracks, the coaches rattled and jingled through the narrow streets of Derby at all hours. They were focussed on

the great centres of refreshment and entertainment and business, too, of that time — as we shall see — the pubs and hostelries, where horses were regularly changed in the early hours of the morning as the timetable dictated.

The 'flying' coaches were the product of the improved turnpike roads of the eighteenth century, which were again made redundant by the establishment of the railways and their massive excursion programmes. The pub was succeeded by the station hotel refreshment bar as a recuperation centre, although the need must have been much less dire for patrons of the better 'classes'.

A piece written near the end of the nineteenth century by Chas J.Payne illustrates the relationship between the fast coach and the transmission of news seventy-five or so years before. He records that earlier in the century there was an old poster in a Derby hotel (unspecified) which advertised the fact that the London to Manchester coach, named 'Defiance', did the journey via Derby on Sunday, 10 April 1814 in twenty-four hours as the first to convey the news of the abdication of *the tyrant Bonaparte* to the town.[16]

In September 1838, the driver of this same coach, Joseph Barrington by name, was fined by local magistrates for driving in a fury on Sunday morning down St Peter's Street.[17] Back in 1815, the rivalry of the various coach drivers from London to be first with the news of the Battle of Waterloo was such that the passengers on one of them dismounted one-and-all in Derby *on account of the furious driving.*[18]

The relationship between coach and pub/hotel is well illustrated in Pigot & Co's 'Commercial Directory for Derbyshire,' 1835. The duo of Tiger and King's Head in the Corn Market is most prominent in the coaching timetable, as the stopping place/staging post for the 'Defiance' and 'Bruce' (London), the 'Standard' (Birmingham), the 'Lord Nelson' (Manchester) and 'Times' (Nottingham).

Among other hostelries, the Bell in Sadler Gate saw the 'Telegraph' (London), the 'Lady Nelson' (Manchester) and the 'Champion' (Nottingham). The Royal Mail for London, Birmingham, Manchester and Sheffield had an office in King Street.

Of course, it was largely those with leisure and money to spare who travelled in the stage coach era. On this aspect, again, the railway wrought a revolution. The wealthy had their private transport, the post-chaise, something which we shall see they tried to carry through into the railway era until the concept of comfortable first-class travel became bedded in.

For the benefit of the 'political' community, the 'Mercury' in particular published advertisements of post-chaise traffic in the form of a weekly list of nobility and gentry passing through town, changing horses or sleeping at one or other of its hostelries, culminating in the week ending 16 September 1835, when the King's Head took in no less than the Dukes of Devonshire, Rutland, Newcastle and Cleveland.[19]

An entry in Glover's 'Directory' for 1858 could almost be an obituary for the coaching service, reduced to an ancillary existence for the railway:

The Royal Mail Coach now runs only between Rowsley and Manchester, through Bakewell and Buxton, leaving Rowsley after the arrival of the

The King's Head Hotel in the Cornmarket, prominent in Derby's coaching days.

10.30am. Train from Derby, and arriving at Rowsley in time for the Train arriving at Derby 8.30pm.
Locally, the same volume advertised:
OMNIBUSES — W.W.Wallis from the New Inn, King Street, calling at The Bell, King's Head, and Royal Hotels to meet every train.

All roads were tending to lead to the station, which in Derby's case lay some distance from the centre of town and thus became a separate focal point for local passenger traffic. A new thoroughfare, Station Street, later renamed Midland Road, had for some time connected the station with the London Road.[20] It was in vain that some coach proprietors lowered their fares to try to compete with the 'iron horse'. Indeed, the W.W.Wallis referred to by Glover started a horse omnibus service to and from the station from as early as about 1840, although it was not until 1877 that a network of horse bus services was established in the town at the dawn of the tram era.[21]

One element of local horse-drawn traffic remained steady throughout our period and, indeed, received a boost from the railways in a form of rational complementary transport system that had something to commend it for this present motor-lorry age. This was the 'carrier' traffic for freight, which again through these decades remained focussed upon the pubs as starting and finishing points. A study of Glover's 'History and Directory of Derby' for 1849 yields the following detail:

From the Rose and Crown in the Corn Market, a carrier service departed on three days a week for Alfreton, Ripley, Burton, Butterley, Chesterfield, Coxbench and Kilburn; on two days for Castle Donington, Hilton, Loughborough, Matlock and Shardlow; and once a week for Bradbourne, Breaston etc and Kegworth.
From the Nag's Head in St Peter's Street on two

days a week for Ashbourne, Milton and Repton; and once for Draycott, Etwall, Matlock, Marston and Sutton-on-the-Hill.
From the Queen's Head in Victoria Street on three days a week for Ashby and Cromford; on two days for Castle Donnington, Church Gresley, Hatton, Leicester etc., Shardlow, Swadlincote, Wirksworth and Wooden Box.
From the Dolphin in Queen Street on six days per week for Heanor, Langley Mill, Shipley, Stanley and West Hallam; on three days for Duffield; and on one day for Brailsford, Codnor etc, Ilkeston, Morley, Sawley, Smalley and Stapleford.

There were many other bucolic starting places and destinations in a close network of local freight routes. By 1858, the operation is listed as *Omnibuses & Light Vans* but still operating from hostelries.

The carriers, from the 1840s backed up in the case of ambitious retailers, wholesalers and customers by the railway, served the shops and work places of the centre's narrow streets. To these streets came also a growing circle of local customers attracted beyond the range of the terrace corner-shops on the edges of town.

Mid-Victorian trade directories provide evidence of an astonishing variety of trades and shops doing business within these streets, reflecting the far more local nature of production at the dawn of the 'global village' era — although Derby, as the — in a geographical sense — strange originating place of manufacture of refrigeration equipment for ocean-going vessels, would play a significant part in its onset at the very end of our period.

Study of the detail of a selected three streets, namely Sadler Gate, Irongate and Bridge Gate as listed in Glover's 'Directory' for 1849, shows the richness of activity in central nineteenth-century Derby. The businesses are listed alphabetically by proprietor/lessee. Analysis reveals the following results:

Sadler Gate (and Bridge):
1 hairdresser and perfumer, 1 hairdresser, 1 veterinary surgeon, 2 tailors, 3 tailors and woollen drapers, 8 butchers (including 1 baker), 3 working jewellers (including one also clock and watch manufacturers), 1 jeweller and silversmith, 2 shoeing smiths, 3 shoemakers (including 2 also making boots and 1 lasts), 2 shoe warehouses (including 1 also for boots), 2 last makers (including 1 also for *boot tree and patten maker*), 4 provision dealers (including 1 warehouse), 7 victuallers including 1 Commercial Inn and Posting House (the Bell, others namely Black Boy, Half Moon, Three Tuns, Lord Byron, Shakespeare and Horse and Jockey), 3 grocers (including 2 tea dealers), 1 upholsterer, 1 malster, 2 printers (including 1 bookseller and stationer), 1 dyer, cleaner, 1 carver and gilder, 1 gardener and seedsman, 3 hatters and hosiers (including 1 furrier), 2 bakers and flour dealers (including 1 confectioner), 1 milkseller, 2 chemists and druggists, 3 plumbers and glaziers, 1 tobacconist, 2 fishmongers and dealers in game, 2 whitesmiths (including 1 locksmith and 1 bellhanger), 1 braziers, 1 brush manufacturer, 1 currier and leather cutter, 1 coach proprietor.

Irongate:
10 drapers (including 3 silk mercers and 2 haberdashers), 4 grocers (including 3 tea dealers and

The Dolphin Inn, under the shadow of All Saints' Church, pictured around 1876. Regular coach services also left this ancient Derby watering hole.

1 confectioner), 2 victuallers and wine and spirits merchants (Globe Tavern and Talbot Commerical Inn), 1 brazier, 2 booksellers, binders and printers (1 office of 'Mercury' and the other a Circulating library), 1 laboratory, 1 optician and instrument maker, 1 cheesemaker and bacon dealer, 1 butcher, 1 banker, 2 chemists and druggists, 1 cookshop, 1 confectioner and biscuit maker, 1 bootmaker, 1 shoe mart, 1 lace dealer, 1 plumber and glazier, 1 silversmiths, furnishing ironmongers, flakdressers, gunsmiths etc, 1 cabinet maker, upholsterer, dealer in pianofortes.

Bridge Gate:
2 brokers, 2 joiners (including 1 builder), 1 currier and leather cutter, 1 dealer in bones, 1 tailor, 1 watchmaker, 3 butchers, 2 shoemakers, 1 sinker maker, 1 spar ornaments manufacturer, 1 weighing machine, 2 flour dealers (1 baker, 1 grocer), 2 framesmiths, 1 whitesmith, 1 shopkeeper, 1 dealer in fruit, 1 greengrocer, 1 dealer in cheese and bacon, 2 Catholic priests, 1 builder, 1 weaver, 1 omnibus driver, 1 model maker, 1 hair cutter, 1 gardener, 1 fitter up, 1 nail manufacturer, 1 needle maker, 1 chemist and druggist, 1 dealer in coal, 1 dyer, 1 soda-water manufacturer, 1 engineer and manufacturer of steam engine boilers, iron boats, tanks, steam kitchen apparatus etc, Wilmot almshouses, 7 victuallers (including 2 beer sellers, 1 shoeing smith and 1 Commercial Inn, Orange Tree, White Hart, Nottingham Arms, British Arms, Fox & Owl, Three Crowns, Roe-buck).

Bridge Gate, virtually obliterated for over twenty years now, is further out than neighbours Sadler Gate and Irongate and, in 1849, near the northern edge of the town. But apart from the marvellous diversity of trades and business evident in these lists, there are obvious and interesting differences between the three streets which must have stemmed at least partly from their location.

Irongate was more 'upmarket', overlooked by the tower of All Saints' and at a more discreet distance by two other 'established' places of worship. It would tend to be more frequented by 'quality' people from the county as the main thoroughfare from the north into the central Market Place. It was obviously a street for quality clothing and also requirements assuming money to spare, such as optical instrumentation, silverware, guns, pianos and, indeed, banking services. It was distinguished by the 'Mercury' offices.

Sadler Gate, around the corner and off the Market Place, was, on the other hand, clearly the venue for buying meat, tailoring, shoes, and especially liquid refreshment. There was obviously a strong craftsman presence, including jewellers and whitesmiths.

Bridge Gate, rivalling Sadler Gate for the opportunities offered for the purchase of strong drink, had closer connections with manufacturing industry and its work-force, although this was clearly only a matter of degree as Irongate boasted three silk mercers, with the Old Silk Mills just the other side of All Saints' rivalling the Italians in the production of fine silk.

There is some interesting detail in all this. Clearly Bridge Gate reflected the ten-years-old presence of the fine St Mary's Roman Catholic Church and its vestry. Also that of the venerable engineering firm of

J.Harrison. A full blast of their advertisements sounds thus:

Manufacturer of all kinds of Wrought Iron STEAM ENGINE BOILERS, for high or low pressure; GAS & WATER TANKS: GAS-HOLDERS; Iron PLEASURE and CANAL BOATS, BARGES, FLATS, and FERRY BOATS; Brewing and Bleaching Pans, or any kind of Vessel that can be manufactured of Wrought Iron.

GAS WORKS ERECTED COMPLETE. All kinds of COOKING APPARATUS, for large or small establishments, adapted for any situation, Roasting, Steaming, Stewing etc. WATER and SMOKE JACKS. Baths constructed of Copper, Enamelled, or other Materials, and heated on the most approved principles; also every other description of Bath furnished. HOT AIR STOVES, COCKLES, Hot Water and Steam Apparatus for Heating Dwelling Houses, Churches, Chapels, Manufactories, and Forcing Houses of any description.

WEIGHING MACHINES, either for road Carriages or Rail-Roads, or small ones for Warehouses. Freezing Machines to freeze from one to three Ice Creams at the same time. Washing and Squeezing Machines. APPARATUS for CUTTING CHAFF for Cattle, to be worked by horse power or otherwise. Steam Boilers and Cisterns, with all their Apparatus for Cooking Food for Cattle. THRASHING MACHINES, to be worked by hand, capable of thrashing one hundred strike per day, (and they can also be applied to horse power).[22]

A truly useful institution, and what a marvellous insight into contemporary state-of-the-art technolgoy for domestic and other regimes!

An intriguing individual entry in the *Directory* is the 'Fitter up' (of what?). And there is an interesting sartorial contrast between the 'Hair cutter' of Bridge Gate and central Sadler Gate's 'Hair dresser' and 'Hairdresser and Perfumer'. Finally, to be noted is the presence in both of these streets of 'Shoeing Smiths', evidence of the overwhelming dominance, still, of the horse away from the railway track.

The very next year after these details were set down, a very different kind of concern came to Derby six years after its inception in the northern mill town of Rochdale. This was the 'Co-op', of course, the new concept being the return of profits made to their working-class customers. The Derby initiative was at first the child of the Carpenters and Joiners' Union operating with the barest minimum of capital from the yard of the old George Inn.

They were able to set up proper accommodation in Full Street from 1858, having quadrupled their membership to forty. They opened in the evenings so that working people could have access to their wares, they were able to expand with four branches amongst the terraces to the west of the centre of town, and they inaugurated a grand new store in Albert Street in 1870. They would continue to prosper and expand up to and beyond the end of the century, the Jubilee Year of what had become entitled the Derby Co-operative Provident Society.[23]

Iron Horses

The early afternoon of Thursday, 30 May 1839 was a truly historic one for the town of Derby. At 1.18pm,

An engraving showing Derby Railway Station c.1842, just two years after it had opened. The employees and rolling-stock are those of the North Midland Railway.

the very first railway train to get here steamed to a temporary wooden platform just south of the present station.[24] It was given a tremendous welcome by a crowd of the great and the good of Derby, supported, according to a 'Mercury' reporter, by hundreds of others *gaily attired . . .cramming every conceivable vantage point* and backed up by the bells of the churches.[25]

The engine 'Sunbeam' and four first-class and two second-class carriages belonging to the Midland Counties Railway Company had started from Nottingham, forty-eight minutes earlier. There, thousands of people reportedly crowded all possible sighting points to see it off with railway guards and policemen in bright new uniforms, the carriages elegantly painted with the company name prominently displayed and a flag to each.

According to the 'Mercury' reporter again, a crowd of railway workers cheered its passage en route and policemen *in their new dresses were stationed all along the line with flags in their hands.*[26]

A second, longer, train pulled by the 'Ariel' left Nottingham just five minutes after the first, to cover the fifteen and a half miles to Derby in forty-four minutes, averaging 21mph to arrive at the crowded wooden platform only one minute after its predecessor. It later returned to Nottingham and came back to Derby the same afternoon, presumably to show its unbuttoned prowess, in only thirty-one minutes, averaging 30mph[27] and a maximum speed of 40mph.[28]

So passed what was probably the most momentous day in Derby's transport history, to be followed on Tuesday, 4 June by the opening of the first public railway passenger service to Nottingham, with four trains each day on weekdays and two on Sundays. The second-class return fare of 2s 6d (12.5p) was about an average day's wage for a worker, although definitely cheaper than the coach.

It was only two months later, on 5 August, that a second company, the Birmingham and Derby Junction Railway, started operating from that wooden platform in a different direction. The equivalent ceremonial train from Birmingham, with nine carriages filled with directors, shareholders and friends, took all of four hours to reach Derby because of site-viewing along the way and were taken to the King's Head in the Corn Market for their traditional cold meal. By this route, with three trains a day to Birmingham and two on Sundays, citizens of Derby could reach the capital by a change on to the London-Birmingham line opened the previous year.[29]

There was, in fact, a third such special occasion, yet another line-opening, grander than those preceding, unavoidably delayed for over a year after the first. On 30 June 1840, the North Midland line into Derby from Leeds was officially opened when a giant train of no less than thirty-four coaches pulled by two engines and hauling five hundred passengers arrived at the end of seventy-two miles in five hours in the early afternoon.

By this time, a reference in the contemporary report to the receiving platform being of stone seems to indicate that the wooden structure had now gone and that the projected grand station was now in use. A band was in attendance and a banquet (cold meat but with wine, as befitting a company with the famous Stephensons on their books) was served to the huge party on the platform.[30]

Clearly, Derby interests had capitulated with a vengeance to the blandishments of the railroad. The prospect of no less than three railway companies proposing to make for the town seems to have caused the opposition to crumble. Derby's strategic position as a central gateway between north and south had won the day. The station, a joint affair of the three companies acting in union, is, however, in a curious position, way off the town centre in contrast to neighbours Leicester and Nottingham.

As we have seen, this had consequences both for the disposition of local transport and the spacial development of the town, pushing it out towards the south. First thoughts were similar to those prevailing elsewhere. The Midland Counties engineer Charles Vignoles aimed his track from Nottingham at the centre, where property between the Market Place and the river had been bought up by his company for a projected terminus there. But there was opposition from alarmed citizens at the environmental impact, and the other companies had different ideas.[31]

In 1836 agreement was at last reached on the final site, on the Borough border with Litchurch parish, causing Vignoles to have to bend his track mightily to suit a new destination.

Work began on station-building in the autumn in 1839, after the first two track celebrations using the temporary platform. A thirty-acre site had been acquired — large enough for a whole railway colony — to include station, workshops, offices, hotel and a then unique group of three streets of workers' cottages in unified style. Because of a fear of waterlogging, the site was raised eight feet with sand and gravel.

The North Midland Railway Company was responsible, being by far the giant of the group of concerns with its architect, Francis Thompson. The builder was a Londoner, Thomas Jackson. Thompson's discrete rooftop triangles, round-headed arches and pilasters bore classical reminders of Pickford's work.

A 'Derby Mercury' report in May 1840, during the process of erection, describes it as a *wonderfully extensive place which astonishes every person arriving there for the first time.*[32]

Meanwhile, the company's line was nearing the end of its three-year slice through the Derbyshire hill-country from Sheffield, taking in the great Clay Cross Tunnel, navvies working continuous 24-hour shifts, finally finishing on 10 June, when over 1,500 of them were served an open-air meal near Duffield Station.[33]

When Derby Station finally opened in the summer of 1840, reporters had plenty to write about with its 350 yards length and an enormous platform, over 1,000 feet long shared by all three companies, passenger shed covered with *light iron roof of 42-foot span,*[34] spacious hall, refreshment and waiting rooms. It joined three series of workshops, again one for each company. The still existing 16-sided Thompson engine-house with central turntable was the doyen of the assemblage which was lit by nearly 750 gas lamps put in by Thomas Crump of Derby.[35]

By the time the station was finished, the Midland Counties had also completed a link to London via Rugby and so Derby citizens had a choice of competing routes to the capital. Quickly expunging any doubts voiced about the viability of such a huge station, it was soon very busy.[36] There was destructive cut-throat competition between the companies, uneconomic fares and even resort to 'dirty tricks' such as one company's train blocking the scheduled departure of another's from the common platform, despite the provision of separate bays.[37]

The only solution was amalgamation, achieved under the guidance of 'Railway King' George Hudson of York, who chaired the first meeting of the shareholders of the new Midland Railway Company in Derby on 16 July 1844.[38]

This however, was not to be the town's last, and certainly not its most traumatic, experience of railway building. This distinction was reserved for the arrival, over 30 years later, of the Great Northern Line. The operation represented a drive into the Midland's territory by its arch-rival, both companies in yet another free-market price-cutting situation, fighting for the East Midlands coal trade and, in particular, the output of the mines in the neighbourhood of Ilkeston and the Miller-Mundy Shipley estate.

It was the line which had far-and-away the most dramatic, even spectacular impact on the Derby urban environment, with a whole series of engineering feats of varying degrees of aesthetic appeal. This work was prepared for by an unprecedented swathe of devastation across the town's north-western residential landscape. The legal basis: an Act of Parliament obtained in 1872 authorizing the company to proceed.

The line originated in an extension of that from Grantham to Colwick, east of Nottingham through Ilkeston and West Hallam to Derby and on to connect with the Staffordshire Potteries via Egginton. It therefore became a prime east-west passenger excursion route as well as a busy coal-hauling line. The contract for building the Derby section was obtained by the native firm of Bent and Woodiwiss;[39] the latter became Derby's mayor twice in succession, two years after the line's opening.[40]

In crossing the Derby scene, the GNR involved the excavation of at least three cuttings, the largest at Breadsall outside the Borough boundary, through Little Chester, and immediately north of St Helen's House; three big embankments, two on either side of Little Chester with two metal iron bridges over Alfreton and City Roads, and across Markeaton Brook with a sequence of associated blue-brick arches over the neighbouring streets.

Then there was the construction of two metal bridges made in the Handyside works right beneath the line on the west bank of the Derwent (one, a severely functional and humble reminder of Sydney Harbour Bridge across the river, with suspended track and separate pedestrian way; the other an ornately crafted arch graced with the Borough coat-of-arms in the corner spandrels in two close-clamped spans across Georgian Friar Gate).

There was also the looping of a short branch line along Darley Grove north of St Helen's House and underneath the river bridge to serve the Handyside works, with wagons passing through a loading bay constructed out on stilts over the river bank on the town side, as revealed in the background of a fascinating 1881 print of Haslam's Union Foundry on City Road.

A huge area of garden and field to the south of Friar Gate was cleared for a new station, colossal warehouse and workshop with brick campanile tower reminiscent of warmer climes. There was also the destruction of Agard Street Chapel and two hostelries, the Golden Fleece and much-lamented medieval Old White Horse Inn on Friar Gate.

The Old White Horse in Friar Gate which was demolished as the new railway bridge and Royal Institute for the Deaf building were erected in 1878-79.

Finally, as if all this were not nearly enough, four whole streets (including Cherry Street) were wiped out and two others were cut short in their prime.[41]

Naturally, public opinion was divided over such massive change. The imposition of a bridge, however graceful in design, on fair Friar Gate was to many an abomination, let alone the destruction of scores of houses, however by contrast humble, mean and nasty for the most part. But apart from the presence of Abraham Woodiwiss, already referred to, the 1871 Mayor of Derby, Samuel Leech, and the Borough Surveyor of that time were secretly on the company payroll![42]

So the town felt the apocalyptic presence of the navvies, so potent the length and breadth of Britain in Victorian times. Many would be admirably Irish but there would also be many local boys. Anyone else with time to spare in Derby north in 1877 might have witnessed a scene similar to the following as described by a contemporary writer:

Runs, as they are called, are made by laying planks up the side of the cutting, on which the barrows may be wheeled. The running is performed by stout young men, round the waist of each is a strong bell, fastened to which is a rope running up the side of the cutting, and turning on a wheel at the top, whilst to the other extremity a horse is attached to the barrow being laden . . .the signal is given to the driver, who leads the horse quickly out a given distance into the field, and thus the man is drawn up the acclivity; the contents of the barrow are emptied, and the horse being led back the rope is slackened and the man runs down the plank again, drawing the empty barrow after him.[43]

The line should have opened on New Year's Day 1878, but inclement weather caused a blockage at the Breadsall cutting.[44] On Thursday, 24 January 1878,

the 'Derby Mercury' carried the report of a special train for officers to make an inspection of the line in preparation for the opening. When they approached what was probably the Breadsall Cutting (although this is not exactly clear from the report):

. . .opinions were divided as to the success of the enterprise. The treacherous grounds had, however, been surveyed by Mr Abott after the violent storm on the preceding night, and pronounced safe. A large staff of men under that gentleman's guidance were awaiting the train and we passed over the 'slip' with perfect safety.

A short run brought us to the outskirts of a Roman encampment at Little Chester (Derventio) and we crossed the river . . .

Darley Grove and its gardens have long since given way before the march of railway improvements; but it was quite a new sensation to find ourselves across Friar Gate and deposited by the train precisely on the spot where our boyish memories centre themselves on once smiling gardens, now the pathway of the iron horse.

Three days later, a serious accident between West Hallam and Ilkeston caused further delay. Two trains, one carrying wood and the other steel which was spare from the construction work, collided with each other on a bend where visibility was poor after they had ignored signals. Three workmen who were hitching a lift on one of the trains were pinned in the driving cab and were severely scalded by steam and water. Two died and seven other workmen in all were injured, with one losing both legs and another a foot.[45] Next day, however, Monday 28 January, the line was opened to freight traffic and finally, at 9am on All Fool's Day, the first passenger train left Friar Gate Station for Nottingham in a snow shower. It was soon to be busy with both freight and passenger traffic.

A year after its opening, the 'Engineering' magazine for 11 April 1879 carried the following report:

Bridge over the River Derwent at Derby

The Great Northern Railway Company not long since completed their new railway across the Derbyshire coalfields . . .The new railway traverses the town nearly from north to south, and besides numerous bridges for the street crossings, it includes two important structures, one carrying the line over the River Derwent, and a handsome caste-iron arched bridge over Friar Gate . . .The (river) bridge has a clear span of 132ft and a width of 28ft 6in between centres of ribs. It carries two lines of railway, and has an overhanging footway on one side . . .The bridge was put together at Messrs Handyside's works, and was erected in position by them over the river. The work was completed in the early part of last year and was tested by three locomotives of 72 tons each on each line, in all six locomotives with a total load of 432 tons.

Something to remember as we venture over its still substantial frame today!

Friar Gate station, although far nearer the centre of town and causing some realignment of public transport so that a horse-tram route for a fare of twopence was started to connect with the centre and the Midland Station, changing at the Royal Hotel at the corner of the Corn Market, was no rival in comfort and size to its competitor. A buffet, two waiting rooms and toilets were provided on an island platform, reached from the road through a subway.

Of greater interest were the accompanying warehouse and workshops, with numerous sidings, each for a particular commodity — cattle, coal etc. The huge warehouse was entered by four of these sidings. It had three levels: a basement, twelve feet below ground for bonded store and offices; a ground floor with two island platforms each with hydraulic lifts and winches; and a storage loft with two grain chutes for loading wagons and ten hydraulic cranes.[46]

What would travel be like for Derby citizens who felt they could afford to indulge in the pioneering days of steam, the days of the Midland Counties rather than the Great Northern? There was a considerable difference right from the start in the standard of comfort that different classes of people could expect on getting into a train at the Midland Station in the 1840s, although, as we shall see, things had considerably altered by the time Friar Gate Station was operating in the late 1870s.

First-class carriages showed the strong influence of stage-coach design, with three compartments only, cushioned seats, windows with glass and, early on, even a guard on the roof to watch the luggage covered by tarpaulin. If very rich, customers could even arrange to travel on a privatized basis in their own carriages put on a truck, their horses placed in either open cattle-wagon or horse-box according to fee.

Second-class passengers could expect no padding for their bottoms and no window protection. The third-class 'coach', however, was in reality a mere wagon, no roof, no seats. The inmates could be soaked by rain, covered in soot, even sparked alight. They must have been even more apprehensive

about tunnel episodes than their second-class neighbours.[47]

Nevertheless, the railways obviously prospered and indeed transformed the life of the nation. Initially, it was the concept of the cheap special excursion which brought ordinary folk into the ranks of those who ventured far from home, if only for a day.

The Midland Counties line was the world pioneer in this respect. The very first was a series of four reciprocal affairs between Derby's neighbours, Leicester and Nottingham, two each way between 10 July 1840, the very first, and 24 August, the date of the fourth. The first two were in the nature of mutual exchange between the Mechanics' Institutes of the two towns, but, adapting the idea, the railway company organized the latter two.

The fourth, from Nottingham to Leicester, attracted no less than two thousand customers carried in sixty-five coaches, forty-nine of them in the second-class category and eight each of the others.[48]

It was, of course, Thomas Cook of neighbouring Melbourne who saw the full possibilities of the idea and organized his very first excursion on the Midland Counties line on 5 July 1841, from Leicester to Loughborough for a Temperance demonstration. Some 570 people paid one shilling each return, with all but one of the fifteen carriages open-topped third-class.[49]

Soon, Derby was to be the focus of attention for the further development of the day-excursion concept. In September 1840, the Arboretum was opened, the first park in Britain to be publicly owned and operated (*see* Chapter 8 — Arboretum). The special attractions put on for the annual festival celebration of the opening proved a tremendous draw for working people from at least a fifty-mile radius through this very first mass-transit medium.

For example, the 'Derby Mercury' for 12 June 1861 carried the following advertisement:

Special Trains from Birmingham, Sheffield, Chesterfield, Nottingham, Leicester, Loughborough, Rowsley, Ripley, Mansfield, Coalville and intermediate stations advertised to run for the Derby Arboretum Anniversary Festival on Monday, 24 June 1861.

Two issues later, 26 June, it reported:

The number of people who came into the town by railway was about 6,000, seventeen hundred less than last year.

This continued throughout our period as a 'Mercury' report on the Arboretum Festival for Whitsuntide 1881 reveals, claiming an estimated four thousand people came in to Derby by the Midland Railway.[50] As for the other available directions, the 'Mercury' carried the following advertisement on 12 June 1861:

Excursions

Weekly to North Wales (Holyhead for Dublin).
Marcus's Special Trains from Derby and Burton, to Liverpool (week-end) to see the Great Eastern Steam Ship in the Mersey."

Also a fortnight later, on 26 June 1861: *Midland Railway Excursions to the seaside — Scarbro', Harrogate, Whitby, Filey, Redcar, Bridlington, Withernsea, Grimsby, English Lakes, Ireland, South Wales, Malvern, West of England, Matlock etc.*

The above-mentioned report on 8 June 1881 went on to list outward excursions, 150 people travelling to London, 300 to Liverpool, 230 to Birmingham, 700 in 'pleasure parties' and an unspecified crowd to Dovedale. This on Arboretum Festival Day, a Whit Monday.

The Great Northern Line, in particular, soon established itself at this time as the great excursion mover to resorts on the East Coast, a little later especially to Skegness. It was also at least partly responsible for a tiny example of a large-scale London phenomenon, which has grown to gargantuan proportions in the present century, namely the birth of the suburban rail commuter, enabled to live in sylvan seclusion on the outskirts of a town and to work at or near its heart. A line of generously-plotted villas was built around 1878 near Mickleover station, itself well away from the village at the time.[51]

Finally, ranging on the broader national scene, of which Derby was clearly not an insignificant segment, railways had wider transforming effects. Their firm bedding-in led to the standardisation of time-keeping, by 'railway (Greenwich) time', which was made the legal requirement for all communities in 1880. No longer would the unmonitored chimes of All Saints' suffice.

As we have seen, the railway's mass-transit possiblities particularly benefited the labouring classes, a fact recognized in the provision by the Midland Railway, in 1872, of seating in third-class carriages, followed three years later by the abolition of the second-class facility. Again, whilst the telephone was available for business use from the 1880s irrespective of railway development, towards the end of the decade 'The Times' newspaper in its Golden Jubliee retrospect of June 1887 eulogized the railways for revolutionizing the sending of news and correspondence.

This was in particular through the electric telegraph service which was taken over by the General Post Office in 1870. That same year, too, saw Gladstone's government introducing the postcard.[52]

Telegram and postcard — these were facilities Derby folk would use and appreciate, home and away, as would their fellow-countrymen and women all over Britain, as essential and valued products of the railway age.

During the last decade of our period, there was a postscript to local transport development in the nineteenth century in the form of the tram. Electrical application did not arrive until a little later to take things forward into the present century; what happened in the 1880s could in one way be regarded as a combination of the coach and the rail — programmed horse-transport.

Horse and Tram

We have seen that it was not until as late as 1877 that a basic horse-omnibus network for the whole of the town was organized. On 6 March 1880 came the first horse-tram run by the Derby Tramway Company on a narrow 4ft-wide track.[53] The grand villas based on longer-distance rail commuting via GNR were, as we have seen, going up on the far north-western outskirts. The working man and woman needed a

humbler service in the pre-bicycle age. The middle-class would, by now, be used to the horse-cab with its jingling harness and clopping hooves, sounds which would have been much more prevalent in Derby streets after the opening of the Midland Station.

This era was gloriously captured by local photographer Richard Keene in a shot of the newly-cobbled Market Place in 1872 with a row of handsome-cabs parked across the middle of the empty square.[54]

The wealthier end of the social stratum would have had their private carriages still. Indeed, nationally, an indication of growing middle-class affluence between 1851 and 1881 was a doubling of the number of private carriages at a time when it required an income of £600 a year (workers might average up to £80) to maintain a modest two-wheeler. Those elegantly wide entrance-arches of our older town buildings were still strongly utilitarian.

There was, however, a less acceptable side to this for urban living, which only the electric tram at the end of the century would begin to eliminate — the smell and dirt from horse-droppings, nostalgic childhood memories for some notwithstanding. This could have been mightily offensive, although as usual more particularly in London where crossing-sweepers were necessary in an age of long brushing skirts.[55] It has been calculated that each town horse produced three to four tons of droppings a year.[56]

An article in 'Cornhill Magazine' of March 1890, on the worker and transport, declared in the habitual patronizing tone of those days that *The Tramcar is his familiar vehicle and he can ensconce himself there in his mortar-splashed clothes without restraint.*[57]

The first grooved tram track had been laid in Liverpool back in 1869. In Derby in the 1880s there were four routes, indicated to potential passengers not by our familiar numbers but by a code of lights:
Red Light: Market Place, Station Street, Deadman's Lane, Alvaston.
Blue Light: Royal Hotel, Victoria Street, Osmaston Road (Cotton Lane).
Orange Light: Normanton Hotel, Normanton Road to Royal Hotel.
Green Light: Royal Hotel to Coach and Horses, Ashbourne Road.[58]

On the Uttoxeter New Road and Kedleston Road, the trams did not supplant the horse-omnibus until electrification over twenty years later, so that the emphasis was clearly on serving the southern and south-western terraced estates. The trams must have been a cheerful sight after dark, lit by two often smokey oil-lamps at either end, with a pungent smell for those inside.[59]

However, as usual things did not go entirely smoothly in Derby. To begin with, there was considerable opposition even to the idea of them, mainly from those with property interests along the proposed routes. The familiar technique of fear-arousal was well to the fore, as the letter by the not-too-disinterested coach-builder, Arthur Holmes of London Street, published in the 'Derby Mercury' on 25 November 1879 indicates:

If the company succeed in getting and keeping the consent of the majority of us to the laying of two lines of rails, and lay them, no coals can thenceforth be shot at our doors, no barrow be unloaded, and no unfortunate inhabitant will be able to step off the pavement opposite to his house without the risk of being killed and cut up in the very face of his family.

We are told, forsooth, that the proposed alterations will facilitate the traffic . . .For my own part I consider the town of Derby, with its cramped streets, altogether unsuited to tramcar traffic; that the tradesmen, wherever the tramways are laid, will be sadly inconvenienced while housing their goods and that they will sustain much loss from their carriage customers being unable to stop at their shop doors . . .[60]

An article in the 'Mercury' of 20 February 1884 shows that the operation was not yet a huge success in Derby, certainly when compared with the situation in a neighbouring town, and indicates also a sabbatarian problem (treated further in Chapter 5). The article also offers a great deal of advice:

To the Derby Tramways Company and their fortunes the public of Derby are by no means indifferent. The tramways have become one of the institutions of the town. The cars seem to be ever with us, and the tinkle of the bells is a fimiliar sound from early morning till late at night.

Every five weeks the number of passengers equals, on the average, the entire population of Derby. Therefore, we may assume that the public will read with some degree of interest the report which we give elsewhere of the half-yearly meeting of the company held last week. It seems that the promoters are not satisfied with the progress they have achieved. In Leicester the population get in and out of the cars once every eighteen days, and if the people of Derby would follow this estimable example all would be well.

But in spite of all their exertions the directors have not succeeded in making the tramcars popular, and they do not suggest any reason for the failure. Some of the shareholders seem to think that the Sunday traffic had something to do with it; but the Chairman made it tolerbly clear that some profit at all events

is made on Sundays and it may also be contended that if the public choose to use the cars on a wet Sunday, the directors are entitled to say that in running them on the seventh day they are supplying a public want, even though in fair weather the need may not be an urgent one.

Undoubtedly there is a feeling amongst many persons against the working of the lines on Sunday . . .For our part, we do not believe that this matter is at the root of the company's difficulty. If they would run the cars at times which could be remembered by the public and, having fixed the times, adhere to them; if they would avoid the continual waiting on loop lines (some memories here), which might easily be done by good management; if the guards would keep a good look-out for would-be passengers in rear; if the cars were freed from the stench of the oil-lamps — if these and a few other improvements, which will doubtless suggest themselves to the management, were effected, there would probably be a large increase in the number of passengers.

What is wanted is that the cars should run frequently, punctually, and quickly. Moreover, if the directors could see their way to adopt the suggestion of Mr Barrs and introduce penny fares as far, say, as Mill Hill Lane, Charnwood Street, and Vernon Street on the respective routes, we are very strongly of the opinion that the experiment would be worth trying.

We can surely identify with much of this. Some of the advice was taken up, such as fare-reduction and a new rule-book in 1887 which contains the following:

The company shall at all times keep every car clean and in good condition.
Every driver and conductor of a car using the Tramways shall behave with civility towards every passenger or intending passenger.[61]

Public transport surely always was, and will be, a live issue, as long as it exists!

Notes

1. *Report to the General Board of Health on a Preliminary Enquiry into The Sewerage, Drainage and Suppply of Water, and the Sanitary Conditions of the Inhabitants of the Borough of Derby 1849.*
2. P.P.Burdett, *Plan of Derby, 1767.*
3. *Map of the Borough of Derby, with Portions of Derby, Litchurch and Little Chester. Surveyed by the Board of Ordnance for the Local Board of Health AD 1852* (Derbyshire Archaeological Society 1980).
4. Various sources including Maxwell Craven, op.cit., Roy Cristian, op.cit. and Census summaries for 1881 and 1891.
5. Roy Christian, *Derby in the Making, Railway Derby,* 1989.
6. Ibid.
7. Maxwell Craven, op.cit.
8. Roy Christian, *The Development of a City.*
9. Roy Christian, *Railway Derby.*
10. Maxwell Craven, op.cit.
11. Roy Christian, op.cit.
12. Ibid.
13. Ibid.
14. Ibid.
15. *Derby Mercury, 2 April 1834.*
16. Article in *Ward & Co's Annual, 1892.*
17. Maxwell Craven, op.cit.
18. *Ward & Co's Annual.*
19. Maxwell Craven, op.cit.
20. Ibid.
21. Ibid.
22. *Railway Companion.*
23. Account based on that in Maxwell Craven, op.cit.
24. Roy Christian, op.cit.
25. *Derby Mercury, 6 June 1839.*
26. Quoted in Roy Christian, op.cit.
27. J.B.Radford, Introduction to *Railway Companion,* op.cit.
28. F.S.Williams, *The Midland Railway, Its Rise and Progress,* 1875.
29. Roy Christian, op.cit.
30. Ibid.
31. Maxwell Craven, op.cit.
32. Roy Christian, op.cit.
33. Ibid.
34. Ibid, quoting *Derby Mercury.*
35. Maxwell Craven, op.cit.
36. Roy Christian, op.cit.
37. Maxwell Craven, op.cit.
38. Ibid.
39. Roy Christian, op.cit.
40. Maxwell Craven, op.cit.
41. Ibid.
42. Roy Christian, op.cit.
43. F.S.Williams, *Our Iron Roads.*
44. Roy Christian, op.cit.
45. P.W.Parkin, *The History of the GNR Co. and Derby Friargate,* unpublished paper, 1971.
46. Ibid.
47. J.Radford, op.cit.
48. Ibid.
49. Ibid.
50. *Derby Mercury, 8 June 1881.*
51. Roy Christian, op.cit.
52. D.Read, op.cit.
53. Maxwell Craven, op.cit.
54. Ibid.
55. D.Read, op.cit.
56. F.M.L.Thompson, *Victorian England: The Horse-Drawn Society,* 1970.
57. Quoted in D.Read, op.cit.
58. Centenary Article, *Derby Trams and Buses* in *Derbyshire Advertiser,* August 1980.
59. Ibid.
60. Quoted Ibid.
61. Quoted Ibid.

At Work — Or Not

THE machinery is dispersed through six rooms, occupying the six storeys. This is all put in motion by the water-wheel, on the west side of the building, and the steam engine. The elaborate machinery consists of many thousand reel bobbins, star-wheels, reels, and spindles; but an adequate idea of the complicated assemblage of wheels and movements cannot be conveyed by words; to be distinctly conceived it must be seen. All is whirling and in motion, and appears as if directed and animated by some invisible power.

So Glover, in his 1849 'Directory of Derby', describes the activity in the most famous place of industry in the town, the Old Silk Mills on the Derwent, just a few yards from the rear of All Saints'.

Certainly it was the oldest, as we have seen, dating from early in the previous century, dedicated by its founders, the Lombes, to the production of fine 'organzine' silk, the raw material of the best silk products.

The mention of six storeys is surely inaccurate, despite the change in appearance the mill had undergone since its early days, such as the replacement of the original vaguely crenellated roof-line by a sloping hipped roof as a result of a fire in 1826. The generally acknowledged number of storeys before the final, much more destructive, fire of 1910 was five.

Whatever the detail, one modern authority attributes to the Silk Mill the creation of a tradition of skilled factory working through successive generations of operatives which would be of enormous benefit to the town during the nineteenth century, when so much new industry was attracted to it.[1]

During our chosen period, Derby became overwhelmingly an industrial and manufacturing town in which the distinctive sounds of powered and working machinery would be inescapable. We have seen how the Derby Canal would have contributed to this during the first decades of the century. Then came the decisive contribution of the railway, building on the foundation laid by the Lombes well over a century before.

If in 1812 the Derby skyline would have featured a few stacks to accompany the Shot Tower as the environmental signature of a new age — there is a record of seven active silk mills in the town at that time,[2] two or three of which, like the oldest of them,[3] might have been experimenting with steam power — then by Victoria's Jubilee it would have been fenced

Derby Silk Mill, the first in England and claiming to be the country's first proper factory. It proved of enormous benefit top the town in the nineteenth century.

with them beneath the inevitable smoke-pall of prosperity.

So that, apart from the equally inevitable slump as a consequence of free-market economics, there was employment in plenty during the Victorian period. And not only for the typical male head of the family but also for all its members if of a suitable age, a qualification not as narrow in scope earlier in the century as it was to become later on.

The story of the silk industry might supply an interesting opening case-study of the vagaries of change, of response to improvement in communications, markets and other constraints and also of working conditions.

Because it was not keyed-in to a mass market like the cotton industry, on the one hand it was fuzzy-edged in that several of the Derby mills combined silk with cotton manufacture, on the other it had to adapt and diversify or go under. This latter fate would have seemed to be the case with the Old Silk Mills themselves in 1887, as they ceased production altogether in 1890.

The great southern (town-end) section, which for two centuries had protruded into the river on a prow-like base separated from terra firma by the entrance to the mill-race (its configuration can be much better appreciated at the present time since the recent 'urban fund' work there), would be in a parlous state as the following account indicates:

Last year (1891) the building was reported to be in a most dangerous condition and incapable of being preserved, so that it became necessary on the part of the Corporation of Derby, the owners, to give orders for its demolition.[4]

In any case, for some time past this section of the Mills had been used as a steam laundry, a further indication of serious contraction regarding its original purpose.

Earlier in the century it was a rather different story. During the first three decades of our period, the silk mills were the principal employer of labour, if the following extract from the 1849 'Board of Health Report' is to be credited:

Since the establishment in 1719 of a silk-throwing mill at Derby, by a mechanic and draughtsman named John Lombe, the chief part of the population have been employed in the silk manufacture; the town has in consequence grown up into the importance which it at present enjoys.[5]

According to an 1847 factory census, Derby had the third largest concentration of silk workers in the country, after Lancashire and Cheshire.[6] The Old Silk Mills were the standard model for all mills wherever they were situated:

There are now (in Derby) several establishments, chiefly of brick construction, four or five storeys in height, where the winding engines . . .are placed in a regular manner aross the three upper storeys, where several thousands of swifts and spindles are put into regular motion by steam and water power. On the lower storeys are placed generally the spinning and twist mills, which are turned by perpendicular shafts, moved by the same power.[7]

Thirty-one mills and workshops of varying size are listed in Pigot's 'Directory of Derbyshire' for 1835 (seven of which under the heading 'Hosiery' might possibly have used wool as raw material) and fifty-three in Glover's 'Directory of Derby' for 1849. The 1830s and 1840s therefore seem to have been vital developmental decades.

Right in the middle came the railway to provide easier access to markets and also competition. When comparing Pigot's and Glover's lists, three characteristics become evident: high volatility, diversification, and location spread. On the first, only

The Shot Tower in the Morledge. Built in 1809 it was a landmark in Derby for more than a century. Molten lead poured through sieves at the top were formed into tiny drops which were rounded as they spun through the air.

eleven of the concerns listed in 1835 were still there in 1849, which might suggest that competition rather than stimulus was the more prevalent influence brought to bear by the railway.

This is not to say that there was no volatility earlier (as a comparison with Pigot's list for 1831 would disprove), only that it seems to have been much more intense after 1835. In any case, the early 1830s were a period of severe industrial strife, as we shall see.

On the second feature, however, a whole new range of product is listed by Glover, such as ribbons, purses, trimmings, twists, braids and twines. Significant change in fashion might also be indicated by the addition of no less than eight specialist 'dyers', in retrospect conspicuous by their absence in 1835.

On the third characteristic, Glover's list of addresses is much more diverse, spread around the town. In 1835 there was a marked concentration of the industry in the north-west sector of Derby, in and near the area of expansion over Nun's Green in Regency times.[8] Many of the mills were along the course of the Markeaton Brook. The majority of later mills were built further to the south-east nearer the station and also the canal. Access to coal supplies with the early nineteenth-century switch from water-power to steam must have been a major factor here.

There were also addresses to the south of centre, along the Normanton Road for instance, as we have previously seen indicated by the 1852 'Board of Health Map'. However, according to Glover, the largest mill, that of Thomas Bridgett, was still in the old sector on Bridge Street. The vast Rykneld Mills, premises shared with James and Charles Peet, employed 750 workers. These mills are, indeed, one of the most impressive reminders of the early industrial revolution in Derby with seven-storey and five-storey blocks, hierarchies of small cast-iron windows, and a faint classical reference in a triangular-pedimented end-gable.

Bridgett himself was an excellent example of upward mobility in industrial society. He had started life as a humble framework-knitter, working in his own home with the domestic machine improved by Jedediah Strutt in the previous century, then an independent hosier, silk throwster (concerned with one of the three basic processes involved in the manufacture of silk). He finally became a mill-owner in 1821.[9]

Not all silk workers were concentrated in mills. According to Glover's 'Directory of Derby' for 1829, there were 700 'domestic workers', as Bridgett had once been, in the town to between 2,000 and 3,000 mill operatives. The domestics concentrated on weaving and 'small-ware'. 'Riband Weavers' featured in the processions for the opening of the Arboretum in 1840.[10]

However, many of these might by then be working in the mills as the domestics were increasingly levered out in the competition. For a time, Derby, with Coventry, was the country's leading ribbon-manufacturing town.

Again, all this was not the whole story. The industry had also to adapt to changing legislation with regard to rules of trade. In the 1820s, Parliament in London abolished, after a run of over a century, the protective customs duties which had prohibited the sale of foreign silk goods in Britain. The Derby mills adapted much better to this change than those in some other parts of the country, according to evidence by Ambrose Moore before the Select Committee on the Act for the Regulation of Mills and Factories in July 1840:

I believe that the silk manufacture is different in its character from what it was before the admission of foreign manufactured silks. All the finer silks for the wear of the higher classes, or a large portion of them, are imported from France, and the manufacture of them has ceased in this country. Instead of that finer silk there has been a large quantity of course and inferior silk brought into use, which was not used before; and some of the mills, especially those in Derby, are working upon them . . .[11]

In the 1860s, however, a free-trade agreement was concluded with France, exposing the industry to the laser-beam competition of French fashion. In 1840, Ambrose Moore had already made a baleful comment on the predilection of the ladies for Paris fashion, for which as imports they were prepared to pay inflated prices:

There is no doubt that if the very same articles had been made in Spitalfields, and they had not happened to be in fashion at Paris, no fashionable lady would have considered them good; she would have said it was bad taste, though it was the same that was bought at Paris . . .[12]

There is no doubting the subsequent decline of the Derby industry. Whilst there was a strong return to the Markeaton Brook with several new mills manufacturing silk-tape in the 1850s,[13] many Derby firms started to go out of business from the 1860s. The Old Silk Mills themselves went bankrupt during the previous decade and Rykneld Mills was a casualty ten years later. In spite of belated new ventures such as Charles Dould and Sons 1874 Spa Lane Mills making furniture trimmings, fringes and tassels,[14] the 'Oddfellows' Companion and Guide to Derby' for 1892 records that there were only eight substantial mills working then, against an 1862 figure of forty-two mills of various sizes.[15]

The largest at the end of our period was the 1842 Bath Street Mills on the west bank of the Derwent, which employed 200 to 300 workers.

The silk industry also provides interesting perspectives on the experience of the work-force during the classic years of the first Industrial Revolution. One salient characteristic of the trade was the high proportion of child and female workers, at least in that section of it concentrated in mills. According to the statistics amassed by the 'Factory Acts Reports' of 1840, the Old Silk Mills under the direction of Mr William Taylor employed 101 workers of thirteen years of age or under, fifty-five aged thirteen to eighteen and not one adult! Two other mills had similar returns.[16] In all, in 1840, 64 per cent of the total Derby silk work-force was aged eighteen or under and 68 per cent was female. According to the evidence of Medical Officer Douglas Fox: _. . .if you do not let children go in until the age of thirteen they would never become so valuable as silk hands as if they had come earlier._[17]

Factory-owner Ambrose Moore explained the infrequency of elderly workers engaged in the silk process thus: _They get comparatively clumsy; they are not so useful as young persons . . .I think unless they were trained when younger than thirteen, they would_ not do it so skilfully . . .undoubtedly it is a fact, that little fingers manage that with greater dexterity than larger ones; unusued to it at an early age, they acquire the knack of doing it.[18]

When the attitude of parents was enquired into, factory inspector Mr Bury alleged cases of false baptismal certificates being obtained by parents anxious to lie about their children's age in order to secure their employment in the mills. He added a plea for birth dates on certificates to be entered in writing rather than in figures, instancing a case in Draycott where parents had managed to alter the figures on the certificate: I got my penknife and cut the certificate out of the certificate book, and holding it up to the light, I found that the child was born in 1828, and that the parent had altered the eight, making it into six, making the child thereby two years older.[20]

Significantly, Mr Bury went on to add: My opinion is that they have been driven to this by the necessity of circumstances, or a desire to get more remuneration for their children.[21]

The Factory Acts Reports contain valuable evidence about conditions of work in the silk industry and, by implication, into prevalent conditions in others. The Factory Act of 1833 had laid down discretionary rules about the length of the working day and had reduced the hours current in the silk mills for children between nine and thirteen years from ten to eight per day.

Whilst Inspector Bury admitted that during the year previous to the inquiry (presumably 1839-40), 'there has certainly been a greater disposition . . .to comply with the Act . . .',[22] Medical Officer Fox's attitude to the reduction in hours did not tally with the inspector's: I think it would have an injurious effect . . .I have made extensive enquiries, I feel well convinced it would throw a great number of those children out of employ altogether, and that those who were not thrown out of employ would, in a great measure, have their wages reduced, and it would affect their physical condition to a serious extent. Many of the families in Derby depend greatly on the employment of children; in a great measure on the employment of children of that age.[23]

He was, of course, backed up by factory owner Ambrose Moore: . . .the silk trade, I give my testimony, cannot bear it; the competition abroad will not allow of our being so restricted. I must maintain there is no necessity for it in the silk employment; it is a healthy employment; no abuse can be proved to exist that does not exist in every house in the kingdom . . .
I believe additional restrictions will fall heavily on the hands; any disadvantages of any sort on us must be taken out of the wages of the work people. It cannot be taken out of the profits of the master, for there are no profits left for it to be taken out of.[24]

On the other hand, the inspector indicated a change of attitude on the part of parents: I am happy to say there is an increasing desire by the working classes to see their children educated.[25]

He went on to give some flavour of what contemporary mill hours meant in practice when pleading for a reduction: I am of opinion that the factory working day ought to be reduced in the summer months from half-past five in the morning to eight at night, and in the winter months from six in the morning to half-past seven in the evening.[26]

Mr Fox, again on the other hand, maintained that the existing hours had no injurous effects on children. He had questioned some of them as to whether they felt tired and the large majority of them said they did not.

When questioned on the effect on children's educational prospects and whether a nine-year-old was capable in addition to the working day of profitably attending evening school, Mr Fox responded: Once or twice a week; they do so in many instances in Derby.[27]. They surely bred them tough in those days!

Silk mill children did escape the severe shift system prevalent in the lace mills of Derby and elsewhere, described at length by Inspector Bury as completely depriving many youngsters so employed the opportunity of any education at all. Lace children were brought to the mill at any hour of day or night and might remain there for up to twenty-four hours at a time.

When asked of the physical effect of such a regime, Mr Bury replied: Decidedly injurious; their very countenance speaks it.

Could there possibly be a more telling response? He singled out Messrs Boden & Morley (whose lace mill was situated near the Cockpit, dated 1825) as being an exception to prove the unnecessary nature of the suffering involved, in that they installed two sets of bobbins and carriages rather than the normal single set, thus dispensing with a shift after eight hours. Lace mills were not covered by the provisions of the Factory Acts.[28]

Moving on to the factory experience itself, there was disagreement before the Factory Acts Committee between Inspector Bury and Medical Officer Fox on the general working environment. According to the inspector: The majority of the mills in Derby are old, rackety low places; they are far inferior to the cotton mills, in my opinion.

The Medical Officer replied (7 July 1840): There are sixteen silk mills in Derby, eleven of which have been constructed within the last twenty-five years, and several within the last five years, and some of them even more recently than that . . .[29]

The inspector compared his experience of the four different kinds of textile mills in his remit: I consider the silk preferable to the cotton; a little, but not much . . .Because there is not so much flying about of the material, and the children do not imbibe it into their chests or lungs as much in the silk mills as they do in the cotton-mills . . .[30]

In his evidence Ambrose Moore stated that the average height of the rooms in his factory was nine feet. Mr Fox gave it as his opinion that the children's health was good: I have observed that the children in the mills are what I should call a set of particularly healthy persons, and I attribute that mainly to their being kept in a wholesome and warm atmosphere, and are well-clothed . . .The atmosphere is generally temperate; it is now and then warm in the winter, from the gas-light.[31]

Nearly ten years later, the 'Board of Health Report' of 1849 passed a very favourable verdict on Derby's silk mills and, indeed, on work places in the town in general:

It said: *The ten or dozen silk mills now in active operation are all well ventilated, and appear to have their interior wall regularly whitewashed; in no instance was there observed a neglect of cleanliness. Generally on each floor are separate water closets for males and females, the construction of which cannot but be approved. The several storeys where the workpeople are employed are warmed with hot water, which circulates through iron pipes, and maintains a regular temperature throughout . . .*

All the inhabitants of Derby are engaged in some profitable employment, and nothing can exceed the order and cleanliness observed in the larger workshops and manufactories; did the same conditions exist in the workmen's families, there would not be much to complain of.[32]

A significant comment here in advance of our study of home life in the town.

If we attempt to watch the children actually at work, the evidence of the Medical Officer provides some insight. When asked how they were generally employed, whether walking the length of the frames to pierce the threads, Mr Fox replied: *Yes, generally; in some instances they have small stools to sit upon but they are generally walking.*

And when asked if they were given boards to stand and walk on if they were not tall enough to reach the bobbins with comfort: *I have not seen such, but I have seen moveable frames for them to stand upon.*[33]

He goes on to give, again, a favourable impression of the regime in the mill, although wise caution might lead to some scepticism about the evidence of an officer clearly on the side of the management.

When asked whether he had not seen sticks in the overseers' hands, he replied: *No. And I speak as a magistrate, I occasionally have causes of complaint, but they are very rare. Once or twice in a year we have complaints of a child having been ill-treated by the overlooker, and we always make it a point to inquire minutely into the treatment of the hands when they come before us. I can speak with great confidence, as far as any information can be procured, that coercion is not used in the mills.*

When asked about specific cases, he remembered: *They are generally young women or girls, who, it has turned out, have been excessively insolent, and the overlooker or persons who were there have taken and put them out of the office . . .*[34]

Many teachers will surely sympathise! When further questioned about the possibility of accidents to children at work, Mr Fox admitted to keeping no record of their number and went on: *I have inquired about them; and I know from that enquiry, and from those that come into the infirmary, that they are rare cases . . . I do not think it is confined to any particular age, except the minor accidents, such as having their fingers trapped; the ends of their fingers.*

Do you mean cut off?

No. Trapped, pinched.

Do you know of fingers being amputated in consequence of these accidents?

In the course of years I have taken them off myself, but they are rare occurrences . . . Those with their fingers trapped were generally children who went for the first time, before they became adroit.[35]

Finally, a look with reference to the whole age-range of the work-force at two further related aspects of their experience of the silk-trade — diversity of jobs and pay. On the first, the 1851 Census Ennumerators' Returns for a selection of streets in the town, but with some particular attention to the north-west sector, reveal evidence of the diversification of the industry in the middle of our period referred to earlier.

The following is a list of the different specialities encountered in the replies of house occupants to the questions of the censor: weaver, throwster, glove-maker, ribbon-weaver, winder, framework knitter, hooking, silk hose seamer, silk warper, cordwainer's apprentice, embroiderer, silk stocking seaming, silk doubler, silk wrapper, silk lace maker, silk dyer, silk mill hand, broad silk weaver, silk girl.[36]

Quite clearly, 'silk worker' represents a very broad generalisation and this would no doubt apply to a similar reference to many other industries in the town with their great variety of skills.

Trying to produce a respectable approximation to rates of factory pay in Derby in, say, mid-Victorian times is a minefield. It is a case of working with fleeting clues from various times, trades and locations — usually outside Derby — to try to arrive at a reasonable figure. Again, working out a weekly rate is one thing, but going on from there to attempt an annual average wage is quite another. In such an exercise the effect of recessional lay-offs in an age when the idea of unemployment pay would have been anathema to the prevailing laissez-faire philosophy must have some cautioning influence on any confident stab at such a figure.

For example, in all the comings and goings of the silk business evidenced in the Pigot and Glover trade lists would the ordinary worker, child, female, male, have experienced bouts of unemployment during changes of ownership, however brief? If so, then the figure for average income would have to stand some adjustment. All this is aside from the problem of conversion into decimalised modern fiscal terms, taking into account 150 years' worth of fluctuating inflation — is it at all a meaningful exercise?

However, available clues are as follows: First, the evidence of mill-owner Ambrose Moore on children's rates at his factory, which gives us an impression of vagueness, possibly Olympian detachment about such mundane matters on the part of management, and also of union-free direct bargaining.

After stating that the absolute minimum weekly wage for a child under thirteen, remembering the hours prevalent at the time, was 2s 0d (10p), when asked what the top rate was for the same age range: *I do not know exactly; I should think it was probably 3s 6d, perhaps 4s 0d . . .*

And when asked about the attitude of mothers when their below-age child got proficient: *A woman came who had four or five children; I happened to be there, and I asked what she wanted. She said they had eaten so much since they came to the mill, that she could not afford to keep them unless we raised their wages.*[37]

On rates for older children: *The scale of wages rises gradually with the age; those of the age of twelve are more valuable than those of the age of eleven . . . those we are at liberty to employ twelve hours if they are only a day older, so as to qualify them to work longer, receive more wages than those we are restricted from employing above ten hours.*[38]

Next, evidence from the Poor Law Commissioners whose new regime from 1834, for families totally unable to cope economically, was characterised by an imperative against relying on parish provision in order to keep the bill down as far as possible.

In 1835, the Commissioners appealed to local employees to take on pauper children for their mills. Thomas Bridgett, as the largest silk manufacturer in Derby, responded to the effect that he would provide work for pauper girls aged ten to fourteen and also some women, at the following rates: 1s 6d (8p)-3s 6d (18p) to age twelve; 3s 6d-5s 0d age twelve to fourteen; and for women 6s 0d-8s 0d, all per week.[39]

Last, in the absence of anything nearer home for adults of the same period, one Leeds spinning mill in 1836 paid out as follows (average per week per hours): men 21s 6d for 72 hours; women 5s 5½d for 66 hours; children 2s 10¾d for 66 hours.[40]

Comparing the rates offered by Thomas Bridgett to pauper women and children in Derby with those received by the female and child operatives at the Leeds mill, the home figures appear very favourable, possibly due to the large numbers needed in the silk industry here compared to the available work-force.

Conversely, the men's wages might have been depressed in Derby by the same factor. Perhaps we would not be far wrong in proposing a rate of around 18s 0d per week for men in the Derby silk mills. A family with four wage-earners at a silk mill (husband, wife, and, say, son of sixteen and daughter of fourteen) might expect a weekly combined income of around 40s 0d.[41]

But we could easily point to a family such as the following from Upper Brook Street (in the vicinity of Rykneld Mills), for whom life must have been truly a struggle: John Leake, ribbon-weaver, age thirty-six; wife Elizabeth (at home) thirty-one; sons John and James, age three and five months respectively; daughter Julia age two.[42] One meagre wage-packet for a young family of five!

If we go forward beyond the 1840s, workers in general could look to a rise in wages across all trades between 1850 and 1870 of fifty per cent if previously badly-paid work is included, by thirty per cent if not. However, the rise in the cost of living more than took away the benefit up to 1865, followed by better times.

By 1870, it has been calculated that working families would have been better off by an average of ten per cent compared with 1850.[43]

But again, bitter trade recessions like that of 1878-9, described by G.Phillips Bevan in an article in 'The Times' on the New Year 1879, as a period of depression and distress previously unknown to that generation and forecasting the wholesale destruction of manufacturing industry, a gain on such a tentative scale could indeed be precarious.[44] Have we been here before sometime?

Other Industries

After this lengthy case-study of what was, at least at the beginning of the Victorian century, Derby's most prestigious trade, a look at some of the town's other workplaces is now overdue.

First, a glance at a variety of industries related to Derby's earlier gentrified Georgian existence, to the age of elegant country and town houses, their costly decoration and fittings and outreach coaches. From Regency times, the Old Crown Derby China Factory was re-sited on King Street, continuing to prosper from discerning customers.[45]

An important industry was that of paint-making or colour-grinding, to which the coming of the railways gave a new boost. There were six firms of some size, with three, namely Mason, Pegg and Leech at the very end of our period, of some consequence.[46] In Regency times, the firm of James Mason was well established on the Markeaton Brook, opening an imposing new works on the Burton Road in the 1870s. The firm of Robert Pegg was based on the Morledge, with a gypsum and plaster department on the Uttoxeter Old Road.

These firms were being overtaken by Jubilee Year by the firm of Leech, headed by two brothers, the elder of whom we have already encountered as an enabling factor for the Great Northern Railway. Also related to the 'county' past was the coach-building firm of Messrs Holmes with their impressive triple-stacked works on London Road. This firm obtained the benediction of the Royal Warrant and also a real queenly visit in 1852.[47]

We have already encountered the founder's grandson as a fairly predictable opponent of the tramcar in 1879. A good example of the firm's laconic advertising style appears in 'The Nottingham and Derby Railway Companion' of 1839: *Manufactory For Fashionable CARRIAGES & HORSES, London Road, Derby. Herbt & Alfd Holmes.* One assumes they had little to prove!

There were also several firms of clockmakers, in particular that of Whitehurst which ended with the death of the last of the line in Queen Street in 1855, carrying the legacy of the circle of practical-minded intellectuals who had graced and stimulated the town's life in the times of Joseph Wright and Erasmus Darwin.[48]

At a time of triumphant competition from the French and the Swiss, the firm of John Smith was started in 1850 on the Whitehurst hearth. The other firm of importance was Edward Johnson and Son, which began shortly after that of Smith.[49]

Finally in this group of trades was the firm of John Davis and Company, manufacturers of mining implements, microscopes and barometers, which we have already unwittingly glanced at in our survey of Irongate in 1849. About 30 years later they expanded into a factory on the other side of All Saints'.

There were also industries which were related to the products of the country house estates around Derby, in retreat before the unstoppable tide of development. The town retained its connections with the countryside, perhaps mutely symbolised by its whole elongated shape along the routeway from the mid-Derbyshire uplands towards the Trent Valley, swelling for an instant in the middle in the Market Place.

There was a venerable firm of tanners, that of Richardson, which started off in the seventeenth century in Smalley to the north, and no less than five prominent cornmillers, maltsters and brewers. Their activities were again concentrated in a zone to the north-west of the centre. The Sowters of Castle Donington, to the south, dominated this scene in the Regency period from their mill in Curzon Street, joined later in the century by Forman's mill.

The Sowters also ran the mill named after them on the river adjacent to the Old Silk Mills at the north end of that venerable site. The Lowe family had a brewery in the Wardwick which was then sold to Alton and Company, who expanded it greatly in the 1870s, so that the twin stacks and triple maltings gables with protruding hoists must have dominated this street so near the centre of town. Lastly, there were the Strettons, who built the magnificent maltings on Surrey Street, off the Ashbourne Road.[50]

A separate industry which rates at least a follow-up mention from Regency times is the manufacture of plaster of Paris using as raw material the prolific resource of Chellaston gypsum. The firm of John Brookhouse was well established on the banks of the Derwent by the beginning of the century. Its huddle of cottage-like workshop roofs and stumpy kilns are the subject of a fascinating painting by H.L.Pratt in 1846 against the backdrop of the early nineteenth-century architectural highlights of the town.[51]

Otherwise, prominent amongst Derby industry were the foundries which received tremendous stimulous from the coming of the railway. We have already encountered the Harrisons of Bridge Gate with their proudly extensive range of products, a firm which had started up in the previous century.

There was one other in early competition with them, further down the slope nearer the Derwent in Duke Street, Weatherhead, Glover and Company. They started in 1818, a time when there would be a substantial demand for iron products suitable for installation and use in houses with the numerous Regency villas going up on the outskirts as the town centre succumbed to the effects of industry.[52]

The Duke Street works, named the Britannia Foundry, early established a reputation for cast-iron windows and garden ornaments.[53] For example, the gothically functional windows of St John's, Bridge Street, built ten years later, were made here. By 1843, the firm was owned by Thomas Wright, under whom it made the cast-iron temple in the gardens at Alton Towers for the Earl of Shrewsbury.[54] However, the arrival of the railway gave the opportunity for the manufacture of equipment and rolling stock for a period of about thirty years until the Midland Railway's own plant ousted all outside competition.[55]

In 1848 the foundry was taken over by Scotsman Andrew Handyside. Under his direction, it achieved an international reputation after exhibiting some of its products at the Great Exhibition of 1851 and receiving a medallion for its efforts there.[56]

From these premises, only a stone's throw from old St Mary's Bridge Chapel, came a series of bridges, stations and port installations worldwide, including examples in South America, Japan, Russia and Australia.[57] Train sheds at St Enoch's Station, Glasgow and the Central Stations at Manchester and Liverpool were followed by the feats on the Great Northern line on the doorstep which we have already surveyed.[58]

Despite all this achievement, today the firm would not be considered a large one, with an 1858 complement of 270 men and boys. Incidentally, the average weekly wage for this payroll was £1. Handyside himself continued to work right up until his death from bronchitis at the age of eighty-one in our Jubilee Year of 1887. His firm continued in existence for a further twenty-four years.[59]

This northern riverside front of the town was the prime early iron-working location in position to benefit from the very early days of the railway before a more general move on the part of newer firms in the middle of our period to trackside sites to the south-east of the centre.

On the opposite, eastern bank of the river to Handyside's was the old already-encountered firm of James Fox. This came up with what, according to one modern authority, could have been the very first 'effective production gear-cutting machine'.[60] From gear-cutting, it turned to railway equipment before a take-over in the 1870s by the giant Haslam combination to be described below.[61]

In 1834, right by the far end of St Mary's Bridge, the Pheonix Foundry was started by James Hayward. Its main output was stoves, grates and ranges, for which, as we shall see, it had more than one competitor but also a richly expanding market with the frantic terrace and villa building of the Victorian years.[62]

For the same purpose, in 1851 another Scotsman, Robert Russell, with local man Henry Fowke, set up the Peel Foundry a little further down river on Meadow Road, opposite the Morledge.[63] Finally, in 1865 came Haslam's back in City Road next to Fox's, which they soon went on to absorb. It began with the production of hydraulic machinery but, much more significantly, went on to dry-air equipment for refrigeration, which was adapted for use on ocean steamers and so transformed the trade in imported meat and in consequence household diet and even farming endeavour.

This was the product, from 1881, of the Union Foundry on the river bank right opposite Handyside's works with its GNR loop-line. From the foreground setting of Chester Green with its fringe of trees, this foundry was an imposing if overly-massive presence, with its procession of tall round-headed windows on either side of an imperious clock tower entrance, and long ranges of workshops stretching riverwards beneath two sentinel stacks. Its complement of workers was almost double that of the Britannia Foundry.

All this development on the east bank of the Derwent, opposite and slightly to the north of the main body of the town, must have had an enormous environmental impact, possibly more devastating to the distant prospect of Derby than any other single change.

In the previous century, the riverside approach to Derby was a particularly pleasing one to travellers. The tower of All Saints rose behind the Tuscan bell tower of the Silk Mill and the picturesque gables of the chapel, flanking the balustered bridge whose elegant arch spanned waters which, in Celia Fiennes', phrase still *ran by the town*. No more: the cathedrals of industry will have shattered this genteel view for ever. There can surely be nothing more remarkable than the hand of time!

There were three other employers of note positioned away from the river in an approximate triangle on this northern side of Derby. Furthest out in Brook

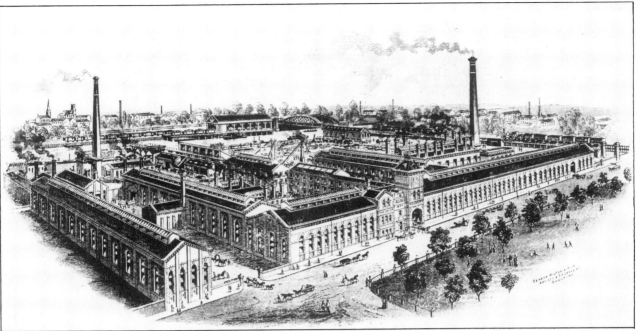

Haslam's Union Foundry in City Road, Little Chester. It was built in 1865, next to Fox's which it soon absorbed.

Eastwood and Frost's foundry on Cotton Lane. With its close proximity to the railway it was not surprising that from 1864, by then known as Eastwood and Swingler, it was making specialist track equipment.

Street and therefore in the thick of the old silk manufacturing zone and also near the Markeaton Brook, was the firm of William Abell, dating from the 1850s, suppliers of silk mill machinery and also attractive cast-iron street furniture.

Around the corner in Nun's Street, then from 1862 in King's Street, was Smith's brass foundry. In Friar Gate, the gas-lighting and piping firm of Thomas Crump had its headquarters, the head of the firm later becoming general manager of the town's Gas Company in the same location.[64]

The firms whose fortunes were more directly bound up with the railway were sited on the Midland Station side of town. The first such foundry came ten years after that famous structure was begun: Jobson's (from Sheffield) in Litchurch Lane, then Cotton Lane. This works specialised in the production of domestic grates like the Phoenix Foundry to the north.

Three years later, in 1852, came Eastwood and Frost's foundry, also in Cotton Lane after a brief flirtation with the crowded riverside Morledge setting. With a number of changes during the next few years, when Frost, a local man, set up on his own making railway-wheel axles, the firm from 1864 became known as Eastwood and Swingler, producing specialist track equipment.

Again to Litchurch Lane in 1860, from down south in Southwark, came George Fletcher to establish the Masson Foundry; it made steam engines and sugar-refining equipment. Lastly, corresponding to Haslam's in the north, although a decade later in 1874, Ley's malleable castings foundry was established under a director who had trained with Andrew Handyside.[65]

No account of employment opportunities in Derby during Victorian times would be complete without some direct reference to the Midland Railway itself. Derby obviously became a railway town, so strong was the contribution of this company to its prosperity and life.

Apart from the contracts with several of the concerns already mentioned, to supply equipment and stock to the Midland in its early period of the 1840s, the fortunes of two others were transformed by the opportunity offered. One was William Bemrose, the Market Place printers whose pay roll of twelve workers employed in 1840 on the basic task of printing and bookselling increased to fifty-seven in 1855 and to 228 in 1871, when a contract for railway timetables was secured. Success necessitated new enlarged premises on Wellington Street, a huge barrack-like enclave of four-storey ranges on three sides and a tall smoke-stack on the fourth, all within another stone's throw of the Midland Station. The other was James Smith, Cheapside tailor only since 1839, who obtained the contract to make the uniforms for the Midland Railway staff in 1844.[66]

The range of repair and maintenance workshops which we saw established around the station in 1840 were not long in turning to the manufacture of the company's own engines and rolling stock after the amalgamation. Two personalities were very much responsible for this development and, consequently, the fact that by 1877, when a new Carriage and Wagon Works was opened, the whole railway assemblage covered an area larger than that of the whole town in the middle ages.

These men were Superintendant Matthew Kirtley and General Manager James Allport. Kirtley came to Derby from the North-East, in 1844 at the age of thirty-one after experience with the world's two most famous early railways, the Stockton to Darlington and the Liverpool to Manchester. He never left his adopted town, continuing to live near the station at 22 Railway Terrace and dying here in 1873. Under his direction the Midland Railway trains came to be hauled exclusively by Derby locomotives constructed in the Company's own works.

Allport was responsible for the policy of building the company's own carriages, starting with just two in 1850. After 1877 came the new plush third-class carriages which replaced, amidst much antediluvian criticism, the old second-class numbers, as it was an article of faith of his that the humble masses should be encouraged to venture far from home through a policy of cheap fares. He also introduced Pullman cars to the company's range after an eye-opening visit to the United States.[67]

By 1887, therefore, the influence of the Midland on the fortunes of the town more than corresponded to that of the Old Silk Mills on those of the Derby of over a century-and-a-half earlier.

Looking back on this brief survey of a vast range of employment opportunities in the fifty years since the railway burst upon Derby, one aspect might easily be forgotten without the aid of prints of the time. Impressions of foundries in particular, and perhaps more especially those in the vicinity of the railway tracks, seem to portray a sky blackened with the outpouring of a host of chimney stacks. Not on the same scale as celebrated views of the 'Black Country' perhaps, but enough for us to reflect upon the environmental impact, including that upon working citizens, of economic growth in the age of coal and steam. It is now also, nearing the end of the succeeding century, a world we, in this respect at the very least, have thankfully lost.

In Dispute

There was obviously plenty of employment in Derby for most of the time during the period of our survey. But not all the time, which, given the imbalance in resources between employer and employed, was very much harder for the latter. Therefore relationships between employer/master and employee were sometimes sour, never more so than in 1833-4, the period of the so-called Silk Mill Lock-Out.

During this affair, Derby was the centre of interest of everyone in Britain concerned in any way with what we have come to refer to as industrial relations. It was a premier trial of strength between employer and employee in the aftermath of an Act of Parliament eight years earlier which had cancelled an earlier law of 1799 against the very existence of trades unions in a time of war against Revolutionary France. Its repeal in 1825 resulted in a mushroom growth of primitive trades unionism, but Parliament in effect held a sword of Damocles over their heads in the shape of a prohibition against any pressure to get workers to join by means of the administration of secret oaths.

Such oaths were familiar in the world of freemasonry but their more general application was looked upon with a world of suspicion by those in authority. Any admission of the practice taking place could be seized on by hostile magistrates and employers in a combination of their own to launch criminal proceedings against union leaders. At the same time, in a period of trade depression, the practical socialist philosopher Robert Owen was attempting a grand combination of the numerous disparate unions covering many different trades on the principal that unity is strength.

It was as part of his umbrella organisation that union members in Derby used an incident at a silk mill in the town - not the Old Silk Mills — as the focus for a trial of strength with the masters. Their hopes concerning the outcome of such a course of action were over-optimistic, possibly naive in the circumstances of the time.

On 21 November 1833, 'The Derby and Chesterfield Reporter' carried the following in its editorial column:

Appearances indicate an approaching struggle between the operatives of this town and their employers, which, we are afraid, will be attended with an almost total suspension of business for a time, unless a compromise take place. During the past week it is said that upwards of 800 of the workmen have joined the Trades' union, and entered into engagements with each other, under an oath, which is imposed upon every member; but the terms of this contract are kept a profound secret.

Their object, however, is understood to be the protection of labour, and for this purpose they have adopted the forms and ceremonies of the Freemasons or Oddfellows. These proceedings, connected with what has transpired at Manchester, Leeds, and other places, have aroused the attention of the manufacturers, who have had several meetings during the week, but nothing has transpired regarding their intentions. It appears, however, the workmen themselves are apprehensive their employers will follow the example of the Leeds manufacturers, and try to break up the Union by refusing to employ any of the members.

On Tuesday last, Mr Frost, the silk manufacturer, discharged one of his hands; for what reason we have not heard, but as soon as it was heard in the manufactory, every member of the Union left his employment, and refused to return, unless the discarded workman was taken on again. With this Mr Frost refused to comply, and they all left, in consequence his works have been standing ever since.

This clear and graphic account of the start of the Lock-Out, or 'Turn-Out' as we shall see it referred to in Union circles, needs some gloss to be fully appreciated. The context of a wider struggle in the North of England should be noted. The workers' fears were fully realised in the Derby affair in the response of the employers, as we shall see.

The reported incident was at the silk mill of Frost and Stevenson in City Road[68] and the alleged cause the sacking of a worker who refused to be disciplined by a fine for faulty work. The precise date of this happening seems to be far from clear. Different secondary sources put it variously as 19 and 21 November 1833. However, if the above report is to be taken at its face value, since the 'Reporter' came out on a Thursday and the report is dated 21 November, the reference to *Tuesday last* puts the date of the start of the Lock-Out as 19 November. However that may be, the effect of the stoppage was registered in the editorial of the same paper a month later, 12 December:

We regret to say that the numbers of the Trades' Union in this Borough, are still 'out'. There are now in consequence about 800 men, women, and children, out of employment. Most of the manufacturers are doing a little, partly with their old hands, but chiefly with new ones. It may, however, be taken for granted, that with so large a number of persons out of employment very little business can be done. The privation of the hands must be very great. We sincerely wish they would abandon everything like compulsion or coercion towards their employers in the terms of their Union, then there could be no obstacle to an amicable return to their employment.

Two points perhaps need emphasising here, the references to the response of the employers in replacing union members with others willing to take their place and also the 'privation' into which the workers' action was taking themselves and their families. The 'Reporter' it should be added, was in general more favourably disposed towards the unionists than its rival the 'Mercury'.

In the meantime, on 23 November, the employers had met at the King's Head in the Corn Market to settle their response. They seized on the secret oath which prospective union members had to take as vitiating their otherwise legitimate purpose. In consequence, twenty of the 'masters' passed a resolution published in the local Press which included the following:

That each of them will cease to employ every man who is a member of the trade Union, and will not receive or take back into his service any man who continues to be a member of that Union or any other Union having similar objects.

That the resolution is adopted on the deliberate conviction that a prompt and vigorous and persevering resistence to the Trade Union is absolutely necessary to protect the joint interests of the master, to preserve the commerce of the County, and to secure the true interests of the workers themselves.[69]

There was, therefore, total divide, no possiblity of compromise. One of the signatories was William Taylor of the Old Silk Mills and it may have been due to the fame of his factory that national interest in the dispute was aroused so quickly.[70] The course of the Lock-Out was extensively reported not only in the local Press but also in the two union journals of the time which had only just been established and in fact would barely outlast the dispute itself, 'The Pioneer or Trades' Union Magazine' and 'The Crisis', the organ of Owen's Grand National Consolidated Trades' Union (GNCTU).

On 28 December, 'The Pioneer' reported a total of 1,447 people involved in the Turn-Out at Derby, all but sixty-two of them belonging to the silk and lace industries and 'small-ware weavers'. The other sixty-two were members of the building trade.

The textile workers consisted of 430 men, 498 women and 454 children. The total number affected was claimed to be 1,800, although there is no other direct evidence known to the author to back up Davison's statement in his 'Derby, Its Rise and Progress' (1906) that many other trades were also involved in the dispute. Considering the total population of the town at the time, however, this was still a formidable number. The strikers received 7s 0d (35p) per week from national union levies.[71]

The practical arm of the employers' resolution was the replacement of strikers by other workers. This, of course, raised the temperature of the dispute considerably. 'The Pioneer' issue of 8 January 1834 carried the following notice, prefacing a list of names:

BLACK SHEEP

Mr Peet, in the small-ware way of Derby, has been to London, and engaged the annexed list of hands, from the neighbourhood of Bethnal Green. He gave them forty pots of strong ale at starting from London. Beds are prepared for them to sleep in the manufactory in which they are to work.

There was also a report, dated 8 January, of an interview with one of the men on the list near Spitalfields, claiming that he (Benjamin Mayblin) had been deceived by Peet into thinking he was going to work in a brand-new factory, hence the adverts.

When we arrived at Derby, Lord, how ashamed I was! We were hooted and hissed by the women and children at the entrance of the factory in a dreadful manner. When we got inside the building, there was an excellent dinner of roast beef etc, but I would not eat a bit of it . . .We were locked in night and day like prisoners on board the hulks. However, I and Sleeth managed to get over the wall yesterday morning, and made our 'lucky' to London; and you'll soon see some, if not all, the others here shortly . . .

The result was accusations of intimidation against strike-breakers, prosecutions and sentences of imprisonment of up to three months.[72] On the evening of Saturday, 8 February there was a skirmish between strike-breakers returning from the Seven Stars public house to their quarters in Peet and Frost's mill and a party of strikers, which ended in one of the latter being killed. At the March Assizes the assailant was condemned to death but had his sentence commuted to transportation for life.[73]

On 2 January 1834, the great Robert Owen visited Derby, as 'The Crisis' reported: *No public notice was given of this meeting, but such is the organisation of the working classes in 'Union', that although but a few hours' notice was given of the intention of Mr Owen to address them, the Lancasterian School-room was crowded to excess before the business of the meeting commenced.*

He, in fact, attempted a reconciliation by meeting both sides separately, but to no avail. Each continued to hold out with dogged determination. 'The Pioneer', on 1 February and 8 March, reported two forms of help afforded to the strikers whose situation must have been getting ever more desperate. The first concerned the produce of the workshops which the Union following Owenite principles organised to gainfully employ the strikers:

TO CORRESPONDENTS

Persons wishing to purchase Derby Union goods are informed that the females of Derby have forwarded to Birmingham a variety of caps, shirts, etc, for sale. Till further arrangements are made, application must be made at the Town-hall Tavern, Ann-street. Petrification ornaments of all descriptions for sale, or made to order.

Native Derbyshire produce in the cause of solidarity! The second report concerned the mobilisation of more general working-class sympathy in the form of the Friendly Societies which were the humble contemporary response to the absence of any form of national insurance:

SUBSCRIPTIONS

At a special meeting of the members of 'The Christian Friendly Society', held at the school-rooms adjoining the Brook-street Chapel, Derby, on Wednesday the 12 February 1834, the sum of £5 5s was unanimously agreed to be given from the funds of the said society, to the relief of the Derby turned-outs: and a resolution agreed to, that the regular contributions from the members of this society turned out of employ, through connections with the Trades Unions, be not demanded, while such members continue out of employ; and that the proceedings of this meeting be inserted in 'The Pioneer'.

JOHN CHOLERTON, Sec.

By March, the resolve of the strikers was beginning to break, as the following extract from 'The Pioneer' of 22 March seems to indicate:

THE PIONEER TO THE MASTERS OF DERBY GENTLEMEN — We are now in a position to soften down a little, and we appeal to you as men, possessing some portion of common sense, whether you think it prudent to carry on this absurd struggle till ruin lays its reputation on your pillow. You know too well

that the men will not disgrace their manhood by complying with your intolerant terms . . .We assure you, on our part, that there shall be no display of victory, no irritating show of conquest . . .It is in vain for you to hope to crush the spirit of Union. Indeed, you have in a great measure been instrumental in forming the Grand National Consolidated Trades' Union.

Some insight into the condition of the strikers and their families that undoubtedly prompted this appeal may be gained by a further consideration of Medical Officer Fox's evidence to the Factory Acts Committee upon the dependence of the silk workers' households on the income brought in by their children.

Mills were now working at least part-time with the aid of the numerous strike-breakers whilst only two days earlier the Derby Press carried reports of the incident which has subsequently become far more famous but which the Derby Lock-Out pre-dates by several months, at least in its inception. This was the case of the Tolpuddle Martyrs, who caught the full rebound from Derby of the magistrate-employer combination in a rural setting against the taking of 'secret oaths'. Derby faded out of the national scene.

The strike is generally believed to have ended on 21 April 1834, when a majority of the participants were taken on again by the masters, although 600 were left in the cold.[74] The state in which the unequal contest left them in can perhaps be gauged by the following extract from a letter by a G.B.Mart, thanking the cordwainers of Northampton for their subscription, published in 'The Pioneer' on 31 May: *I do assure you there are at this time several hundreds of people in this town that have not the means to obtain a morsel of bread.*

However, one modern commentator maintains the strike actually lasted two months longer into June, although the present writer has been unable to uncover any clear evidence for this[75]. Could the following letter, also by G.B.Mart, published in 'The Pioneer' on 17 May indicate a longer struggle than has hitherto been generally accepted?

The masters here boast that they have crushed the Union; but I assure you it is not the case. There were nine hundred men in Union in Derby during the Turn-Out, who were never discharged from their employment; and I do think the masters dare not discharge them . . .Several of the petty despots say, that if they could find out who the leaders were, they would send them after their brethren of Dorchester.

On the other hand, Mr Mart does refer to the dispute in the past tense here. Also of interest is the cross reference at the end to the Tolpuddle Martyr case, tried and sentenced to transportation at Dorchester.

As a postscript to this inevitably brief account of a major incident in Derby's history, it may be worthwhile sampling the opinion of someone who might, from the evidence before us, be described as an educated citizen of the time, obviously a man of means, not directly involved, but with the perspective of the 'political' set, those who prided themselves as having a stake in the country without necessarily wishing the existence of too many holders of stakes.

In other words, perhaps we have here the view of the equivalent to the average informed voter of the time on this very important issue. He is perhaps replete with anti-union prejudice and resonating with one of the less pleasant aspects of the decade we ourselves have just lived through with its concept of 'the enemy within'.

It is a long letter published in 'The Derby and Chesterfield Reporter' for 23 January 1834, occupying a whole column, signed *A PEACE MAKER* and dated 21 January.

He begins by finding fault on both sides of the Derby dispute but spends half the letter blasting the effect of the quarrel on the country and its integrity. On the one hand: *There is, I am convinced, a great fault to be found with many masters; in many cases they have not given their workmen a fair remuneration for the overplus of labour they have exacted from them; indeed I have seen many instances where a poor man has risen up early, and late taken rest, for a bare maintenance.*
On the other: *There is in these Unions a spirit of tyrannical dictation, which in a free country, cannot be tolerated . . .*

He maintains they cripple the commerce of the country and that the joiners and bricklayers who call a 'turn-out' are better paid than *many of the clergy and gentry of the kingdom.* Unions lead to the moral degeneration of many young men: *The place of meeting is generally a public house; thus the hitherto sober man is insensibly led into habits of intemperance, and his ears become habituated to those sounds of blasphemy and obscenity which once he would have shuddered to hear.*

Above all, the strife between masters and men is putting the country at peril. As a result of an extensive European tour some years previously (*I was in Russia, Poland, Germany, Austria, France and Italy*) he is convinced there is universal detestation of Britain because of her prosperity. War against her would be very popular, hence dissention is putting the country at mortal risk!

And a final indication, although not from Derby, that the Lock-Out may perhaps have been part of a general 'spirit of the times' which might even have caused the faintest tingeing of the atmosphere in a country house or two on the edge of the town: the 'Derby Mercury' for 7 May published a reprint of a circular letter to 'The Times' in London from Sarah Browne, Secretary to the Grand United Lodge of Operative Ladies' Maids, under the heading *Strike amongst the Ladies' Maids* (an area of four miles' radius from Grosvenor Square was mentioned).

Ms Browne gives notice to employers of a response to *the ruinous effects of a destructive fashionable competition,* imposing on behalf of her members such conditions as: *No sister shall brush, plait, or dress her lady's hair, or wait upon her in sickness — except for such remuneration as each sister shall deem it expendient to ask. No sister shall be called before ten in the morning, nor shall any sister remain in a service where she is refused a fire in her own room, an arm chair, a subscription to a circulating library, the free use of her lady's clothes, and as many followers as she may wish to retain.*

She concludes: *It only remains for me to add, that your lady's maids, members of this society, will cease to answer your bell, though you may ring it ever so often, should you decline to act upon the new*

regulations; and, further I think it right to apprise you, that in that case they will no longer think it necessary to keep any family secrets with which they have made themselves acquainted.
What more could one say?

The Silk Mill Lock-Out clearly involved the old mill on the Derwent to a minimal degree. We can only speculate whether the payroll there set down by the 'Factory Acts Committee Report' six years later, with its total complement of workers of eighteen years and under, applied also to the time of the dispute and in turn was likely to render its participation unlikely.

In itself, the dispute was a tragic failure; but given the undemocratic nature of Government at the time and the disposition of the economy to dip and rise periodically in distressing slump and boom, it could not be the last incidence of unrest during our period. The Lock-Out must at the very least have raised awareness of on-going issues enormously, having regard to relative remuneration for effort, distribution of wealth and the underlying causes of the ills of the time.

Much of this residual insight must have been tapped by the Chartist Movement for extension of the vote during the 1840s. There was a visit to Derby on Sunday, 26 June 1842, of the great Chartist leader Feargus O'Connor, editor of the Movement's journal 'The Northern Star', to address a meeting at the Theatre, Bold Lane.[76] The 'Derby Mercury' evidently did not see fit to send a reporter along, possibly because of the invasion of the Sabbath.

At this time also, there was great distress amongst those textile workers, in particular the framework-knitters, who had for so long resisted the meagre blandishments of mill employment and were now in desperate straits. Charity was the only conceivable remedy to those in authority. In 1839, Mayor John Sandars started a fund for their relief, or at least those whose pride was sufficiently flexible as to accept it. This, as we shall see, was not a universal psychological trait. But overall, as the historian Asa Briggs has pointed out, the late 1830s and the early 1840s was a period of social and economic crisis, alleviated by a boom in the mid-1840s.[77]

There was trouble again in 1861, this time on account of another textile group who had refused for whatever circumstances or reasons to read the signs of the time. These were the weavers who, in February 1861, evidently fought back against uneven competition by picketing Bridgett's monster silk mill.

In a report of a court case on 27 February, the 'Mercury' states that three weavers were charged with *unlawfully intimidating by means of certain language, and otherwise obstructing, Joseph Cooper, thereby endeavouring to force him to depart from his employment.*

As part of his evidence Cooper stated: *I am one of the men that have gone to work for Bridgett & Co. I went last Thursday morning, the reason being that I have a wife and eight children who were all starving. I was offered 22s 6d a week, and all I could earn above that sum. I took it. After dinner I was going to work again, when I saw Milner and a great crowd at the corner of Peet's manufactory. They 'bah'd' me, and when I went into a shop for some snuff in*

Bridge-street, Milner said, 'Give the ------- some poison to stop his head up.

The reporter noted the crowd of weavers in court approved of the light sentence of binding over for the sum of £10 at the express wish of the employee. But there was more trouble in April when a crowd attacked a strike-breaker and his host. In the evidence of Sergeant Green as reported in the 'Mercury': *There was a mob of a thousand persons, and the man's windows and door had been battered with stones (in Whitecross-street) that lay about in all directions. I and the officers walked with Mr Bridgett to the mill, and stones and brick-ends were showered upon us all the way. A part of a brick struck me on the shoulder and cut my coat.*

The strike was evidently still on in June as the 'Mercury' carried a report on the 5th of that month of a brutal assault on a strike-breaking weaver who had come to Derby a week previously to work at Bridgett's mill again. It happened near Kedleston Street as he was returning on foot from a Saturday afternoon outing to Allestree.

Other reports and a letter from the local Union secretary provide evidence of a dispute with Bridgett's over stoppages from pay and of layings-off which had the result of bringing down the average wage paid out to well below the going rate alleged by the employers. Mills were also working on the Bank Holiday at the request of the weavers, presumably in order to supply them with enough raw material to give them a bare subsistence.

In general, according to Briggs, the 1850s and 1860s were a period of great economic growth.[78] It was succeeded in the late 1870s, as we have already seen, by yet another slump. Sadly, poverty and unemployment were still there in our Jubilee Year of 1887. On 19 January the 'Mercury' reported a meeting in Becket Street to discuss what was obviously a crisis. In contrast to the Mayor, who had previously given it as his opinion that there was no necessity for the doling out of relief, his deputy admitted that the *distress seemed to be increasing day by day.* A member of the Board of Guardians (ie of the poor Law) reported that: *A large number of men were out of employment. There had been a scarcity of employment during the past summer and autumn, so that many persons had nothing to fall back upon now the inclement weather had thrown them out of work, but he knew there were scores of men who would dispose of all they possessed before asking either privately or publicly for assistance.*

A Mr Kelly asked: *What was the use of his taking a gallon of soup from the Morledge to his house in Kensington-street if he had no coals to warm it up.*

It was resolved that a deputation should see the Mayor: *The Guardians were in a difficult position and did the best they could. There were now 340 receiving out-door relief more than last year, and then the number was extraordinary. Besides this they had been compelled by force of necessity to turn thirty or forty married men out of the workhouse to make room for older people. It seemed very hard to offer men the stone yard, but there were certain lines laid down for them to go upon, and they had no alternative.*

A deputation attended by 400 people waited upon the Mayor at the Town Hall the next day, 14 January, to persuade him to re-open the Charity Fund started by his predecessor of forty years earlier. He resisted, contending that a soup kitchen was more appropriate. At the same time, the Charity Organisation Society reported seventy-nine requests for relief during the previous twelve months, of which thirty-one were ruled out as undeserving.

The soup kitchen was opened in the Morledge that evening, with 400 tickets-worth prepared, but in the event a lot was left over. However, 520 tickets were distributed for the following Tuesday (18th). The cost of the soup kitchen was £30 a week and £20 was set aside for children's dinners.

Here we have a glimpse of the underlying void beneath the work-force of Victorian Derby in an age innocent of the Welfare State. On whatever high note we may choose to end our survey of this extraordinary Victorian town story of growth and activity, we should never entirely brush the shadows from our minds, the agenda of social justice even yet only partially addressed. But perhaps it is now high time we looked at what are today the most visible achievements of this three-quarter century, and mainly in central Derby.

Notes

1. Dr W.J.Richardson, article in *The Derbyshire Advertiser*, October 1954, quoted in H.Butterton, op.cit.

2. J.Farey, *View of the Agriculture and Minerals of Derbyshire*, 1811-17.

3. Frank Nixon, *Industrial Archaeology of Derbyshire*, 1969, with reference to Cotchett's mill on the same site (Bill of Sale, 1802).

4. *The Oddfellows Companion and Guide to Derby*, 1892.

5. Report to the General Board of Health, op.cit.

6. J.V.Beckett, *The East Midlands From A.D.1,000*, 1988.

7. *Report to the General Board of Health*, op.cit.

8. H.Butterton, op.cit.

9. Maxwell Craven, op.cit.

10. H.Butterton, op.cit.

11. *Reports from Select Committees on the Act for the Regulation of Mills and Factories*, 1840, Vol.1 British Parliamentary Papers, Irish University Press.

12. Ibid.

13. Frank Nixon, op.cit.

14. Ibid.

15. J.V.Beckett, op.cit.

16. *Reports from Select Committees, op.cit.*

17. Ibid.

18. Ibid.

19. Ibid.

20. Ibid.

21. Ibid.

22. Ibid.

23. Ibid.

24. Ibid.

25. Ibid.

26. Ibid.

27. Ibid.

28. H.Butterton, op.cit.

29. *Reports from Select Committees, op.cit.*

30. Ibid.

31. Ibid.

32. *Report to the General Board of Health*, op.cit.

33. *Reports from Select Committees*, op.cit.

34. Ibid.

35. Ibid.

36. H.Butterton, op.cit.

37. *Reports from Select Committees*, op.cit.

38. Ibid.

39. WEA extra-mural class research report in *Derbyshire Miscellany*, Spring 1972.

40. J.F.C.Harrison, *Early Victorian Britain 1832-51*, 1971.

41. H.Butterton, op.cit.

42. Census Ennumerators' Returns, 1851.

43. Woodward, *The age of Reform 1815-70, 1960*.

44. Quoted by Roy Christian in an article for the *Derby Evening Telegraph* Centenary Edition Supplement, July 1979.

44. Maxwell Craven, op.cit.

45. Ibid.

46. Ibid.

47. Ibid.

48. Ibid.

49. Ibid.

50. Ibid.

51. Ibid.

52. Ibid.

53. Roy Christian, op.cit.

54. P.W.Parkin, op.cit.

55. Roy Christian, op.cit.

56. P.W.Parkin, op.cit.

57. Ibid.

58. Roy Christian, op.cit.

59. P.W.Parkin, op.cit.

60. Frank Nixon, op.cit. quoted Maxwell Craven, op.cit.

61. Maxwell Craven, op.cit.

62. Ibid.

63. Ibid.

64. Ibid.

65. Ibid.

66. Roy Christian, op.cit.

67. Ibid.

68. *Derby Mercury* 27 November 1883 and Pigot's *Directory of Derbyshire* 1835 (Pigot 1831 has the address as Chester Rd.).

69. Centenary Article by A.Sturgess, 1934.

70. Ibid.

71. Ibid.

72. Ibid.

73. Maxwell Craven, op.cit, after Davison, op.cit.

74. Ibid.

75. Article by Graham Stevenson in 150th Anniversary Booklet, 1984.

76. Davison, op.cit.

77. Asa Briggs, op.cit.

78. Ibid.

I am also indebted to Mr Stevenson for drawing my attention to the Union journals of the time.

Important Buildings and Streets

GRADUALLY the Derby skyline came to reflect some pride in what the product of industry could facilitate, as well as the means of doing so. New cupolas, towers, domes and spires joined magnificent old All Saints' in contrast to the smoke-stacks as focus for the approaching visitor.

The streets of the town centre received more than mere cosmetic treatment in order to reflect its thrusting prosperity. Broadened thoroughfares became flanked with sequences of masonry shaped in some considerable style and which brought brief echoes and reflections of the capital city to a provincial town.

Derby's important structures might be classified into the well-honed divisions of civil and ecclesiastic, representing very different aspects of the age itself. The nineteenth century saw the central urban scene in many towns and cities transformed by imposing, sometimes colossal, monuments to civic pride. They symbolised the achievements of reformed administrations active, in far less circumscribed fashion than has sadly become the norm of late, within their rapidly expanding areas of command. This was especially so in the Midlands and the North, in a hundred pumping hearts of the first Industrial Revolution. Images of St George's Hall in Liverpool and of the mighty civic 'seats' in Glasgow, Manchester, Leeds, Bradford or Birmingham swell in the mind in humble acknowledgement of the peculiar Victorian splendour.

The scale in Derby was far more modest, but still enough to form most of the highlights of our urban scene, backed up by the sometimes odd towers and pepper-pot turrets of educational and medical institutions, to say nothing of soaring flights of more spiritual fancy.

There were two Guildhall-building episodes in Derby, in 1828 and again in 1842. The structure with which the Town Council members began the century was nearly one hundred years old when, in 1827, they had the opportunity to buy a central plot on the south side of the Market Place on which to put up a new one.

The old version, actually the third there, stood out into the square, restricting the open space available for market activities. So it was demolished and an architect, Matthew Habershon, engaged from London to design the fourth in the Derby succession.[1] From contemporary prints it appears to have been an attractive building, on the model of an ancient Greek temple — all the rage at the time — with four central free-standing pillars with twirling ionic caps holding up a triangular pediment and central clock, all supported on a base-trio of tall round-headed arches. The top of this base within the pillars made a balcony fronted with iron railings, whilst beneath it the three arches, the middle one larger, gave access for carriages to a court. This served as police headquarters and beyond that was a new market area with permanent stalls.

But on the night of 21 October 1841, Habershon's building caught fire and was so badly damaged that yet another guildhall was required. The base of the damaged building could still be used, but the rest of the new structure was completely different. The new architect was Henry Duesbury. Whilst at least one modern commentator finds the result less distinguished than the impression left us of its

Henry Duesbury's Derby Guildhall, built following the disastrous fire of 1841.

46

predecessor, the present writer finds it more distinctive and less blandly similar to a hundred imitation Greek essays all over Britain.

In front of the central archway, Duesbury placed a tower almost 104 feet high which immediately gave it a place on the Derby skyline. The section above the roof of the main block, itself proud with four urns, featured twin belfry lights topped by a clock and capped by a cupola and vane. In contrast to the sequence of first-floor windows in Habershon's design, a stage-set of relief carvings was provided by a sculptor referred to in the 1843 Glover's 'Directory' as 'Mr Bell'. The whole makes a striking appearance in H.L.Pratt's

painting of 1847, set against the rest of the building blocks around the square, likely to be griming rapidly among the proliferating stacks.

Over twenty years later, on Tuesday, 16 February 1864, was laid the *elegantly lettered foundation stone*[2] of the structure which would represent in Derby what was possibly the essence of Victorian originality in architecture, the marriage of design and modern engineering. This was the Market Hall, to squat grandly behind Duesbury's clock-tower. Habershon's covered area behind the previous Guildhall had become unsatisfactory for its purpose.

The first touch for the new building was supplied

The Derby Guildhall of Matthew Habershon was the fourth such building in the Market Place. It was built in 1828, on the south side of the square. On the night of 21 October 1841 it was so badly damaged by fire that yet another guildhall was required, although the base of the damaged one was used in the re-building.

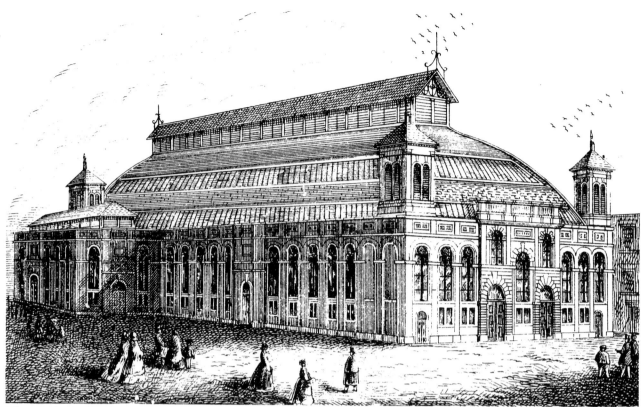

The exterior of Derby Market Hall, designed by T.C.Thorburn, the Borough Engineer, and opened in 1866, by which time his successor, George Thompson, had overseen its completion.

by the Mayor Thomas Roe, the ceremony described thus in a report in the 'Derbyshire Advertiser' for 19 February 1864:

A couple of hours of sunshine in the afternoon of a changeable and stormy day, and a procession consisting of volunteers, Policemen, Town Councillors, Aldermen, the Mayor, supported by two clergymen, followed by the architect bearing the plans of the Market, the Clerk of the Works carrying a polished mallet, and a Chamberlain with the presentation silver trowel on a crimson silk cushion, guarded by sundry members of the police force disguised in long cloaks and three-cornered hats, armed with ancient halberds, with a hundred workmen in their everyday dress, a few more policemen and another company of volunteers, with a good-humoured crowd of lookers-on.

The design of the new building was by Mr T.C.Thorburn, the Borough Engineer. However, because he obtained a new post as Borough Surveyor of Birkenhead before completing the plans, his deputy and successor, Mr George Thompson, was entrusted with the enterprise and was responsible for the final appearance. The offical opening did not therefore take place until 1866. Thompson did, indeed, make some alterations to the original design and was wholly responsible for the interior.

Kelly's 'Directory of Derbyshire' for 1895 contains the following description of the Market Hall:

The building is of red brick with stone dressing, and has four separate approaches: the interior contains 40 shops, each 12 feet square, besides a clear space of 186 feet by 86 feet for stalls; the entire length of the building is 210 feet by 112 feet in breadth; the roof being constructed of wrought-iron ribs, resting

upon 22 pillars 20 feet in height, and covered in with glass and slate.

Behind it was a new fish market and, adjacent to the old so-called Lock-Up Yard, the police station continued in existence. It was apparently a common sight to see the members of the Borough Force doing their physical training on the cobbles there! On the opposite side of the Market Hall, next to a poultry market, live poultry, rabbits, dogs, cats, aquarian fish and many other creatures were to be seen.[3]

Such were the humble and lively scenes on either side of the high Victorian triumph which was the subject of a eulogy published in the Derby Mercury on 16 May 1866, a fortnight before its official opening:

The performances of the Messiah will form a fitting inauguration of one of the finest halls in the Kingdom. Those who have watched the gradual development of the beauty of the new hall will rejoice at the effect which has been produced by the decoration suggested by Mr Owen Jones. The result is most pleasing mainly because the colours are not only well blended, but also because they throw out in an effective manner the striking outlines which arrest the eye.

On the 29th of this month the new hall will be opened by the performance of the greatest composition left us by the immortal Handel, and, in order to influence our readers at a distance to patronise this remarkable inauguration, we state that the building is one of the finest of its kind in the Kingdom, and its erection reflects the highest credit on the spirit and enterprise of the town, though the whole appearance prompts a feeling of regret that so splendid a hall cannot remain available for musical and other assemblages . . .

There are 37 spacious and commodious shops on

*the ground floor which will be principally occupied
by butchers. The galleries extend round the building,
and are 12 feet in width: they are protected by a neatly-
designed, ornamental cast-iron railing . . .The body
of the hall will be filled with stalls of various
descriptions and of the most approved design . . .A
benevolent lady residing in Derby has presented the
Corporation with a handsome and costly drinking
fountain, which it is intended to erect in the middle
of the large hall. We may add that the estimated cost
of the Market Hall complete with fittings, will be near
upon £20,000.*

Which turned out to be an underestimate of about
one-third!

An aspect of Victorian provincial culture is well
illustrated in this extract and which we shall again
encounter in our survey of leisure, the dominance of
George Frederick Handel from the previous century
in the musical life of the time. A fuller description
of the opening ceremonies for the Market Hall will
form part of the final chapter of this book. Of course,
the new building was certainly not destined to become
Derby's concert hall. It quickly became a place of more
mundane occasions as intended, like its predecessor
on the site, as the following plea for mercy in the
'Mercury' for 9 September 1863 against marauding
prams just six months before the stone-laying
ceremony shows, and prompting the speculation
whether such entertainment persisted within the new
hall:

PERAMBULATORS IN PUBLIC

*We have been requested by the Borough Magistrates
to caution the proprietors of perambulators against
pushing them through the market. By a lucky reading
of the law, it has been ruled that perambulators are
not carriages, and therefore the nursery-maids push
them with impunity — and sometimes with
impudence — along our footpaths. But in our long
sufferance we need not be called upon to endure the
presence of these objectionable vehicles in the public
markets. The complaints have been made with such
frequency that some notice must be taken of them
if the nuisance is continued after a public caution.
The petite carriages are generally supposed to be used
for the conveyance of juveniles in order that they may
enjoy the salubrity of Duffield Road, or the brisk
breezes of the hills that lead to Littleover; but the
mothers of Derby never contemplate, we should think,
sending their children into the crowded area we dignify
with the name of the New Market, where fresh air
is by no means plentiful. There, however, every Friday,
numbers of these annoyances have to be encountered,
to the terror of elderly persons whose proverbially poor
feet render them particularly alive to the painful fact
that if 'the French gout is only taste, the English gout
is feeling'.*

Looking at the problem for a moment from the
maids' point of view, it must have been a splendid
way to mix business with pleasure as a lead-up to
the weekend!

Around this central core were a series of building
projects for varied objectives during a period of fifty
years which considerably altered the appearance of
the heart of the town. The most extensive was the
first, representing in effect Derby's first essay in town-
planning on however limited a scale. It amounted to

the re-casting of one of the centre's most important
road junctions, that of the Corn Market with Victoria
Street. The scheme was completed in 1841, only a year
after the Midland Station and the year before the latest
Guildhall. It amounted to the erection of four
buildings in a unified architectural style in an arc
around the corner of the junction. It was really
consequent upon the periodic flooding of the
Markeaton Brook, which until four years previously
had openly run along its route to join the Derwent,
as we have seen, at right angles to the Corn Market,
where it had been crossed by the stone-balustered St
Peter's Bridge at the junction. The street at right angles
to the Corn Market had been really little more than
a brook-side pathway, actually called Brookside until
1837.

That year of the Queen's accession, the Borough
had taken the decision to culvert the brook from St
James' Bridge further up from the river and so cover
it over and make a proper street of it. This, in turn,
led to the clearing of the varied collection of buildings
which occupied the Corn Market-(now) Victoria Street
junction around the old St Peter's Bridge in order
to extend an already active building site on the west
side of the Corn Market so that it would come right
around the corner overlooking the now buried bridge.

The old White Lion Inn had until recently stood
on the active site, where the Derby & Derbyshire Bank
had engaged another London architect, Robert
Wallace, to build them new headquarters. This scheme
was now overtaken by the clearance of the whole
corner-junction site. A competition was announced
by a new company got up for the purpose, called the
Atheneum Society, with Council worthies including
two of the Strutt dynasty prominent, to design club
rooms, a hotel and a Post Office. Wallace won it from
fifty-one other designs and so he was able to extend
his concept for the bank all around the corner. The
Post Office came next to the bank in the Corn Market,
sharing frontage with the Royal Hotel right on the
corner, with the Atheneum club rooms facing west
along Victoria Street at a right-angle.

On the whole, it is an impressive piece of urban
architecture, centred on two large-scale columns with
ironic-twirl caps for the hotel on the corner above
a baluster-topped entrance and with a smaller upper
storey. This was imposingly crowned with the royal
coat-of-arms, and the plainer-fronted Atheneum,
although decorated with processional sculpture by a
London artist, concealed, within, an imperial-sized
ballroom and a lavishly-plastered interior.[4]

The Atheneum ballroom, however, was not the first
elegant interior to be produced by the Victorian age
in Derby. Again in the year of the Queen's accession,
a new hall for the Mechanics' Institute, which had
been established in 1825, was opened on 18 October.
The building containing it was in the Wardwick and
had been bought by the Institution five years earlier.[5]
According to Glover, it boasted a library of 6,000
volumes, a museum and 'philosophical apparatus'.
He describes the hall thus:

*An elegant and spacious room in the Grecian style
of architecture, with fluted pilasters (grooved flat
pillars), 75 feet long, 40 feet wide, and 35 feet high,
lighted by 16 windows, 12 branch gas lights and a
handsome chandelier. The room is ornamented with*

The Royal Corner at the junction of the Corn Market and Victoria Street. The group of buildings included the Athenaeum, Royal Hotel, Post Office and Derbyshire & Derbyshire Banking Company. The Post Office was moved along Victoria Street in 1869.

many valuable paintings, presented by Joseph Strutt, esq.[6]

We shall encounter Strutt's art collection again later in this chapter. One other point of note in this description is the reference to a 'Grecian' or classical style. Taken in conjunction with the pillars of the Royal Hotel and the urns adorning the Guildhall, we see the Victorians' general adoption of stylistic details of the ancient Greek and Roman classical world, sometimes as reinterpreted by the Italians of the sixteenth century, as being the appropriate face of 'wordly' civic concerns. This was in contrast, as we shall also see later in this chapter, to their choice in building for religious and educational purposes.

In 1861, another distinctive addition to the Derby skyline appeared, modestly echoing Duesbury's Guildhall cupola of twenty years earlier. The Corn Exchange, on another if lesser junction of streets,

Albert and Prince's, was designed by Benjamin Wilson, a Sheffield architect, who produced a round drum shape for the corner site with a copper dome above, all topped by a tiny open cupola.[7] The main body had a less attractive warehouse-like appearance though the row of round-headed windows matched the drum entrances.

Almost a further twenty years were to pass before the next building of note was opened with massive celebrations on 28 June 1879. This was the Free Library and Museum on a site in the Wardwick which had previously been occupied in part by a large house where the books that were to form the core of the public loans collection had been housed until then, namely Lockett's House.[8] The construction was also partly dependent upon the belated culverting at the back of it of the central section of Markeaton Brook west of St James' Bridge in the 1870s. Again a competition was held for the design, won by R.K.Freeman of Bolton, with a style described as 'Franco-Flemish'.

Certainly there must have been a touch of fantasy, a vague flamboyant continental feel about the imposing entrance which thrust an antiquated rocket of a tower complete with booster turrets and gables to keep more exotic company at a higher level with

The Free Library and Museum, opened in 1879 amidst great celebrations. This is how it looked before the alterations of 1915-16.

the Guildhall clock. The protruding bowls with round-topped windows on either side of the entrance archway were capped with steeply sloping roofs crowned with decorative iron. The extension which came three years later in 1882 with more rejoicings to form a public art gallery was more humbly reminiscent of native English building. Tall rectangular windows yielded something to Hardwick Hall separated by checker-board brickwork and with a crenellated roof. The architect this time was John Storey.[9]

It was all made possible by the generosity of the town's MP Michael Thomas Bass. He had offered nearly £5,000 towards the cost of a new public library over ten years earlier in 1868, provided the Council obtained a site, but he had been refused. Even then it was nearly twenty years since Parliament had passed the first Public Libraries Act in 1850, encouraging town councils with a population of over 10,000 to provide a library by means of a special minimum rate. Bass increased his donation to £8,000 when agreement to go ahead was finally reached and Freeman's design approved. The foundation stone was laid by the MP on 25 October 1876 after a procession of Freemasons and musical entertainment from the orchestra of Nottingham's Theatre Royal.

He it was, of course, who performed the opening ceremony in June 1879 when, after being met at the Midland Station and being dined at the Midland Hotel by the Mayor and Corporation he processed through handsomely decorated streets, led by six bands. There were speeches, concerts and, apparently, theatre.[10] Finally, Thomas Bass donated a further sum to help pay for the extension in 1882 so that library, museum and art gallery could be housed together.[11]

Regarding the contents of the three sections, they had been gathered from various sources in the town and beyond. Lockett's house contained 13,000 volumes by 1871, including the libraries of the Mechanics' Institute and the eighteenth-century Philosophical Society started by Erasmus Darwin.[12] Between the laying of the foundation stone and the official opening, that collection was supplemented by nearly 3,000 books and pamphlets about Derby and Derbyshire from the Duke of Devonshire.[13] The paintings came from Joseph Strutt's house which, as we shall see, had recently disappeared in street improvement and where earlier in the century the public had been invited to view his advertised collection of Italian masters on Sunday afternoons for a modest charge. According to Glover's "History and Gazetteer of the County of Derby," Strutt's collection included works by Rembrandt ("Head of a Jewish Rabbi"), Reynolds, Titian, Wright, Canaletto, Rubens, Poussin, Gainsborough, Van Dyck and Hogarth.

The museum collection had been housed for public viewing on the same terms at first in the Atheneum after its opening in 1841, then in the Mechanics' Institute. The natural history objects had come from private commercial displays in the Piazzas and King Street. The museum also included a room with panelling from that in Exeter House, now over twenty years gone, in which Bonnie Prince Charlie and his war council had decided to call off his hitherto triumphant advance towards London in 1745. This

Bass had bought from the son of the House's last resident with the expressed intention of embellishing his pet project.[14]

Finally, on Becket Street off the Wardwick and on the parallel lanes where the tide of building inexorably rose throughout the century up to the ridge to the south of Brookside/Victoria Street, four buildings, the two later of them distinctive and very different in style and purpose, were also built towards the end of our period. The earlier two were directly opposite each other on Becket Street and were built as the offices of the new public bodies which were during our period the result of the Whig and Liberal reforming governments laying down enhanced duties for local authorities.

First came the offices for the Poor Law Guardians Board in an impressive continental-looking style in 1868 and enhanced in 1893. Four years later, in 1872, it was joined by the offices of the Derby School Board. The first of the larger-scale projects, in 1878, the year before the opening of the Free Library, was the Derby School of Art, opened in a rich Gothic (pointed-arch) style this time, the work of F.W.Waller.[15]

It again brandished an entrance-tower, this one flanking the doorway, opened out with tall rectangular windows and a broached Rhenish-looking cone of a roof with deeply overhanging eaves. To either side spikey gables and turrets accompanied coupled pointed windows. In total contrast, in 1886 on neighbouring Babington Lane, the Grand Theatre and Opera House opened its doors. Again a continental look, but this time no semblance of castle or church, very much a pared-down version of imperial Parisian, with a grid of rectangular window above the long foyer entrance and high in the centre three small circular apertures underneath a decoratively carved classical triangle. By the very end of our period, however, it was again a construction site with a replica skeleton only beginning once more to emerge from the ashes of its first month-long existence.

In April 1886 it had burnt down like Habershon's Guildhall and would not open permanently until 1888.[16]

It may be fitting to end this survey of the chief pieces of the public set, against the backdrop of which the drama of everyday life in central Derby was played out, to stay a moment with the reporter of the 'Derby Mercury' for Wednesday 31 March 1886, musing with very evident pride on the opening of the original Grand Threatre and Opera House, the work of Andrew Melville, on the Thursday previous, 25 March. The very first observation is interesting in the inference it is possible to draw from it about contemporary attitudes towards certain types of amusement. Theatre would seem to have fallen foul of the puritanical aspect of the Victorian mental world, no doubt linked to the sabbatarianism we shall shortly encounter, as something not altogether morally sound and healthy:

At long length the anxious hopes of such of the Derby people as look upon the drama as a healthy and legitimate means of instruction and amusement have been realised. After many abortive attempts and false starts, the project for the erection of a first-class theatre received a sudden and strong impetus when Mr Melville appeared on the scene last autumn . . .Not withstanding the severity of the winter the

work has been carried on almost continuously and a liberal use of the electric light has enabled the men to do a geat deal of work during the night . . .it is a theatre of which any town might be proud, and that it will bear comparison with any theatre in the provinces, not only for its handsome appearance but for the admirable — we might almost say perfect — arrangements for the accommodation of the public and for the production of plays . . .Great public interest has been taken in the progress of operations, and during the past week or two especially crowds have stood in front of the building, and many who could obtain the privilege have visited the interior . . .The doors were opened at half-past six on Thursday and large numbers began at once to crowd into the pit and gallery at the extra charge which prevailed until seven o'clock . . .The Mayor and his family were conducted by Mr Melville to one of the two boxes . . .Meantime the curtain — a handsomely painted arrangement, much more pleasing to the eye than the old-fashioned green baise — had been down, and the band were tuning up their instruments. A few minutes after half-past seven the orchestra, consisting of a dozen performers, under the leadership of Mr S.Tate, struck up the National Anthem, in accordance with the loyal custom which prevails in the theatrical world. All the audience of course rose, but many of the 'gods' showed the backwardness of their education in this kind of thing by keeping their hats on . . .the curtain was run up and disclosed the drop scene. It is a charming picture, representing the town of Ancona, with the Arch of Trajan in the foreground. The disclosure of the scene produced a spontaneous burst of applause, and in response Mr Alfred Whyatt, the painter came forward and bowed his acknowledgements . . .

The audience contained all sorts apparently, even a goddam republican or two!

Building Churches

The other feature in the public face of the town worthy of attention was the host of new churches thrusting their towers, steeples or bellhoods in all directions. They reflected a fundamental concern of the age. On the one hand, a desire to hold high a banner of faith tarnished by the easy-going world-embrace of the Georgians and blighted by the alien demands of industrialisation or, later, the challenge to its very validity from the ideas of Charles Darwin; on the other, to present the claims of moral discipline to the mass of new urban dwellers adrift from all ties of tradition through economic circumstances. All this played its part in the Victorian enthusiasm for the Gothic pointed-arch style as the fitting way to express the imperative of faith in stone. The aspiring upward movement of the eye when confronted with tower, spire, buttress and pinnacle was the original inspiration of the medieval world, the age of faith. So the Gothic style was taken up by the Victorians. We have seen its typical application as the morally elevated style allied to the demands of education in the College of Art, in contrast to what was deemed suitable for hotel or theatre, where classical pillar or triangular pediment was appropriate.

So numerous churches and chapels added their punctuation to the increasingly crowded horizon. Derby was no exception to the characteristic dominance of religion in the mental world of most middle and upper-class Victorians. They regarded the observance of Christian worship as vital to the well-being, even existence of society. In England as a whole, in the period 1851 to 1881, over 2,000 Anglican churches were built, and the number of Roman Catholic churches doubled. There was an increase of 50 per cent in the number of people taking Holy Communion in Anglican churches over the same period, the same increase among Methodists and over 40 per cent among Baptists.

The Nonconformists in general, including the above two denominations, also the Congregationalists, Unitarians, Presbyterians and Quakers, were closely associated with the heavy social controls of temperance and the 'frozen Sunday'.[17] But then, the defence of the concept of the Sabbath or 'Sabbatarianism' was a rallying point of a high proportion of Anglicans as well. Derby and Derbyshire were a stronghold of this belief. We have already come across it in the 1880s in connection with the explanation for the relatively low profits of the new tramcars in the town. Fifty years earlier, however, the 'Derby Mercury' for 26 February 1834 published a *Petition to Both Houses of Parliament, and also an Address to the King (William IV) by the Clergy of the Town and County of Derby on the Observance of the Sabbath.*

Interestingly, they begun by expressing *most heartfelt grief at the awful desecration of the Lord's Day by all classes of their fellow subjects.* The Georgian hangover was still very much with them and the gloomy edge of the high tide of Victorianism had not yet settled upon the urban scene. The Arboretum rules of 1840 would even encourage enjoyment of the park on Sundays, much to Joseph Strutt's credit. The clergy then lay down the basis for their attitude to Sunday behaviour in that Christ asserted as *Lord of the Sabbath, that works of necessity and mercy should be performed on that day.* It is not a question of choice. Christ was affirming the Fourth Commandment, which was as unbreakable as the other six, and *the profanation of this day tends only to the increase of impiety, profligacy and every kind of vice.*

Finally comes the evidence for their concern. To start with, as the strong clerical arm of Derby reaches even into London, the Government itself is taken to task for . . .*the holding of Cabinet Councils by his Majesty's Ministers* (on the Sabbath), *a practise, they beg most respectfully to submit, calculated to bring down the displeasure of Almighty God, rather than his favour, on their deliberations, and affording also, a most pernicious example to all ranks of Society.*

Then they target the rest of the country, including presumably many of the citizens of their home town, for . . .*the unhallowed assemblage of multitudes of persons with their Carriages and Horses for purposes of pleasure, in the Royal Parks, and even during the hours of Divine Service — the circulation throughout the country of Sunday Journals — the keeping open of Club Houses, Taverns, Public Houses, and Tea Gardens — the following of Trades and other worldy occupations — the transmission of Mails, by which the Government forces many hundreds of persons to desecrate the Sabbath, the allowing of public Conveyances and Posting on the high roads, the plying of Canal Boats, and also of Steam Boats with parties of pleasure; and the unnecessary sailing of ships from their ports.*

So it was obviously all going on and they wanted a ban on it in order . . .*to secure to all, the unmolested enjoyment of the privileges of the Christian Sabbath . . .*

It was a losing battle. Social control of this kind would not work. Those higher up the social scale may have made a strong habit of hearing and reading sermons. They may have been joined, according to C.F.G.Masterman writing a little after the end of our period in 1902, by most working men in Victorian times in belief in God, at least as far as the idea of a tolerant Deity who would *assuredly compensate him in the next world for the many good things denied him in this;*[18] and also by the working class in general in demanding a good funeral, often of a lavishness beyond their means so that in February 1875, 'The Times' of London could complain of *awful hearses drawn by preternatural quadrupeds, clouds of black plumes, solid and magnificent oak coffins instead of sepulchral elm, coffin within coffin, lead, brick graves and capacious catacombs.*

But regular church attendance was not a strong characteristic of the labouring classes in towns. Where Derby stood on this is not clear. Certainly the evidence presented to the Factory Acts Committee seems to show that in 1840 the overwhelming majority of working-class parents here sent their children off to Sunday School. But nationally, the larger the town the greater was the degree of non-attendance at church. The overall average attendance of 75 per cent would certainly justify the number of churches erected in Derby during the period.

But in the 1851 Religious Census we find the comment on contemporary church congregations, *how absolutely insignficant a proportion of the population is composed of artizans.*[19] Clergy were looked upon as 'gentlemen', a significant proportion of pews were still rented (as, indeed, descriptions of some of the Derby churches in the Trade Directories make clear), and the 'Sunday best' rule in clothing must have been a trial to large numbers of people. They would attend in their hundreds on the great Festivals of the Church Year and also for family ceremonies, but in May 1871, 'The Times' was moved to declare: *The Church of England is the religion of the higher classes, most of the middle, and, in the rural districts, of the labouring classes.*[20] And most working men, having few pleasures apart from drinking and little leisure time on weekdays, were not likely to be drawn to the Nonconformists' negative social programme.

But despite all the protestations of the clergy, Derby Sundays were no doubt overwhelmingly peaceful for the most part. There were indeed spies about, as the following exact from a letter to the 'Mercury' dated 11 March, signed *Advena* and published 19 March 1834 indicates:

SIR — it must, I am persuaded, have been a pleasing reflection to every pious inhabitant of Derby, that on a late occasion, his Town and County stood in the foremost rank of those who met to assert and defend the sanctity of the Sabbath. In the same degree it must produce a painful feeling when any are found persisting in the open profanation of the Sacred day.

Such desecrations there unhappily are; and I wish to point out one of them to public notice, that those who are guilty of it 'may be ashamed', and desist: I have observed that for several Sunday mornings lately there have been men at work in some of the market gardens in the outskirts of the town . . .

'The Mercury' for 30 April that year also indicates some support from the sellers of ale:

OBSERVANCE OF THE LORD'S DAY — The petition to parliament from the keepers of public houses and beershops of Derby and Neighbourhood, praying that public houses may be closed during the whole of the Sunday, has been signed by seventy publicans.

This cannot be a high proportion of the total at the time but it does show that some people were not getting enough rest. Licencing hours were not tackled during our period, which was probably tough on many families whose economic circumstances could not stand the drink drain. There seems little doubt that given the enormous weight of the religious-moral order, a quiet Sunday was consonant with the feelings of a great majority of the people of a provincial town. At the end of our period, of course, tramcars would assist family visiting and other suitable pursuits away from immediate hearth and home.

Whatever the overall picture, the religious instinct gave Derby, as probably most towns in this period, many of its architectural landmarks, though perhaps reminding some souls, then and now, of the 'cultural Stalinism' of medieval times. There was also the preservation of the heritage of previous centuries and enlarging existing structures to respond to the surge in population.

So, according to Glover's 'Directory of Derby' for 1858, the chancel of St Peter's was *thoroughly restored* in 1851, . . .*fitted up with open stalls*, presumably instead of ancient box-pews, and a new stained-glass window and organ put in. The same source records that a new organ and bells were added at St Werburgh's in 1850, this after a complete re-build finished only four years earlier in 1846 to a design by the archiect H.I.Stevens, of whom more in a moment in connection with the completion that very same year of his most notable Derby project.

The highlight of Victorian ecclesiastical building in Derby must surely have been the duo of St Mary's Roman Catholic Church and St Alkmund's C of E Church on either side of Bridge Gate, though many in their respective congregations might not have been pleased at the conjunction, matching the civic pair of Guildhall and Market Hall. Seven years separated the two projects, though that of St Mary's was never strictly completed.

It should also have had a spire, something by which the architect of St Alkmund's, Henry Isaac Stevens, was able to cap, at least physically, the work of the far more distinguished Augustus Welby Pugin on St Mary's. Instead, a print of about 1860 is able, by dint of the artist's standing by the riverside just down from St Mary's Bridge on the opposite bank to the Bridge Chapel and thus oblivious of any industrial developments behind, to present us with the new contrasting slender end-on profile of St Alkmund's rising step-wise by chancel, nave and towerbase to the long tapering spire, and, at right angles, the rich lines

A.W.Pugin's St Mary's Roman Catholic Church in Bridge Gate, built in 1838-39 and enlarged in 1853. It is pictured here from St Alkmund's Church Yard, a beautiful Georgian square that was swept away in 1967.

and pinnacles of St Mary's tower with nave moored horizontally alongside. Thus a new grouping for the Derby silhouette on the other side of the great pillar of All Saints' from the Guildhall.

St Mary's dates from 1839, St Alkmund's from 1846. The first was of national architectural importance at the time as the very first large church which Pugin, the architect then in the news, had had the opportunity of designing and so putting his strongly held convictions and principles into effect due to the backing and resources of the Earl of Shrewsbury of Alton Towers fame. The Catholic community nationally was 'over the moon' about it, as a letter from Cardinal Wiseman dated 11 October 1839 shows:

It is without exception the most magnificent thing the Catholics have yet done in modern times in this country, and is quite worthy of ancient days. The church is all of stone with three aisles, a glorious tower and a very rich sanctuary ornamented with beautiful stained windows and rich broad hangings, all given, as well as very splendid vestments by Lord Shrewsbury . . .On the whole it would not have done dishonour to Rome.[21]

It was well received in the architectural press at a time when it was apparently fashionable to be highly critical. One critical notice declared it was a *painfully beautiful structure* because it showed up the feebleness of the established church's contemporary efforts in this

The 1846 building of St Alkmund's Church, originally founded in the tenth century. This, too, was razed to the ground in 1967, to make way for the inner ring-road.

field.[22] Glover's 'Directory of Derby' for 1849 records that the foundation stone was laid on 28 June 1838 and that

This church, when completed according to the original design, will be among the most imposing and Catholic which have been raised since the Reformation. It is built entirely of an excellent bright stone, and the style is of the earliest decorated kind which prevailed about the commencement of the reign of Henry the Sixth.

There could be no clearer statement of the Victorian propensity for the precise backward glance in artistic matters. Glover gives an interesting description of the setting of the church at the time, especially in view of what was to happen to it in the present century:

It would hardly be possible to have chosen a plot of ground more suitable...Though occupying a most central position, it is nearly surrounded by the gardens of Edward Strutt, esq., MP., one of the representatives for the town, and is therefore, protected from the noise to which great thoroughfares are usually exposed. The ground is also hilly, and requires thirteen steps to conduct us to the doors ...

On the matter of the design which was fated never to be carried through, Glover adds.

The tower is 100 feet high to the top of the embattled parapet, and 117 to the top of the pinnacles, and when it is found possible to raise the spire, it will add 100 feet to the height . . .Considerable expense has been incurred in the foundations, and in the tower itself, for receiving finally the spire, which has been very much admired for its beauty, being richly ornamented with crockets, figures, niches ETC., ETC., but at present this noble addition cannot be made; in the meantime the tower itself must always be pronounced exquisitely beautiful; so much so, that many have believed the building more attractive and symmetrical without the spire.

Finally, turning to details he praises the large window above the entrance at the base of the tower, and continues:

. . .Above this window, in a large and highly ornamental niche, stands the ever blessed mother of our Lord. The figure is about 6ft 5in high, and the infant Saviour is represented reclining in her arms, having in his hand a lily, the emblem of purity . . .

The interior is beautifully fitted up. The dedication took place on Wednesday, 9 October 1839 . . .

The opening did not pass off without incident, however. Lord Shrewsbury and the architect, after arriving for the High Mass, refused to stay for it because they were horrified to see that the bishop had gathered an orchestra for the occasion and also a choir that included some female singers, not appropriate medieval procedure. Accordingly, *they drove away in high dudgeon.*[23]

Elsewhere in Glover, there is a note that the new church had *500 sittings, 70 of which are free,* suggesting that the number of subscribers and regular members would leave comparatively little room for the occasional visitor.

St Alkmund's was larger, seating 1,200 and *more than one half the sittings are unappropriated.* The first stone was laid on 6 May 1844 and it was designed in fourteenth-century Gothic style (about a century earlier than Pugin's model). Apart from the lofty spire at the west end it boasted a large and elaborate stained-glass east window looking towards the river, *charged with heraldic bearings, foliage ETC*[24]. Of the interior, Glover records in 1858:

. . .The nave is divided from the aisles by a series of clustered columns with elegant foliated capitals, from which spring the deeply moulded arches . . .The chancel arch is lofty and well proportioned, and springs from massive clustered columns. In the chancel is a beautiful altar screen with illuminated texts ETC . . .[25]

Before embarking on a brief round-up of the more minor examples of a prolific church-building era, perhaps we may descend Bridge Gate and re-cross St Mary's Bridge for a quick glance at an interesting Roman venture on Nottingham Road on the site of the Old China Works on the other side. There in 1846, the Convent of St Vincent de Paul was built, presenting according to Glover's 'Directory' for 1858, *a most elegant and striking frontage, extending upwards of 300 feet in length.*

It was in the Gothic style of course but the *health, comfort and convenience of the inmates, have been most thought of by the architect.* It consisted of *large poor schools,* chaplain/superior's residence, vestry chapel with *some beautiful stained glass and much decoration,* cells of nuns around the chapel gallery, library, reception and a *noble suite of rooms devoted to educational purposes, especially for the training of young persons in the important art of teaching young children.*[26]

First in the catalogue of Anglican churches was St John's, Bridge Street, described by one local historian as indeed the first in Derby since the Reformation of the sixteenth century.[27] It was to serve the first scene of industrial expansion on Nun's Green. We have already noted its connection with the Britannia iron foundry. Glover's 1849 'Directory' notes that

It is lighted by 22 Gothic cast-iron windows; has a double embattlement, and the six projecting buttresses on each side the nave are ornamented with caps and consols.

Inside, attention is drawn by the tall graceful trio of lancet windows with lace-frill at the top in an arc at the far apse end. Holy Trinity, London Road, came next on the other side of town on the old Castlefields estate at the time of the demolition of the manor-house. Dating from 1836, Glover describes it as Gothic, with square tower at the west end *terminated by four domed pinnacles* and of brick with stone dressings. The emphasis continued to lie with the growing southern-south-western sector with Christ Church, Normanton Road in 1840. According to Glover, it was *on the highest point of the town.* The architect was Habershon of Guildhall fame, this time changing naturally to the required Gothic style using stone and western tower and spire.

On 11 June 1849 the foundation stone was laid of St Paul's, Chester Green, right on the northern edge on the east bank of the Derwent this time. Designed by a Liverpool architect and of decorated Gothic style like three-year-old St Alkmund's, Glover writes of it:

The roofs are open timbered, which, with the stalls, are stained and varnished. The tower is a substantial and well-proportioned structure, and though like the whole building, but sparingly ornamented, possesses with it, in an eminent degree, the suitable simple, yet graceful characteristics of the country churches of the middle ages.

Then, on the other side of the river again just down Queen Street from his larger work, in 1857 H.I.Stevens was engaged once more to completely rebuild St Michael's on the collapse of the old church. Again an effort in fourteenth-century Gothic style, the new tower at nearly 60 feet high was slightly over the old one but nestling comfortably between the neighbouring peaks of St Alkmund's and All Saints'.[28]

Back to the south-west of town, in 1866 came St James-the-Great of stone and 'Early Gothic' and, five years later, the image we stayed with in the opening chapter, St Luke's. The architect here was local Frederick Robinson, who built in stone, again 'Early Gothic', finishing with that 140-foot *saddle-roofed tower.*[29]

With suburban expansion off Kedleston Road to the north-west, St Anne's was opened the next year 1872 in Whitecross Street, of plain brick with distinctive pyramidal bell-hood, in a peculiar

St John's, Bridge Street, the first in a catalogue of new Anglican churches to be built in Derby in the nineteenth century.

Victorian version of what was described as 'Late Gothic' styling.

In a final flourish of Derby's most prolific age of church building ever, the 1880s produced no less than four more, all but one in the Gothic style. The exception was Norman St Thomas the Apostle in Pear Tree Road, built in 1881 to serve the strong tentacle of new development in that south-western area, described by Kelly in his 1895 'Directory of Derbyshire' as being of *brick and Coxbench stone*. However, to the east in the same year next came St Andrew's, Litchurch, now completed nearly twenty years after its inception in 1867 as the 'railway church', to designs by another architect of national distinction in Sir George Gilbert Scott. It served the population in the immediate neighbourhood of the Midland Station. Both main body and spired tower were lofty and the row of upper windows above the lean-to-aisles were of quintessentially Victorian design: each within a broad but shallow pointed alcove, a sequence of six adjoining circles around a slightly larger central one filling an enveloping circular whole. Kelly notes that it ended in an apse and had eight bells. Last came St Chad's, Mill Hill, of stone and 'Early Gothic', similarly St Barnabus in Radbourne Street in 1885-6.

The reaching back towards the medieval period in all this ecclesiastical building was obviously compulsive, reinforced by the two larger Nonconformist projects, as they also were far from idle either.

Earliest was the 1860 Victoria Street Congregational Chapel which dominated the westward prospect from the Royal Hotel with its stone Gothic styling and yet another tower and spire. Next year came the General Baptist Chapel on Osmaston Road, features ditto. However, their 1842 adaptation of the classically styled 1751 Evans' family town mansion of brick and stone in St Mary's Gate was in keeping with a more general Nonconformist leaning back to the Georgian era in styling. Kelly, in his 1895 Directory, states that the St Mary's Gate Baptist Chapel *stands in a large courtyard entered by a fine stone gateway with gates of wrought iron of elegant design, which are much admired.*[30]

In fact, there were two other large chapels which bucked the general Gothic trend and reverted to the classical style so prevalent in the previous Georgian century. First was another complete re-build, to cope presumably with vastly increased numbers, of the Westleyan Methodist Chapel in King Street just the previous year in 1841 and just around the corner from brand-new St Mary's. Almost opposite would soon appear St Alkmund's. The chapel entrance was at the end of a forecourt, with a quartet of pillars with the simple Greek Doric top below a quintet of round-headed windows separated by flat pillars, with the more elaborate Ionic twirl top, on the first floor; centrally above, a shallow triangle. The total design in stone was by a Leeds architect.

Then near the end of that crowded manic church-building decade, H.I.Stevens again, in 1848 designed an earlier Congregational chapel at the junction of London Road and Traffic Street on the southern edge of the centre. This was even more like an Ancient Greek temple, fronted with grand columns with the most elaborate of the classical toppings (Corinthian) holding up the required triangle. In 1861, the Wesleyan Methodists did somethign a little different in their London Road Chapel, *of red brick with stone dressings and a gabled front, flanked by two turrets surmounted by short spires.*[31]

The 1867 red-brick Congregational Chapel in Normanton Road again marked some sort of departure from the norm with its *two dwarf stair towers at the western end, one of which is surmounted by a small dome.*[32]

In 1870, the Primitive Methodists built their largest chapel of both brick and stone in Kedleston Street. Lastly, again on Normanton Road, the Wesleyan Methodists in 1882 built a chapel described in Kelly's 'Directory' of 1895 as the 'Early Gothic' as usual but *with an octagonal tower 90 feet high.*

At Street Level

If this catalogue has seemed overlong, perhaps it will by that have served the purpose of further emphasising what must have been a heavy atmosphere of 'conformity' in the general religious sense, in the psyche of the town, something no doubt replicated all over Britain. The various churches provided focal counterpoints for the community to the civic centre, helping to bind the very sense of community at a time when the counter-pull of cheap mass long-distance travel was barely thinkable and in any case would itself long be a neighbourhood affair of one sort or another. This sense would be formally expressed far more often than in our succeeding century by large-scale celebrations which we shall recall in the last chapter of this book.

But it must have had its oppressive aspect to some, condemning of deviation from the normal state of things, as evidenced in the story of the Silk Mill Lock-Out. However the compensatory, if perhaps patronising, urge to perform charitable deeds great and small must also not be forgotten and features in the story of Derby's heritage of Victorian buildings.

In the fifty years of the Victorian period, from the 1830s to 1880s, the street setting of the important buildings of the centre of the town was transformed. Ancient thoroughfares were widened, completely new ones laid out. It needed to be done, as many were of mere medieval width struggling to cope with the large increase of horse-drawn traffic resulting from the town's enormous development during these decades.

For example, the lower end of Irongate was only sixteen feet wide at its junction with Sadler Gate and therefore required two horse-traffic policemen to prevent sheer chaos.[33]

Taking the brand-new streets first, we have seen how Victoria Street was created out of Brookside in the 1830s, complete by 1839. There was, however, one important scheme begun much earlier in 1825 and completed in a second stage in 1855 and this concerned easing the western approach to the town from the Uttoxeter direction. Uttoxeter New Road cutting across from the Old Road at Rowditch to Curzon Street was the result of a turnpike trust development, enabling a prime site for late Regency villas with easy

access to the town centre. The section beyond the junction with the Old Road continued the arrow-like direction of the first 30 years later. During the 1840s in the meantime, the section of the Markeaton Brook between the Corn Market junction and the river was covered over to produce Albert Street.[34] Meanwhile, Derwent Street was driven through from the Market Place to the Nottingham Road by the first new road crossing of the River Derwent since medieval times. An elegant stone bridge named after the adjacent and soon to be demolished Exeter House[35] replaced the ancient wooden tolled footbridge there in 1850.[36] The designer was Richard Trubshaw from neighbouring Staffordshire.[37] In the 1860s, Sowter Road was made to improve the link past the Old Silk Mills between the Market Place and St Mary's Bridge and hence both river crossings.

Away from the river, Macklin Street was created out of old Cross Lane, of Farington's acquaintance, running parallel to Victoria Street in the same decade.[38] In 1871, St James' Street was made out of what in reality up until then was a mere squalid little 'narrow lane' connecting the upper end of Corn Market with Victoria Street. Both sides of this major shopping creation were new, designed by architects who worked in a variety of styles as evidenced in the details of the doorways, windows and eaves, including Gothic on the one hand and 'Paris Opera' with classically-based details on the other.

At the Victoria Street end, another London-based archiect was engaged to design a new Post Office, working in the style of an Italian palace, middle floor featuring triangle topping to windows and horizontal facing at ground level.

Finally, at right angles, the culverting of the Markeaton Brook was continued westwards between St James' and Sadler Gate Bridges in the 1870s, as we have seen in connection with the building of the Free Library. On top of the culvert was created the Strand, the pet project of Sir Abraham Woodiwiss. It was completed in 1878, the year before the opening of the library.[39]

It may be recalled that Woodiwiss was also concerned during these years with the construction of the Great Northern Railway line through north-west Derby, also opened that same year. He would soon be mayor twice over and in 1881 buy, extend and considerably alter The Pastures mansion beyond Littleover and the current edge of town. The Strand, meanwhile, formed a handsome sinuous new thoroughfare with flanking buildings done in the classical style. In 1880, an arcade was driven through between the new Strand and ancient Sadler Gate.[40]

The widening process was just as extensive and important. The major projects were those of Queen Street and Irongate north of the Market Place and St Peter's Street to the south. Later, in the 1880s it was the turn of Wardwick, whilst the Market Place itself also received attention. Each of these elements involved large-scale demolition so that old and possibly revered elements of the urban scene in Derby were fated to disappear.

Queen Street came first in the early 1850s, causing the unorthodox positioning of H.I.Steven's tower to St Michael's Church. Then, in 1866, a start was made on Irongate, after a delay caused by the Corporation's

St James's Lane, pictured from the Corn Market. The course of Markeaton Brook was covered here in 1836 and the lane widened to form the present St James' Street in 1871.

reluctance to pay for the whole project when much of its use was by County people wanting access to the Market Place and also the necessity to demolish one complete side of the street.[41] The money had to be raised by public subscription and it was the eastern, riverward side that was fated to go.

It was accomplished in two sections, the lower part nearer the Market Place by 1869, the upper two years later. Because it took until the mid-1880s to sell all the cleared sites for new building, the street must have presented a sorry broken-toothed appearance during this time on top of all those years of demolition preceding it. The situation did, however, lead to an interesting variety of building styles being employed, including both pointed-arched Gothic and imitation-Italian. Stevens and Robinson were among architects involved and there was good iron and plasterwork detailing. There was some continuity in business, with firms such as Bennett's and Haywood's reappearing for the future.[42]

The work on St Peter's Street was begun when that on Irongate was nearing completion. This again involved one side of the old street facing demolition; it was the eastern riverward side that again suffered, including Joseph Strutt's former home, Thorntree House, to be replaced by a stylish new bank building, the Derby Commercial, done in mid-century continental Parisian style facing west up Victoria Street. A similar treatment was accorded Wardwick at the end of the 1870s after the completion of the Strand. With the eastern side again went most of the Mechanics' Institute, though not the grand Lecture Hall. The Institute was, however, replaced.[43]

One effect of these central improvements was the creation of at least a single urban 'space' which could, without too much fantasy, be compared with metropolitan glories. This was the junction of Wardwick, Strand, St James' Street and Victoria Street. Looking west and away from the primly assembled façade and spire of the Congregational Church, a perhaps bemused citizen might now gaze at two curving sequences of round-topped and square-headed windows neatly grouped through three or four tiers between flat pillars (pilasters). These patterned curtains of stone then met the steadfast straight lines of St James' and the Post Office. The confection was topped with ranges of balusters and, in the Wardwick, a fretwork of iron tracery offsetting neat pyramids of slate. At the very heart of the junction the curving grip of Wardwick and Strand made counterpoint with a squared-back introduction to St James'. In all, this was no mean achievement for a provincial town.

With the completion of the first part of the Irongate project in 1869, a start was made to extend the northern edge of the Market Place opposite the Guildhall. By 1871 the Shambles, Rotten Row and the Old Piazzas had all gone, following which the Market square itself was cobbled. In this last process of re-surfacing, the long rows of market stalls billowing across this time-honoured space disappeared as well.[44]

So ended a prolific period of street refurbishment to complement a series of varied individual public buildings. The centre of Derby was now very different from the scene it had presented in Regency times: still the same basic alignment of streets tending north-south but with new crossing routes like Albert, St James' and Derwent Streets for a more efficient grid and accompanying a central river-crossing. All were widened to cope with crowded horse-drawn traffic and lined with at least reasonably stylish buildings with something of an international flavour.

Taking in the whole town in its extended form from 1877, by 1882 Derby contained 362 streets and it was a continually enlarging unit. The mid-1880s saw the joining up of Little Chester in the wake of the GNR upheaval and producing a new amenity in Chester Green itself by 1886.[45] The essence of modern Derby was virtually complete by Victoria's Jubilee.

Notes

1. Maxwell Craven, op.cit.
2. Article in the *Derbyshire Advertiser*, December 1959.
3. Article by Frederick Longdon in *Derby Evening Telegraph*, 11 October 1982.
4. Maxwell Craven, op.cit.
5. Glover, *History and Directory of Derby*, 1849.
6. Ibid.
7. Maxwell Craven, op.cit.
8. Maxwell Craven, *The Derby Townhouse*, 1987.
9. Maxwell Craven, *Derby, An Illustrated History*.
10. Article, *The Changing Face of Derby No.25, The Derby Trader*.
11. Maxwell Craven, op.cit.
12. Ibid.
13. *Derby Trader*, op.cit.
14. Maxwell Craven, op.cit.
15. Ibid.
16. Ibid.
17. D.Read, op.cit.
18. C.F.G.Masterman, *Into The Abyss*, quoted in D.Read, op.cit.
19. Quoted D.Read, op.cit.
20. Quoted Ibid.
21. M.Trappes-Lomax, *Pugin: The Portrait of a Mediaeval Victorian*, 1932.
22. Phoebe Stanton, *Pugin*, 1971.
23. M.Trappes-Lomax, op.cit.
24. Glover, *Directory of Derby*, 1849.
25. Glover, *Directory of Derby*, 1858.
26. Ibid.
27. Roy Christian, *Devlopment of a City*.
28. Glover, *Directory of Derby*, 1849.
29. Kelly, *Directory of Derbyshire*, 1895.
30. Ibid.
31. Ibid.
32. Ibid.
33. Roy Christian, op.cit.
34. Ibid.
35. Maxwell Craven, op.cit.
36. Roy Christian, op.cit.
37. Maxwell Craven, op.cit.
38. Roy Christian, op.cit.
39. Maxwell Craven, op.cit.
40. Ibid.
41. Roy Christian, op.cit.
42. Maxwell Craven, op.cit.
43. Ibid.
44. Ibid.
45. Ibid.

Authority

WHO were the people responsible for taking the important decisions which, in many cases, led to the sort of changes occurring in the town we have been looking at, and what was the effect of their decision-making on those who put themselves, voluntarily or not, in a completely dependent position in relation to that responsibility?

There were two milestones in this particular aspect of Derby's story during the period of our survey, at least as regards the creation of a framework for the exercise of local power in the community, although other laws from Westminster led to the setting up of other groups of officers wielding more limited powers over their fellow citizens.

The first milestone Derby shared with all other towns in the country in the shape of the Municipal Corporation Act of 1835, which was a product of one of the great reforming governments of our history (joined later by the Liberal administration of 1905 and the Labour one of 1945). This insisted on local government becoming dependent on limited democratic choice. The second was the Derby Corporation Act of 1877, enabling the extension of the Borough's boundaries and adjusting the Council's arrangements accordingly.

Until 1835, Derby was certainly no approximation to a democracy. It had what Maxwell Craven has identified as an 'odd bilateral' system.[1] It was a closed system. There was a more formal regular part with a Mayor and a 'bench' of aldermen who were composed of and chosen by a limited number of self-appointed 'burgesses' or well-to-do citizens. Then there was an additional part tacked on to this ancient two-centuries-old machinery and dating from two special Acts of Parliament in 1768 and 1792. These had set up an ad hoc group of so-called Improvement Commissioners to carry out their terms releasing the Nun's Green area on the west of the town for building, as we have already seen.

The aldermen came from a closely-knit group of long-established prosperous families, tied by inter-marriage. Their products were rewarded with repeated Mayoralties: two families held eleven each in the hundred years up to 1835, a period when only thirty-six families supplied all Derby's Mayors.[2] The commissioners, by contrast, were the heads of newer thrusting business families, Strutts, Foxes, Evanses. However, because the two sets also inter-married to some extent, the municipal government was not entirely devoid of energy, as our next chapter will

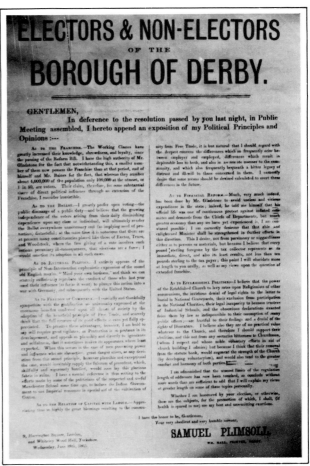

The election address of Samuel Plimsoll, elected in 1868 as Derby's second Liberal MP and runner-up to M.T.Bass. He represented the town until 1880.

make clear. Also, the members of the regular oligarchy running the town were not devoid of connections with humbler Derby families.[3]

The Municipal Corporation Act, the provisions of which came at a time of rapid expansion in the 1830s leading up to the arrival of the railway, defined the Corporation so as to consist of a Mayor, elected each year, twelve aldermen elected every third year and thirty-six councillors. The title 'aldermen' was a continuing indication of the assumed sexual consitution of the wielders of power in the locality, as at the centre! Either the councillors, elected from six wards or districts (Bridge, Becket, Castle, Derwent, Friar Gate and King's Mead), or their constituents directly, could choose the aldermen. A constituent had to own £1,000-worth of property or be chargeable for a rateable value of at least £30.[4] A Corporation also had to have seven permanent officials, including Town Clerk and Coroner, and there were also a number of additional ones such as Superintendant of Police and Charity Commissioners.[5]

In fact, as Maxwell Craven has demonstrated, the 1835 Act made little difference to the nature of the power-wielding elite in Victorian times, though after 1850, when a 'rank outsider' in the person of Piazzas pawnbroker William Goodwin became Mayor, it was rare for someone to hold the office more than once, and only as a mark of special distinction. Typical holders were still 'gentlemen', attorneys, company directors or bankers.[6] There was obviously a broader representation of industry during the period. For example, the heads of the following firms attained the status of alderman or Mayor: Leech (paint), Sowter (millers), Wheeldon (maltsters), Forman (maltsters), Haywood (ironmongers) Russell (foundry), Handyside (foundry), Smith (brass-founders), Fowkes (foundry), Haslam (foundry) and Woodiwiss (railway-contractor).[7]

Kelly's 'Directory of Derbyshire' for 1895 summarises the later change thus:

By the 'Derby Corporation Act, 1877', the Borough, from the 1 November 1877, was extended, and divided into eight wards, and appointed to be governed by a Mayor, sixteen aldermen and forty-eight councillors. The additional wards would cater for Litchurch and Chester Green.

Derby's parliamentary representation of two seats during the Victorian period was entirely in what might be described as the 'reforming' interest. There was only one Tory or Conservative MP for the Borough during the period 1830-88, namely William Thomas Cox (1865-8). All others were Whig or Liberal. The canvas is dominated by Michael Thomas Bass, who was returned consecutively on no less than seven occasions from 1848-85, nearly a forty-year span, as Liberal. Also notable were Edward Strutt, returned as a Whig (pre-Liberal) four times from 1830-47, with a fifth result

later declared void and in favour of Bass, and Samuel Plimsoll, returned three times 1868-85.[8]

Bass was a prolific benefactor to the town: apart from his interest in the Free Library and Art Gallery he had also given a Recreation Ground in 1867 with costs of preparation included, on the banks of the Derwent just north of Midland Station. On 17 October 1884, six months after his death at the age of 85, a statue of him was unveiled at the Corn Market end of the Market Place.[9] It now stands in Museum Square.

There was attached to the municipality one office of the Crown in similar fashion to that of Lord Lieutenant to the County today. This was High Steward, hereditarily reposed with the Dukes of Devonshire.[10] In the nineteenth century there was still a widespread and real deference to aristocracy, at the apex of the pyramid of county interest beyond the confines of the busy industrial borough world, perhaps reminding Derby of its previous close gentry connections as a county town most clearly imaged in the Assembly Rooms and the houses of Friar Gate. And so, from time to time, the readers of the weekly journals were regaled with up-dates on the current duke's activities as one of the living peaks of the political landscape. In the 'Derby and Chesterfield Reporter' for 28 November 1833, we read:

The Duke of Devonshire left Devonshire House on Wednesday morning sennight, on his way to Paris, to pay a visit to his sister, the Countess Granville, and thence to Naples for the winter. His Grace, it is expected, will remain abroad until the month of March next.

In the 'Derby Mercury' for 26 March 1834 we find:

TUESDAY'S POST London, Tuesday 25 March THE DUKE OF DEVONSHIRE — His Grace will probably arrive about the middle of May, and not sooner. The Duke gave a pledge to the King that he would, if health would permit, be at Court on the 22nd, the day appointed for the celebration of His Majesty's birthday.

The Poor

Looking at the system from entirely the other end of the social scale, there were three aspects of authority where those who were, through more or less fault of their own, in a state of direct contact or unwilling dependence on its representatives. These were in the spheres of Poor Law, Criminal Law and Policing. In an age when the standard response to great and evident need was the dispensation of charity, any state provision was in the nature of a fending-off operation. There were, as we have seen, charity commissioners at a local level and the Mayor was responsible for emergency feeding in the form of soup-kitchen and children's dinners at times of acute distress from unregulated market economics.

But there was also the Poor Law system, nationally reformed in 1834, to cope with a growing problem, of possibly modest proportions in Derby at that time but which must have been increased considerably by the result of the Silk-Mill Lock-Out. What we are dealing with here are those, estimated nationally by William Booth right at the end of our period in his book 'In Darkest England' (1890) as being one in ten of the population, who were in a state of almost helpless poverty and dependence, in fact in a

Michael Thomas Bass, the Liberal MP for Derby who dominated the scene for 40 years.

demoralised state. If we judge by some local commentators writing in the pages of the 'Mercury' and 'Reporter', the situation in Derby may not have been all that bad, certainly nothing like that in London and possibly a handful of other large cities.

For example, in 1832, the total number of inmates in the five parish workhouses of the unreformed system (All Saints', St Alkmund's, St Michael's, St Peter's and St Werburgh's) was only 198 against a total Derby population of about 30,000.[11] The trouble was that the 'reformed' system introduced in 1834 was designed to off-load the new workhouses of all who were not sick, unemployable through infirmity or old. It has been caluclated nationally that between 1865 and 1880, the percentage of the population catered for in this way fell from 4.5 to 3.2, because officially no one could be helped other than inside a workhouse.[12]

But there was a large number of 'working-class' people — below the highly-skilled artisan group — for example, printers, building workers, trades with apprenticeship rules — who consituted 'the poor', not always destitute but living in fear of that desperate state, a real trap-door into oblivion for them through unemployment, accident, illness, old age, meaning the workhouse. We have already encountered the periodic desperation associated with the decline of old trades such as framework-knitting and consequent activating of soup-runs. And in the lower reaches of the recipients, there was *the residuum* as John Bright called them in the 1850s,[13] who after 1834 had to go into the workhouses if they wanted 'community help'.

The 1832 Derby figures already quoted could be misleading. It has been calculated that under the old system, in 1803, just under ten per cent of the town's population actually got help, because they could then receive what was known as 'outdoor relief'. Admittedly, that was in the short intermission in the middle of the French Wars when their effects would be all too evident in the face of high food prices. However, in that year, 1,060 people got help, 308 of whom were under fourteen, 225 over sixty years of age or disabled, 254 occasionally, that is, presumably, those fit normally but unable to get regular work.[14]

These figures may overlap with the work of the nine Friendly Societies in the town at that time, in effect the self-help insurance against disaster of those in work. By 1816 there were apparently fourteen of them, the majority centred on pubs.[15] But there was a 'dummy' run in Derby for the post-1834 regime which received the approval of the Government's Commissioners when they came on their tour of inspection to pave the way for the new legislation. This was at St Werburgh's parish, where they refused to pamper the poor, due to the efforts of a Mr Henry Mozley who managed to reduce the amount handed out by fifty per cent between the early 1820s and 1830s, when the parish population had increased by 1,000. Mr Mozley was applying the workhouse test of so-called 'less eligibility', people who wanted help had to go there or get nothing.

Men who were fit were often put to stone-breaking for the roads as the St Werburgh's assistant overseer for the poor was also overseer for the highways. Only the old and 'impotent' were willing to stay long in St Werburgh's workhouse. Anyone who was given help had his/her name published every six months

together with the mothers of illegitimate children and fathers in arrears with maintenance.[16] We saw in chapter three that Thomas Bridgett was willing to employ pauper women and girls at his mill. This was after John Moody, the overseer of the poor at St Werburgh's, wrote to the Poor Law Commissioners in 1835, saying that people were willing to work in the mills for less than the parish would give them because it was indoors and therefore warm, not like out on the cold open road.[17]

Apart from this, the unreformed system did have its critics. For example, again a little before the start of our period of survey, William Hutton in his 1791 'History of Derby' villified the old Derby workhouses:

> ...they are completely destructive; they are nurseries of idleness, the corrupters of manners, the receptacles of vulgarity, the sink of rudeness, the destroyers of health, the slaughter-houses of infants, and the plagues of old age.[18]

Between 1837 and 1841 the changes in response to the new law were carried out. St Alkmund's workhouse was closed down, the others specialised in looking after different categories of pauper. All Saints took on males only, St Peter's females and vagrants. St Werburgh's took only children. The implications for the integrity of the family unit will be noted. In July 1837 came the order for all unmarried men from St Peter's to make their way to All Saints'. In July 1838 all boys under fourteen were sent to St Werburgh's (the workhouse was situated in Friar Gate). However, apparently children were not sent to the mill and a school was provided, as evidenced in the 1841 Census returns which note a Mr Henry Cummings, aged twenty-five, as headmaster.

On 18 April 1837 the decision had been taken to build a single new workhouse for all Derby paupers. A site of two acres was found on Osmaston Road, actually in Litchurch, with estimated room for 500 inmates. Here it remained, on the site taken over much later in the century by the Royal Crown Derby Porcelain Company, until 1877 when it removed to a new site on the edge of town on the Uttoxeter Road near Mickleover. The rules for the institution were approved by the Board of Guardians, set up by law to administer the Act of Parliament, on 11 June 1839. They included the following: no smoking, beds to be made first thing each morning, rooms cleaned, windows to be left open as far as the weather permitted; two wicker-work cradles to be provided to contain six children each for the women; boys to attend two hours' schooling, morning and afternoon, to learn shoemaking and tailoring in between those periods and to do gardening in the late afternoon; hoops and swings to be provided for the children. In addition a library was started.

As we have seen, families were separated into single-sex groups. Children had to separate from their parents at the age of fourteen. Stays were, apparently, often short, of a week, or two weeks or sometimes a little longer, perhaps supporting our earlier generalisation of the all-pervasive presence of the basement trap-door, though many inmates were there temporarily under a specific removal order because they had come from a parish outside Derby. For example, this entry in the books for July 1837:

Thomas Axam, aged 13 years, belonging to Marston,

Bedfordshire, had been sent off by boat by the Relieving Officer at the expense of 9s 1d.

Often, discharged families were to be found applying for relief once again a month or so after discharge, probably because of illness, death, unemployment or eviction from lodgings. Many inmates when discharged would have no furniture or even possessions and therefore would be dependent on relatives near or far. It would be a hopeless condition. While children whenever possible might be found apprenticeships, adults could not expect such help, resulting in a sense of hoplessness from an utterly degarding situation, the rigour and social stigma of workhouse existence.[19]

It was all much more efficient, of course. But at least in Derby the law was administered with some flexibility and humanity. Every Tuesday evening the Board of Guardians met to consider requests for outdoor relief. There were many applications from people bereaved, a husband, wife or child had died. Very often a coffin was supplied or burial fees paid, although the coffins had to be of a set standard, for example in the thickness of wood used, and to cost 6s for children and 9s for adults. Again, there were many applications from framework-knitters suffering from the competition of the mills. For example, this entry in the books for 7 August 1838:

Joseph Day, 66 years old, framework-knitter applied for relief. He has been in the workhouse some time ago; he states that his earnings are from 3s to 5s per week, out of which he has to pay Frame Rent, Lodging and Maintenance; he has no relations that could do anything for him.[20]

However, the Guardians' humanity had its limits. Samuel Lucas, a representative of the Bricklayers' Union, when enquiring about the effects of the Lock-Out in 1834 reported the following:

. . .a poor widow named Walker, who resided at Court 1 River Street,

. . .because her son 'smelt' of Trade Unionism, was denied all Parochial Relief. He had seen her and found her living on potato peelings.[21]

It should not be forgotten that in addition to the official relief channels there is also evidence of charitable giving by church congregations.

The subjects of this possibly far from universal humanity on the part of official and other bodies must be accounted Derby's share of the 'residuum', those for whom there could be no trickling down of the benefits from Victorian entrepreneurship. The artizans, the aristocracy of the working class, did get their 'trickle'. They had a level of elementary education and literacy which enabled involvement in social, religious and political movements of the day. They gained more than an average share of the estimated 41 per cent increase in money wages between 1850 and 1871 (representing a nine per cent increase in 'real' wages).[22] But those we have seen utterly dependent on authority through poverty of goods and probably spirit were brutally characterised by Sir James Kay-Shuttleworth in 1866 as *the dangerous classes who prey upon property, or sell their virtue, or are ready to take advantage of any tendency to tumult . . .the classes who stagnate in the obscure and unhealthy parts of great cities.*[23]

When turning a little later on to the Reform Bill

Riots should we be tempted to take this judgement into consideration as applying also to aspects of Derby life?

It is in fact impossible to say how much such elements contributed to the larger-scale set-pieces in Derby's nineteenth-century epic. The 'laissez-faire' state of the law in Regency times would have contributed to such a possiblity. There was the reflection of totally unworried good-living on the part of its chief 'servants' on the one hand, and the combination of total severity in sentencing, utterly lenient juries and toothless policing on the other. Certainly, the fact that all those who were sentenced to death at Derby Assizes during our period and were actually from Derbyshire were 'working class' does seem to suggest the probability of poverty being a factor in domestic crime at least, since five of the total of thirty executed were for the murder of wives by husbands and one of a husband by his wife. Poverty, accompanied by long hours of work and poor housing must have contributed to the heavy incidence of domestic crime, with murder often preceeded by heavy bouts of drinking and the tavern the more obvious escape from drudgery than a cheerless home.

With 233 public houses, ten hotels and eighty-nine retailers of beer to choose from in Derby in 1884, heavy drinking played a significant part in half the recorded murder cases.[24] On the other hand, nationally, drunkenness and crimes of violence actually rose in prosperous times, whereas by far the commonest form of crime, offences against property, fell during such times and rose during depressions. There was a twenty per cent difference between crime peaks and troughs, with 1868 and 1880 as peak years.[25]

The Law

As with other aspects of the town story, there was a gradual increase in regulatory efficiency in the relationship between authority and offenders during our period. Judging was very much a part of establishment society in Regency times, if the announcement by the County's High Sheriff in September 1817 is anything to go by that he. . .*intends to meet his friends at Little Eaton, at half-past eleven, and come into Derby at noon. He will meet the Judges at Osmaston toll-gate at half-past three, and proceed thence to the County Hall. Dinner at the George at five.*[26]

County Hall in St Mary's Gate was altered internally in 1827, so that not only trials could be held there but also balls, dinners and other entertainments. One thief was apparently sentenced to fourteen years' transportation for plying his trade inside the very Assize courts.[27] This incident also indicates the response to what we, in the present century, would file as 'petty crime' in the absence of efficient means of crime prevention. From the 1820s on, both custody and policing were improved so that recourse to sheer terror was not so necessary.

Theft certainly kept 'Derby Mercury' and 'Reporter' scribblers reasonably busy throughout the period. For example, the 'Reporter' for 2 January 1834 noted:

Some time between Wednesday and Friday in last week, a fat-horned ewe sheep, marked on the rump with a W., belonging to Mr William Morley, was stolen

WINTER ASSIZES,

TUESDAY,   DEC. 20, 1859

SENTENCES OF THE PRISONERS

Tried at the ASSIZES held in DERBY, on TUESDAY, the 20th day of December, 1859, before the Right Honorable SIR CHARLES CROMPTON, Knight, one of the Justices of our Lady the Queen, assigned to hold pleas before the Queen herself.

The Hon. EDWARD K. W. COKE, of Longford, High Sheriff.

George Hobson, aged 28, soldier,
Charged with marrying on the 19th October, 1857, Elizabeth Bennett, his former wife, to whom he was married on the 10th February, 1850, being then alive—Ilkeston. 15 months

Henry Brown, aged 35, labourer,
Charged with burglariously breaking and entering in the night of the 25th August, 1859, the dwelling-house of John Newton, and stealing one smock-frock, one sack bag, one cheese, a quantity of bread and cheese, and a bag his property—Brackenfield. 4 years' penal serv.

Geo. Leary, aged 21, collier; James May, aged 21, collier;
Were charged with assaulting on the 17th September, 1859, Richard Turner, putting him in bodily fear and danger of his life, and violently stealing from his person nine shillings, a purse, a knife, a leather strap, a key, and a quantity of herrings, his property—North Wingfield. 15 months each.

Maria Ferneyhough, aged 18, Millhand,
Charged with endeavouring on the 12th September, 1859, to conceal the birth of a child—Burton-upon-Trent. 1 month

Charles Walker, aged 49, Druggist,
Charged with maliciously stabbing, cutting and wounding on the 3rd October, 1859, Ulysses Brown, with intent thereby to do him some grievous bodily harm—Codnor. 15 months

7—Thomas Hoult, aged 23; 8—Thomas Moody, aged 26, Labourers; 9—Wm. Hoult, aged 25; 10—Antony Coates, aged 26, Colliers; 11—James Todd, aged 25, Smith,
Charged with burglariously breaking and entering on the 14th October last, the dwelling-house of William Watson, and stealing a book, gilt wood stand, glass shade, and various other articles—Chesterfield. Tod 15 months, others 6 months each.

12—Henry Amos Mansfield, aged 22, Tailor,
Charged with stealing on the 31st of October, 1859, a gun, the property of Hugh Seville; also, with stealing a cap the property of William Henry Jennings—Hartington 3 months

13—Ellen Jones, aged 23, Hawker,
Charged with stealing two silk dress pieces, the property of John Wray Lister—Ashborne. 6 years' penal serv.

14—John Simpkin, aged 59, Shoemaker,
Charged with having in his possession two counterfeit florins and five counterfeit half crowns, with intent to utter the same—Derby. 4 years' penal serv.

15—John Spence, aged 32. 16—Jane Lee, aged 29.
17—Margaret Clarke, aged 29, Hawkers.
Charged with stealing from Thomas Lane, a purse, seven sovereigns, and seven halfcrowns.—Ashborne. Spence, 15 mhs.; Lee, 9 months; Clarke, 12 months.

18—Sarah Alldridge, aged 58, Chairwoman,
Charged with wilfully murdering a newly-born child on the 5th of Dec. inst.—Ilkeston. Discharged.

19—Thomas Richardson, aged 47, Stonemason,
Charged with riotously and tumultuously assembling, with divers other persons, on the 13th Dec. inst., and with force beginning to demolish and destroy the dwelling-house of William Knight.—Chapel-en-le-Frith. Discharged on his own recog.

JAMES H. SIMS, Governor.

HALL, PRINTER, DERBY.

from a close in Spondon Meadows. It is conjectured the sheep was conveyed away in a cart.

A fortnight later on 15 January, the 'Mercury' reported the successful prosecution of a more central case at the Borough Assizes held at the Guildhall on Tuesday 9 January:

Stealing From the Person
John Williams, aged 15, charged with stealing from the person of Maria Adkins, in the parish of All Saints', one purse and nine shillings, the property of the said Maria Adkins.

Maria Adkins said, that on Friday, 6 December, she was in the poultry-market when someone called to her, and she was pushed; found upon examiniation that her purse containing silver had gone; her attention was directed to the prisoner, who held the purse; he was taken into custody. John Allen, constable, produced the purse containing 5s 6d; another witness was called who spoke to the robbery. Guilty. To be transported 7 years.

On 20 March 1860, the same paper noted a comment by Mr Justice Crompton at the Crown Court on Monday, 18th, in his address to the Grand Jury:

He was sorry to see several offences of the foregoing character (burglary, rape, manslaughter) *in the calendar, most of them committed by boys of 15 or 16 years of age. It was a crime which appeared to be on the increase, and severe measures must be adopted to check it.*

Obviously the more efficient methods of response to crime current from the late 1820s on were not the whole answer. However, by this time transporation as the normal punishment for theft and the scaled-down reaction to more 'serious' crime, which included robbery, assault, attacks on property and arson, was being phased out, resulting in turn in harsher prison regimes on the same principle as that current in workhouses, to encourage a desire not to return and so create accommodation problems.[28] Nearly thirty years earlier, Glover, in his 1833 'History of the County of Derby', noted the *number of convicts transported from the borough jail during the last six years* (1827-1832) as forty-two males and eight females. It was apparently usual, then, for the judge at the end of the Assizes to commute a number of death-sentences to transportation. The result, a few weeks later, would be the sight of a coachload of convicted prisoners leaving the town for Botany Bay, as for example in May 1819 when nine were recorded being conveyed to the hulks of Sheerness as transit point. Incidentally, public whippings were still being carried out at this time, with one instance recorded in 1817.[29]

To illustrate the scaling down of the use of transportation as a punishment and therefore also of the severity of the sentencing system as a whole, it is instructive to examine some statistics given by Glover in his 'History and Directory of Derby' for 1849, and therefore the last decade but one before its total discontinuance in the 1860s.

Glover states that in the seven-year period 1843-49, the following transportation sentences were given at the Derby Assizes: 45 for 7 years, 81 for 10 years, 12 for 14 years, 48 for 15 years, two for 21 years and 21 for life. The 'troughs' and 'peaks', whichever way we choose to characterise the annual sentencing totals,

during this period were as follows: for 7 years, there was a range of two in 1846 to 12 in 1848, for 10 years of five in 1847 to 22 in 1843, for 14 years of none in 1847 and 1849 to five in 1844, for 15 years of none in 1848 to 23 in 1843, for 21 years, only two in 1844 for the whole period; and for life, none in 1847, 1848 and 1849 to 12 in 1843.

Quite clearly this terrible sentence was used more sparingly in the later years as confirmed, with one exception, by a review of the annual totals for all these sentences: 69 in 1843, 42 in 1844, 26 in 1845, 17 in 1846, 13 in 1847, 21 in 1848 and 15 in 1849.

The supreme penalty was, of course, public execution, with the theory behind it that spectators would be impressed by the experience with the inevitability of the dreadful punishment for the awful crime of murder. In July of 1817, transportation was the option accorded to only six out of ten accused and convicted men from various Derbyshire villages, not for murder but for setting fire to ricks, breaking and entering and horse stealing. The four convicted of arson were sentenced to death, to be hanged in front of the County Goal in Friar Gate on 15 August. The 'Mercury' report stated that the condemned were undisturbed by the sad solemnities by which they were surrounded and when the proceedings were interrupted by a heavy shower of rain *two of them deliberately retreated to the shelter of an umbrella which was expanded on the drop, and a third placed himself under cover of the doorway.*[30]

There was actually something worse, the punishment for treason by which the condemned were subjected to additional post-mortem indignities. Thankfully the only instance of this in Derby during our period, indeed the last in Britain, was again in that fateful year of 1817 in the judicial ending of the so-called Pentrich Revolution. The trial of its leaders, notably Jeremiah Brandreth, for their rebellious march on Nottingham as part of what they believed would be a national uprising for a more democratic government, resulted in their betrayal by a spy of the regime and in County Hall's most famous occasion.

After the special Assizes in October, Brandreth and John Turner were executed, whilst other of their colleagues suffered transportation. After the bodies had been exposed for an hour on the gallows, they were cut down and beheaded before the waiting crowd which reportedly recoiled in horror when the executioner held up Brandreth's head and shouted the time-dishonoured phrase, "Behold the head of a traitor." The last resting place of the truncated bodies was in St Werburgh's churchyard.[31]

The death-crowd gave vent to its feelings in Friar Gate, where the gaol was situated on the site of what is now the Howard Hotel, once again only 18 months later in March 1819 at the execution of Hannah Barking. She was a seventeen-year-old convicted the previous September of poisioning a fellow servant-girl from Litton in North Derbyshire. Hannah was reported again as being strangely indifferent to her fate:

At the moment, when she was launched into eternity, an involuntary shuddering pervaded the assembled crowd, and although she excited little sympathy, a general feeling of horror was expressed that one so young should have been so guilty, and so insensible.[32]

From 1827 the prevailing spirit of improvement decreed a more humane method of execution with the construction around the corner in Vernon Street, where, as we shall see, a new County Gaol had been built, of a new trap-door-type gallows-drop. This replaced the old tree-and-cart gallows method by which the removal of the cart had left the condemned suspended. It coincided with successive reductions of the application of the death penalty under the reforming Home Secretary Sir Robert Peel which ended in 1837 with its abolition for the crime of burglary.[33]

This did not mean that executions failed to provide a popular public attraction any more. On the contrary, the drastic reduction in the number of such occasions during Victorian times combined with improved communications may have contributed to an increased pulling power as the mid-point of the century approached and even passed! Between 1812 and 1837 (the Queen's accession) there were eighteen executions in Derby, whereas between 1837 and 1882 there were only eleven. The latter figure is in addition to two women whose sentences were commuted.

In compensation, executions featured as special excursion train venues and many people living at a not-too-great distance would walk miles to the scene. It is estimated that no less than 50,000 people attended the execution of Samuel Bonsall, William Bland and John Hulme on 31 March 1843 for a murder committed at Stanley Hall.

The executions of John Platts on 1 April 1847 and George Smith on 16 August 1861 were each attended by an estimated 20,000 people. The 'Derby Mercury' describes the triple execution in 1843 thus:

The concourse of persons was by far greater than on any similar occasion in Derby. The crowd, as seen from the scaffold, presented a densely packed mass of human beings covering the whole spacious area in front of the prison, and extending through the whole of Vernon Street and into Friar Gate. The roads, gardens, yards, windows, housetops, in fact every possible situation commanding a view of the drop had its separate crowd of gazers.[34]

A crowd of particular note gathered to witness the execution of Anthony Turner of Belper on 26 March 1852 for the murder of a woman. According to the 'Derby and Chesterfield Reporter':

A large proportion of the spectators consisted of women and children, the women especially being very numerous. We also noticed a great number of females with babes at the breast. One woman in Vernon Street had no less than eight children with her. They were all dressed up for the occasion, and no doubt she thought she was giving them an intellectual treat. Indeed the scene resembled a pleasure fair more than anything else.[35]

Derby's last public execution was on 11 April 1862 when a reduced crowd of 10,000 in Vernon Street watched the end of Richard Thorley for the murder of a woman in Court No 4, Agard Street. According to the 'Reporter' one optician in the town was inundated with requests for telescopes and opera glasses to improve the view of certain spectators.[36] And

so ended a long and dreadful episode in Derby's legal history.

Police and Prison

What of more direct methods of crime prevention, even detection? In 1812 there was obviously nothing that could be remotely described as a police force, as the following notice in the 'Derby Mercury' for 9 January and 6 February 1812 make clear:

NOTICE is hereby GIVEN, in consequence of the daring and repeated Attacks made upon the House and Premises of John Brentnall, at Locko Grange; and there being no Public Road through his Yards, STEEL TRAPS and SPRING GUNS will be regularly set upon all the Premises, as well as in and upon all the Woods and Grounds belonging to W.D.Lowe, Esq.

A decisive motivating event for change was probably the Reform Bill Riots in 1831. This gave an incentive like nothing else towards the setting up of a regular organised Town Police Force. In common with Nottingham and Bristol, Derby felt the full force of rejection of the modest step towards a democratic system of government, proposed by the Parliamentary party of Reform, the Whigs. Derby's representatives, Edward Strutt and the Hon.F.C.Cavendish both stood for the Whig interest.[37] A weekend of mayhem lasting from late on Saturday evening, 8 October, after the arrival of the London mail-coach with the news that the House of Lords had turned down the Bill from the Commons proposing an extension of the right to vote, until the morning of Monday the 10th resulted in three deaths and several thousand pounds' worth of damage to property.

After an initial tolling of bells at All Saints', St Peter's and St Alkmund's, a mob wrecked the premises of Mr William Bemrose, purveyor of books, music and instruments in the Corn Market, returning three times to do a more thorough job. Other groups had set about many other objects of resentment including Markeaton and Chaddesden Halls on the outskirts. Armed with an uprooted cast-iron lamp-post one large group of well over a thousand rioters broke into the Borough Goal in Friar Gate and released not only those the Mayor had managed to get arrested the previous evening but also the twenty-three regular prisoners as well.

They continued around the corner into Vernon Street, where the governor of the County Gaol had to order armed guards on to the wall and eventually to fire on the mob. The result was the first death of the troubles, a young man of seventeen, shot in the stomach and reported by the 'Derby Mercury' of 13 October to have *possessed a good character and had taken no part in the proceedings.* The other two fatalities occurred on the Monday when, after the soldiers from Nottingham requested by the magistrates had restored a semblance of order in the centre the previous (Sunday) evening, another crowd of varied intent gathered in the Market Place. Stalls for the signing of a petition supporting reform were smashed up and the magistrates reluctantly took the decision to have the Riot Act read and ask the military to clear the square.

When the crowd already in the Market Square attempted to get away from the advancing line of cavalry armed with guns and drawn sabes, they collided with others still streaming in through the narrow street entrances. One man was shot and another fatally injured in the crush. An eye-witness of the first related:

As we were returning a shot was fired. The ball passed through my hat and struck a man who was on the pavement about two yards distant from me. I did not at first know what had happened to my hat. I turned to look and saw the man down. I heard him groan and saw him bleeding.[38]

In February 1836, the Borough Constabulary was formed in the immediate wake of the Municipal Corporation Act and the more distant one of the Riots. It consisted of eight constables backed up by ten watchmen for night duty. By 1843 a superintendant had been provided for with twenty constables under him.[39] In 1856, Parliament passed the County and Borough Police Act putting in central grants to local authorities who wanted to set up an adequate force including an inspectorate.[40]

The result in Derby was a complement of four sergeants paid at 24s per week, ten constables on 19s, eight on 17s and seven on 16s. There were, however, complaints heard by the Council two years later about alleged indiscipline, in particular with respect to convictions for drunkenness among members of the Force.[41]

The 1877 Borough extension would have led to a further increase in numbers: the 'Derby Mercury' report of 13 July 1881 on the visit of the Prince of Wales to view the Royal Agricultural Show mentions a Borough Constabulary of ninety men on duty that day, commended for their admirable service.

What happened to prisoners who were fated to remain in Derby for the duration of their sentence? The town was the site for the County as well as the Borough Gaol and there was a certain amount of exchanging between them until an amalgamation was effected in 1840 on the site of the new County Gaol completed in 1826 after three year's construction work at the end of Vernon Street, then on the very edge of Derby.

Until 1826, the County Gaol was in Friar Gate in a severe version of the classical style put up in 1756 and designed by a Warwick architect. It had the quadruple pillars of St Helen's House holding up a broad triangular frontage with forbidding-looking round-topped windows on the ground floor and even more forbidding square ones above. Inside, it had a central domed hall with two corridors radiating from it in order to separate the major from the minor offenders, and four cells for women. By 1821 it held three times the twenty-one long-stay prisoners it was designed to hold, reflecting the fact that the custodial system was not keeping pace with the 'requirements' of a rapidly expanding general population.

In 1826, when the move to Vernon Street came about, the Friar Gate Gaol was sold to the Borough so that its previous squalid little place of custody in Willow Row could be rendered obsolete.[42] Not before time according to Glover's 'Directory of Derby' for 1831, which records that *there was no chaplain nor any divine service performed in the prison, nor rules for its government, nor employment of any kind.*[43] Both gaols also accommodated debtors and there was a so-called 'House of Correction' in the Guildhall for minor offenders.[44]

The new County Gaol in Vernon Street, designed by Francis Goodwin, who went on to be architect of St John's in Bridge Street not so far away, followed the new guidelines of Sir Robert Peel's 1823 Prisons Act, with separate sections for debtors, felons and people 'on remand', and the further separation of men and women with more individual cells.[45] There were balconies reached by numerous steel staircases and wire nets between. Additions were made in 1880 - a new dining-room and women's block, with hospital, reception area, laundry and workshop. A chapel was also added, with rows of benches and raised seats for the warders and a 'pen' for the governor.[46] The Reform Bill Riots had had their effect on the prison, too, as Glover's 'History and Directory of Derby' for 1849 relates:

Since the riots in October, 1831, eight martello towers have been designed by Mr Mason and built by Mr Thomas Cooper, at the cost of £1,540. These are furnished with fire-arms.

Glover goes on to give more details of the original structure, its situation, officials and the prisoners' diet:

This Prison is in an open and airy situation in the outskirts of the town of Derby. It is enclosed with a brick wall 25 feet in height, with 145 courses of loose bricks on the top, and defended by flanking

The new County Gaol in Vernon Street, pictured before the addition of the Martello towers which were built following the Reform Bill Riot of 1831.

towers, loop-holed for musquetry . . .The gateway is a bold and commanding edifice, exhibiting the strength of character which the Doric order (the earliest and plainest style of Greek architecture) is capable. The governor's house stands in the centre, and overlooks the whole. It is one of the most complete prisons in England.

According to Glover, the Keeper of the prison earned £360 per annum in 1832, and £500 in 1849, well-paid by skilled-worker standards let alone those of the humbler industrial worker and as befitted a post of some responsibility. The Chaplain was paid £150 a year, the fourteen male turnkeys 20s per week, the two female turnkeys 14s per week, and two watchmen also 14s per week. The diet consisted of:

Breakfast a quart of gruel, made from two ounces of oatmeal, and a portion of bread; dinner, one pound of boiled potatoes, and a portion of bread; supper, one quart of gruel, made from two ounces of oatmeal, and a portion of bread. One and a half pound of good wheaten bread, and one quarter of an ounce of salt per day.

Surely no comment is necessary on such a list! During the 1840s the average cost of food per prisoner was actually pegged at 2s 11d per week.[47]

All in all, for general reasons already mentioned, the regime at Vernon Street would have been more strict than that of its predecessors. It ended at least the formal ending of the era in which the standard of a prisoner's comfort depended on the financial power of his/her friends outside. The influence of reformers John Howard and Elizabeth Fry was evident. There was instruction for the prisoners in reading and writing, daily prayers, no spirits or more than a pint of beer per day and no gaming, all rules indicative of what had gone on before. There was an emphasis on solitude and silence to reflect upon misconduct, no mutual conversation, and more confinement in cells than hitherto.

There was, in fact, a more relaxed attitude in Derby than in many other places and so we find Surgeon Douglas Fox requesting urgent attention to heating in the form of *steam conveyed through pipes* on the part of the management. There was indeed a response the following year. In 1839, Fox reported on *the extreme cleanliness and good ventilation of the prison, together with temperance on the part of the inmates.* He had also to report in 1837-8, however, of one old lady whose life was *evidently shortened by the depressing effect of long confinement there*, another who finally succumbed to ill-health as a *scrofulous and feeble subject* and a third who hanged himself with no prior indications given. Two years later, he reported three more suicides, hanged with a sheet, throat cut with a razor and the third found dead in the cell, *Died by invitation of God.*

By this time wool-picking had been introduced for prisoners whose health and physique would not stand up to the 'wheel' or stone-breaking.[48] For those who could not get exempt from the normal regime, there was liberal use of the treadmill, as the 'wheel' is better known, involving the estimated possible climbing of the equivalent of 7,500 feet in a day, or of the handcrank, fixed to a cell wall for individual punishment exercise with up to 10,000 revolutions per day.[49] It was a suitable complement to the workhouse for those who for the most part had presumably reacted with less regard for the law than to their particular circumstances.

Notes

1. Maxwell Craven, opt.cit.
2. Ibid
3. Ibid.
4. Ibid.
5. Ibid.
6. Ibid.
7. Ibid.
8. Ibid.
9. Ibid.
10. Ibid.
11. Ibid.
12. D.Read, op.cit.
13. Quoted Ibid.
14. WEA extra-mural class research project report, *Derbyshire Miscellany*, Spring 1972.
15. Maxwell Craven, op.cit.
16. *Derbyshire Miscellany*, op.cit.
17. Ibid.
18. Quoted Ibid.
19. Ibid.
20. Ibid.
21. Quoted A.Sturgess in Centenary Booklet on Silk-Mill Lock-Out 1934.
22. Quoted D.Read, op.cit.
23. Quoted Ibid.
24. P.Taylor, *May the Lord Have Mercy on Your Soul*, Derbyshire Heritage series, 1989.
25. D.Read, op.cit.
26. Quoted Davison, op.cit.
27. Ibid.
28. P.Taylor, op.cit.
29. Davison, op.cit.
30. Quoted E.G.Power, *Hanged for a Sheep*, Derbyshire Heritage Series.
31. J.Stevenson, *England's Last Revolution*.
32. *Derby Mercury*, quoted P.Taylor, op.cit.
33. P.Taylor, op.cit.
34. Quoted Ibid.
35. Quoted Ibid.
36. Ibid.
37. Maxwell Craven, op.cit.
38. Quoted E.G.Power, op.cit.
39. Roy Christian, article in *Derbyshire Advertiser*, 2 May 1951.
40. D.Read, op.cit.
41. Roy Christian, op.cit.
42. Maxwell Craven, op.cit.
43. Quoted Ibid.
44. Ibid.
45. E.G.Power, op.cit.
46. Article in *Derby Mercury*, 2 September 1921.
47. E.G.Power, op.cit.
48. Ibid.
49. P.Taylor, op.cit.

Foundations

PERHAPS it is now time to examine some of the many strands which, when woven together, give the basis for judging what we may call the quality of life in Derby during this seventy-five year period. This may be compounded of facilities upon which we ought to be able to rely at all times and others that minister to dire emergency.

This is apart from the most basic facility of all but which has always, it seems, and continues to be, denied to far too many people — men, women and children — a decent roof over a minimum of private space, a home. The picture presented is one of a slow groping forward on the part of the 'city fathers', prodded occasionally by the agents of central government and helped by individuals and groups of goodwill, towards an acceptable standard of community life in the latter part of the nineteenth century, when expectations were of necessity rising under the twin prongs of industrialisation and urbanisation as goads of the modern world.

First, a word of praise from a visitor of some stature in 1828, Sir Richard Phillips, who was moved to observe:

. . .I have never seen better shops in a County town — the streets were delightfully Macadamised — and great cleanliness indicated a good police . . .[1]

In view of certain aspects of our survey thus far, we may be allowed a hint of scepticism as to the acuteness of these statements apart from the comparative aspect which only he as a contemporary could realistically make. As he leads us to speculate, he may well have been prejudiced in the town's favour by association with its luminaries of the recent past, including the painter Joseph Wright.

Policing could not have been a very strong point in 1828 as the Reform Bill Riots were soon to bring to light, admittedly in common with other towns the nearest of which boasted both a castle and military base. The quality of the arm of the law at that time might well have had to be judged at close quarters by the company of watchmen, who as we have seen were incorporated in the first official police force for night-duty. Vintage memoirs of old Derby leave us with an amusingly indulgent picture of their qualities, although of unspecified date:

The writer well remembers one of these watchmen's boxes at the bottom of Lodge Lane, and the watchman himself is in his mind's eye at the moment — a solemn man enveloped in several coats, with marvellous decoration and protection in the way of capes which overlapped one another in thick, bulging folds. His boots were fortified with huge nails, and his neck and mouth were guarded against the night chills by a very large shawl or small blanket. The lantern carried by this carefully preserved individual was eighteen inches long at the least and nine inches broad, the sides being of horn and unprovided with an attachment for darkening. On the top of this lantern was a swivel, and by it the apparatus could be attached with cord to one of the huge buttons of the watchman's coat. Picture this ponderous guardian of the peace rambling along the few streets at the rate of a mile an hour or less, keeping doubtful characters well posted as to his whereabouts by his noisy tread, his rattling lantern, and his occasional cry of the time of night or state of the weather.[2]

They were, however, with the handful of constables, appointed by the Justices of the Peace and under the control of the Improvement Commissioners until after 1835.[3]

Phillips' comment on the streets was perhaps 'on better grounds'. It was even supported by a favourable report from none other than the great Robert McAdam himself, most famous road engineer of the time. Derby was, indeed, good coaching territory at the beginning of our period, fit enough for a visit from Grand Duke Nicholas of All the Russias, shown the 'lights' in December 1816 by the Duke of Devonshire whilst staying at the King's Head and admiring the view from the not-so-ancient Shot Tower.[4]

The second of the special Nun's Green Acts of Parliament, it will be recalled, was specially engineered to provide the money, from the proceeds of releasing land for development, to pay for the paving and lighting of the streets. This would be in respect of the more central ones, where the more important citizens, including the Commissioners themselves, would have their houses. The poorer ratepayers opposed the move but the Commissioners, as the active arm of the Town Council, were an energetic group. Between 1824 and 1827 they organised the numbering of the streets, a basic but very necessary facility.

We have seen how later on, under the 'reformed' administration, the main streets were widened at the same time as entirely new ones created. This process was replicated further out, too, most notably in the widening of the Normanton Road to 40 feet in response

The Corn Exchange in Albert Street, photographed by Keene in 1861. Derby was then lit by gas-lamps of the type seen in the centre of the picture.

to the surge of residential terrace building in that sector of the town.[5]

There had also been sufficient resources to make a faint start with the lighting of the streets by gas. This was long after its introduction to such places as London and Birmingham. According to Davison, a prod from a little nearer home was the decisive immediate spur to action, in the form of a report in the 'Derby Mercury' in 1819 on lighting up in Nottingham: *Thousands of people walked the streets to see the new lights.*[6]

At a meeting just a fortnight later, a resolution was made to obtain the Act of Parliament necessary to form a gas company.[7] This was done in 1820 when the Gas, Light and Coke Company was set up between the Markeaton Brook and Friar Gate, where its

headquarters was built. There were two gasometers by 1826.[8] Then, on 19 February 1821, the Market Place was lit by gas for the first time, according to the 'Mercury'...*most brilliantly illuminated by Gas Light placed in the centre, where a beautiful column, or, rather, Candelabra, supported a very handsome lanthorne.*[9]

In 1825, the Commissioners acted again to extend the experiment with a further recourse to Parliament backed up with a borrowing facility to pay for it.[10] However, there was no glowing light anywhere in or near any of the major public buildings of the town other than the Guildhall, with the exception of Bold Lane Theatre until 1831,[11] when the Corporation spent over £560 on illuminating the main centres of attraction and public concourse. By July 1830, 210 gas lamps were alight compared to 110 of the old oil lamps. In the meantime, the Gas Company was forced to reduce the price charged for its product by individual firms installing their own apparatus in response to what they considered an excessive monopoly rate. A second gas works was built in Litchurch and after the extension of the Borough, the combined concerns were, in the 1880s, producing 200 million cubic feet of the stuff, which does sound a fair amount. Gas was to remain the provider of light for the rest of our period as electricity was still at the demonstration stage in Derby by 1887.[12]

So the record of the Improvement Commissioners had been a reasonable one during their regime in the first half of the century. They fell down, however, in the matter of public health and sanitation, the time-honoured basis of civilised life itself. This issue, indeed, finished them as they were abolished as a body when Parliament decided to impose national standards by means of the Public Health Act of 1848.[13] On the surface, despite the existence of a public health inspector in Derby from 1808, there had been many complaints about the state of the streets and in particular about Markeaton Brook's being a receptacle for much of the filth of the town, despite its periodic willingness to flood.[14]

The year 1849 undoubtedly marks the first chapter in the story of Derby's health provision in modern times. It was then that appeared the 'Report to the General Board of Health on a Preliminary Inquiry into the Sewerage, Drainage, and Supply of Water, and the Sanitary Conditions of the Inhabitants of the Borough of Derby, 1849'. This revealed a horror story. The town may have had its General Infirmary, but the Commissioners had simply not realised the unprecedented situation created by unregulated building in response to the demands of factory employment in the first wave of industrial revolution and the consequent need for a new sanitary regime. The damning conclusion on Derby was as follows:

Notwithstanding the vast sums of money that have already been expended in making sewers, no efficient arrangements have been carried out to prevent that vast accumulation of filthy matter on the several yards and courts belonging to private individuals, and which is found to be productive of excessive disease and premature mortality.

Few towns have more need of the provision of the Public Health Act being supplied to them than Derby. In furtherance thereof I must recommend that there be an establishment of a local Board to be composed of the Mayor, Alderman, and Burgesses of the Borough, and the Council of the Borough, to exercise and execute the powers, authorities and duties required.[15]

Obviously the Commissioners had been strung up on the horns of the classic Victorian dilemma of interference with individual liberty even where it was patently detrimental to the common good. The 'Report' listed the following requirements:

Regulate the laying out of new streets.
Lay new sewers and waterpipes.
Convert privies into water closets.
Abolish cesspools.
Clean up lodging houses.
Remove slaughterhouses to the edge of town.
Maintain and clean the roads.

Collect the refuse.
Supply water.
Ventilate the public buildings.
Clean up tenements and houses.
Prevent overcrowding.[16]

It added up to a pretty comprehensive agenda if ever there was one, and it took the Council forty years to come within sight of completion!

The new sewers referred to in the report's conclusion, all constructed during the 1840s and listed earlier in the document, included: from Morledge to Wardwick, Curzon Street, Bold Lane, Agard Street, Sadler Gate, Brook Street, St Peter's Street, Green Lane, Ashbourne Road. On 21 December 1848, the Board had listened to a submission by a doctor and two surgeons to the effect that the town's health had definitely improved over the past ten years as a consequence of the work on the sewers. The death rate was now 1 in 42 compared to 1 in 37 in 1840. The reason why it was still so high was the effect of the new housing put up without mains sewerage for the huge increase in the population of working people during the present decade. They comprised seventy-five per cent of the extra 10,000 people added to the town in the 1840s.[17]

The death rate was high, unacceptably so, Elsewhere in the report comes the statement that during the three years 1840-42, whereas the average mortality for the whole of England was 2.2 per 100, in Derby it was 2.6 per 100. Perhaps this was not too bad for an urban area as we shall see in a moment, but the stigma of being above the average in this particular field was not good either.

In 1840, epidemic diseases carried off 250 people, not plague proportions but still a steady five per week. To put the picture into another perspective, whilst it was still true that in contrast to its eighteenth-century self, as a reasonably healthy community containing within its fabric many gardens and open spaces for private use, Derby was now much more lethal, compared with the situation in the five largest towns outside London it was perhaps not too far off the scale. It has been calculated that in the decade up to 1841, the death rate in these five places ranged from an incredible 20.69 per cent to an even more incredible 30.8 per cent! This was due to foul air, new streets of back-to-back terraced houses without drains, privies, water supply or ventilation. In essence, it was down to weak administrations, producing a situation in which every second child died before the age of five: the terrible state of the poorest countries in the latter part of the twentieth century.

The Royal Commission on the State of Large Towns in 1845 declared only one town in fifty had good drainage and only six had a good water supply. Manchester, for an extreme example, had only thirty-three privies for over 7,000 people in one area. There were national cholera epidemics in 1832, 1848-9 (which was the immediate inspiration of the present inquiry) and again in 1853-54.[18]

To take the true measure of what this meant in Derby for the real unfortunates who suffered the consequences, it is necessary to endure a few scraps of the voluminous testimony submitted to the Board. They surely speak for themselves and render comment superfluous:

Rotten Row looking down Irongate. The removal of the old buildings on the left extended the area of the Market Place as improvments to the town centre continued in the nineteenth century.

...*Mr Douglas Fox, surgeon, gave it as his opinion that diarrhoeas, low fevers, and other diseases, were mainly attributable to the general want of drainage and cleanliness; he asserted that near the Mark Eaton Brook the waters were so charged with sulphurated hydrogen that at Mr Lowe's, the draper, all the white paint and letters in the space of a short time were turned black, and that the newly finished painting with white lead, in the rooms used by the family, was equally injured. The slaughter-houses he also described as badly arranged, and productive of much evil; in several, the pumping into carts without any precautions being observed affected the entire neighbourhood where they were situated...long habit in such occupations renders persons almost unconscious of the disagreeables with which they are surrounded, and they become careless with regard to cleanliness or propriety.*

There are several principal streets, and about 352 courts occupied by the labouring classes; and it is necessary to call particular attention to the fact that the Local Act contains no provision whatsoever for the drainage, sewerage, supply of water, paving or cleansing Etc of these numerous overcrowded habitations . . .the numerous occupiers cannot of course come to an amicable arrangement to perform this necessary duty, and as the public thoroughfares are alone under the Commissioners, the owners cannot demand redress, and they will not undertake the performance of all that is necessary for the health or cleanliness of their tenants.

. . .In No.7 court, belonging to Mrs Armstrong, are 21

dwellings, with 2 privies only, discharging into the Brook.

The same arrangements exist in No.5 court, where are a small gasholder and a retort furnace, the refuse also running into the Brook . . .

No.1 court, Bow-Lane has only 2 privies to 18 houses, over one of the former is a living room. The inhabitants are continually out of health, and in summer the air is much contaminated . . .

No.13 court, Walker Lane. In the house occupied by Joseph Adams, the contents of a privy and a pig-sty find their way through the walls, and render the appartments extremely disagreeable . . .

Siddal's Lane. In the playground of St Peter's Infant School there is an oozing through the wall from an offensive piggery and dung-pit in the adjoining premises, which belong to Mr George Bagnol, who has been summoned on two occasions and fined; yet the powers vested in the present Commissioners cannot enforce him to abate the horrid nuisance so peculiarly injurious to infantile existence.

(Bridge Street): Court No.4, abuts upon Peel's mill. All the houses viz.14, are half-houses, back to back, and the paved way between the privies is only 3ft 4in wide. One family of the name of Ball lost six children with typhus fever; they resided in the house adjoining the cesspools, some of the windows looking over the Brook.[19]

Improvement as we have seen was slow. The trouble was that early Victorian legislation was in the main permissive rather than mandatory. It was not until 1866 that the first compulsive Sanitary Act was passed

A pleasant county market town. Derby from Nottingham Road c.1860, showing St Mary's Bridge and the churches of All Saints' and St Alkmund's.

and it was again not until the Public Health Act of 1872 that sanitary duties and a Medical Officer of Health, were set up.[20] This was again the result of a Royal Commission into sanitation, the report of which made a connection between physical and moral pollution. It stated that a large proportion of the population of town and country drank polluted water also that . . .*accumulations of filth* (were) *widely vitiating the air.* The working classes were rendered sick and poor . . .*by a tainted atmosphere and unhealthy dwellings.*

Smoke pollution went uncontrolled.[21] However, whilst smelly drains were a common feature of urban living throughout Victorian times and it remained a daily battle to keep homes clean from polluting dust, the increasing use of water-closets began to solve the domestic sewage problem by rendering it a public one.[22]

Here in Derby, things were not much further advanced by the time of the 1872 Act. A critical report in the journal 'British Architect' in June 1882 gave evidence of *totally unventilated sewers*, common reliance on cesspools, and preferred dependence on well-water rather than the distrusted product of the municipal waterworks which were set up in the very year after the Board of Health Report, at first as a private company.

After its taking over by the municipality in 1880, a major expansion was undertaken to improve on the modest 1881 service to over 15,000 homes, but with 1,000 still unconnected.[23] The Corporation, however, had apparently turned down five different schemes

of the Borough Engineer, reacting to yet another Act of Parliament concerning river pollution, for a more efficient sewage system in the 1870s.[24] Untreated sewage still went into the Derwent and also Markeaton Brook until the making of the Strand. Things were far better done in Litchurch itself; the only definite improvement as regards the whole town effected by Jubilee Year was the banning of cesspools and the setting up of a refuse disposal unit on Stores Road in 1882.[25] Overall, not an entirely happy story!

Flood and Fire

Markeaton Brook seemed a very central character in the struggle for better things, a tempter to bad practices for the most part, a villainous force on very special occasions. Some of its very considerable powers were taken away by the culverting activities between 1837 and 1845, but only after a second attempt, as we shall see. It was by no means rendered impotent. It was not unknown also for the Derwent itself to flood badly, Chester Green suffering inundation on two occasions during our period, in 1868 and 1886.[26] But it was the Brook that caused trouble for the centre of town and, on All Fools' Day 1842, veritable catastrophe.

Its powers would have been well-known in 1812. William Hutton, venerable writer of Derby history, had observed in 1791:

I have known this little spirited brook, whose common depth does not exceed 5 inches, rise from its bed about 6 feet below the ground floor to within 18 inches of the chamber.[27]

The 1842 event took place because the culverters of Victoria Street had failed to imagine the effect of a sudden period of exceptionally heavy rain. This is evident in the report in the Wednesday 6 April edition of the 'Derby Mercury':

Between one and two o'clock on Friday morning last, Derby was visited with, probably, the most calamitous inundation either within living memory, or of which there is any record . . .

The suddenness of the inundation is matter of some surprise, since, late on the evening previous, there were no very evident appearances of any material rise in the brook which flows through the town . . .The rain came down a complete deluge, and as the culverts of the brook course in Victoria Street would not admit more than one-third of the waters that rushed along them, all the lower streets were speedily inundated.

In response, the Council had to order the construction of a better culvert from Ford Street in the west, right the way down to the Corn Market junction to complement the work at that time underway on the street destined to be named after the Queen's consort.

It is worth pausing to look at what took place during those terrible twenty-four hours and led to the Council's determination to ensure there would be no repeat performance. A tablet was afterwards placed in the Corn Market to mark for all time the height and depth of the water's advance. People had woken up to find the main streets under water together with the shops and houses. A policeman on horseback had raced the flood down Agard Street, Brook Street and Willow Row in the early hours but failed to wake up their inhabitants because he was considered a prankster with a mind to the calendar!

It was too late to save the contents of the cellars en route. Horses, cows and pigs were to be seen swimming pitifully in the streets. Valuable furniture was washed away. A woman was drowned in Brook Street. Down in the centre, two tides swept down Sadler Gate and Wardwick and met in the Corn Market which was submerged under six feet of water. Some shopkeepers lost everything and when the water eventually subsided some pavements were impassable because of a congealed mass of rice, starch and flour! The gas supply was cut off, looters turned out in the darkness next night and lots of toughs attracted into town by the Easter Fair created mayhem.[28]

K.Keys provides a reminiscence of the disaster in 'Ward and Co's Annual' for 1892:

I was living with my parents in Willow Row at that time. I remember watching the water surging down the street, when a rather eccentric cow-keeper, named Dudley, who lived in an adjoining court . . .passed by, mounted on the back of one of his cows, and driving the others in front. He had paid little attention to his toilet; on his head was a night-cap. So comical he looked on the cow, that I can recall the scene as though it was only yesterday. As he approached Sadler Gate Bridge the current was so strong that had it not been for Mr Horsley's (a bookbinder) presence of mind in letting down a sheet for him to cling to, the comedy would have ended in a tragedy. He pulled himself up into Mr Horsley's house, while the cows ascended the bridge, and stayed there till the waters subsided.

Apart from the pure gold of the tale itself, what a delightful reminder of the modest size still of Derby in those days and the proximity of rural pursuits with the vision of a group of cows at the bottom of Sadler Gate!

There was one useful service provided by the Markeaton Brook through its sinuous course across the very midriff of the town and that was the unstinting supply of almost freeze-proof water to aid the parish fire brigades in emergency calls. Not enough, again, for major catastrophes, like the one on Trafalgar Day not six months before the watercourse's rebellion, the burning down of the Guildhall in October 1841.

However diligently the watchmen might brandish their rattles, the primitive horse-drawn equipment was not swiftly enough marshalled and could deploy far too little pressure to counter such a blaze effectively or that of the Silk Mill roof fifteen years earlier. It was not until 1883 that the parish services, including formerly independent Litchurch's, were amalgamated into a Borough Brigade and even they, although backed up by pressured water mains, could not save the Grand Theatre from conflagration in 1886. Eventually, two years later, they were to be equipped with their first steam fire-engine so that right at the end of our period a new era was dawning for fire-fighting.

Living and Learning

The victims of disasters or more ordinary emergencies would be admitted to the Derbyshire General Infirmary on London Road which we visited at the beginning of this survey. The 'Derby Mercury' continued to publish a weekly record of 'business' there, of which the following from 2 March 1812 is a fairly 'hum-drum' example:

Derbyshire General Infirmary, 2 March.
In-Patients admitted 4, Out-Patients admitted 5
Ditto discharged 0, Ditto discharged 4
Ditto accidents 0, ditto accidents 0
Ditto dead 0, On the Books 169
In the House 37, Innoculated for Cow Pock 8
Admitted into the Fever House 2

Its services were complemented from 1830 by a clinic and dispensary in a house in Bridge Gate which had actually been started over thirty years previously by Dr Erasmus Darwin and a group of like-minded practitioners concerned at that time about medical facilities for the less well-off. The chief worry had been small-pox and advice had been given free. With the General Infirmary now available, the Bridge Gate establishment continued on a subscription basis. Two-hundred subscribers were able to provide advice and prescriptions for ten times that number during the year 1830-31.[29]

Other hospitals for more specialised purposes were founded later in the century. First, in 1851 came the County Lunatic Asylum at the far side of Mickleover on a 79-acre site in open country. Previously there had been an asylum at Green Hill House, on Green Hill off Green Lane, but this was closed after a sad incident in December 1848 when one inmate murdered another there. The new establishment was intended for 300 patients and later extended to over double that size.

The architect chosen was the designer of the

'Private Establishment for the Insane' on Green Lane, Derby. An advertisement of 1842 described the house and premises as being 'delightfully situated on rising ground.'

Guildhall, Henry Duesbury, who worked a Victorian approach to the Tudor style of the sixteenth century, with patterned brickwork, broad gables, towers about the entrance and other taller, slender and more lordly pepper pot ones rising out of a quiet frenzy of stone-balled balusters.[30]

Of Duesbury's work and purpose, Glover in his 'History and Directory of Derby' for 1849 writes while it was yet in process of building:

. . .we believe the first to design an Asylum which shall facilitate and be adapted to the treatment of the insane by means of kindness, companionship, and watchfulness, rather than coercion, punishment, and confinement. To effect this object, the wards or residences of the patients (twelve in number and accommodating 300 patients) are placed in the best position, facing the south, and over looking the beautiful valley of the Trent, and the distant hills of three adjouning counties.

Finally, in 1883, a Children's Hospital was opened on North Street off Duffield Road, designed this time by Alexander MacPherson in much more cottagey style: modest porch protruding from a plain front, a row of tall rectangular windows on the first floor below two further ones within a steeply-pitched central gable.[31]

The education of the young was a strong Victorian concern. Nationally, it has been calculated that before 1870, when the Forster Education Act passed by Gladstone's government provided for the setting up of elected School Boards in areas where there was no elementary schooling already in existence, thirty-nine per cent of working class children of up to twelve years of age attended no school, although up to seventy-five per cent of them may have been able to read passably.[32]

The 1870 Act was intended to supplement the efforts of religious bodies, which were strong in Derby. According to the evidence put before the Factory Acts Committee, a very high percentage of the children who worked in the silk-mills attended Sunday schools.[33] By the testimony of medical officer Douglas Fox, as we have seen earlier, the silk-mill children would not have been rendered incapable of benefiting from learning by their long hours of factory work, although his view was in general disputed by the factory inspector:

Do they then generally appear distressed or fatigued by their labour or are they cheerful and inclined to engage in play? - They appear very cheerful, and almost invariably begin to play. I have seen no instance of children coming out from work who would arrest your attention from being fatigued; they appear playful and begin to play the moment they come out of the factories.[34]

Whether Sunday schools would count in the modern estimate is another matter, although if not they might well explain the reading statistic. Nearly all Derby churches had Sunday schools by 1840, including one attached to the Unitarian Chapel in Friar Gate started by William Strutt. St Peter's Church ran three of them. But several Nonconformist (Lancasterian) and Church of England (National) Day Schools were also started, beginning in 1812 with one attached to a mill in Full Street founded by Joseph Lancaster and equipped by Strutt and another (National this time) opened in Lodge Lane by Dr Bell for 230 boys and girls. The latter moved to Bold Lane five years later after a fire.

Others followed: H.I.Stevens designed three of them, including a Church of England Infants School, between 1839 and 1870. There was also a school for the very poor or so-called Ragged School in 1849. Most schools made a small charge. For example, the Wesleyan Sunday School in Chapel Street, attached to the King Street Chapel, asked for three shillings (15p) per quarter for reading instruction, although they provided slates, pencils, ink and a copy of Wesley's catechism for free. In 1879 was founded the Derby Deaf and Dumb Institution, pioneering education for children with these very special needs. By 1887 the founder, Dr William Roe, was working towards the setting-up of a purpose-built school in Friar Gate.[35]

The Derby School Board was founded in 1870 and several so-called Board Schools were built during the following decades. The most impressive in visual terms was that on Ashbourne Road, of red brick, high fenestration and a massive but rather forbidding tower.

For better-off children, ancient Derby School itself was enjoying a prosperous era leading to a move in 1863 to lordly St Helen's House which eventually suffered a far from distinguished supplement to its Georgian splendour for the purpose in the form of a massive but numbingly plain north block on the site of the Strutt family stables and completed fifteen years later.[36] There were also private schools for the seriously well-off, as the following advertisement in the 'Derby Mercury' for 2 January 1812 may illustrate:

Notices of Schools and Academies
CLASSICAL and COMMERCIAL SEMINARY,
Nottingham Road, Derby.
J.CHILDS begs leave to announce his REMOVAL from his LATE Residence, to a more eligible Situation, adjoining the Road from hence to Nottingham. For the convenience of his Day Pupils he has engaged a Central Situation for his School Room, in a large Building in the Irongate, belonging to Messrs Cox and Weatherhead. The above Room is spacious, and the highest Floor in the Building, which cause a combination of more Light and Air, than if it were lower. Board and a Commercial Education, £22 per year.
Ditto Ditto with a Classical Ditto £25.
J.C. takes this opportunity of publicly and gratefully acknowledging the liberal Encouragement he had, in so short a time, witnessed; which has exceeded his most flattering expectations.

For adults, there was a circulating library on a subscription basis at the beginning of our period at the premises of printers in Queen Street, later Amen Alley.[37] From 1825, the Mechanics' Institute provided courses of lectures in company with like foundations in towns all over the country. From 1836, members would have the advantage of the impressive new lecture hall which we saw earlier on. By 1839, the Derby Institute had 740 members, including fourteen women! There were classes in reading, writing, arithmetic, drawing, music, French and chemistry, in addition to a weekly discussion group on literary and scientific subjects.[38] To catch the real flavour of this admirable institution, an advertisement in the 'Mercury' on 4 December 1832 is worth a scan:

LECTURES ON
COMPARATIVE ANATOMY
DERBY MECHANICS INSTITUTION
The Committee have great pleasure in informing the Members of
the Institution, and the Public generally, that
Mr.S.W.FEARN, SURGEON,

Will commence a Course of TWELVE LECTURES on
Comparative Anatomy
And the laws which regulate the Animal Aeconomy,
In the Lancastrian School Room,
On TUESDAY EVENING, the 10th of December.
The Lectures (which will be illustrated by many specimens of various Skeletons, Dissections and elegant preparations) will begain at 8 o'clock, and be continued every Tuesday until the Course be completed.
Tickets of Admission (which are transferable)
Course 6s each, and to a single lecture is to be had at the Mercury and Reporter Offices; and from the Secretary Mr W.Wilson.
N.B. The Members will be admitted on showing their Tickets.
27 November 1833.

For citizens of Derby interested in the clues to the story of their town and its surroundings, from 1841 the Atheneum Club housed the Town and County Museum, with an entrance fee of 6d (2p).[39] We have already seen how, from 1879, the Free Library and Art Gallery subsumed the various collections of books, geological and natural history specimens, historical objects and 'Old Master' paintings from private sources around the town.

In more specialised vein, in 1850 the Bishop of Lichfield established a teacher-training college named Bishop Lonsdale after him on the Uttoxeter New Road to respond to the urgent need for new teachers, even twenty years prior to the arrival of the Board schools. It was once again designed by H.I.Stevens in a less flamboyant form of Victorian sixteenth-century styling than Duesbury's Asylum, boasted interior Minton tiling and proclaimed its purpose 'For the Training of School Mistresses' over the doorway.[40]

In this connection, we should not forget the work of a foundation of the previous decade, the Convent of St Vincent de Paul on the other side of the Derwent with its teacher-training wing with the needs of the poorest in society in mind. Finally, as we have seen, in 1878 came the College of Art on Green Lane, a worthy building in which to move on with the inspiration of Joseph Wright.

Public Spaces

We shall take a more detailed look at one of the most important responses to the pressure of a newly industrialised population, namely the setting aside of space for public recreation, in Chapter Eight. But perhaps equally important at this time was space for the dignified repose of the dead, an acute problem in years when epidemics due to the lack of proper foundations for the living, in the dread form of cholera, swept through towns and cities with the zeal of a phenomenon from the Book of Revelations. The most famous example of all of such provision is Undercliffe Cemetery in Bradford, its sentinel cypresses posting guardian spears around departed luminaries high above the town they moulded in life.

Derby's spaces are far humbler, although the earlier on the south side of Uttoxeter New Road and soon to be accompanied by the inspiration of Bishop Lonsdale on the north side would eventually contain the fascinating monuments of all the worthies of the community. It was opened in 1842 on a site of 4.5 acres. On the opposite side of town, and a more obviously elevated site which in its enlarged form in 1887 must have presented an imposing view of the modest company of Derby's architectural highlights, a new cemetery was opened in 1855 in fifty acres on Nottingham Road with plenty of opportunity to expand to the ceaseless tune of Father Time.[41]

The older cemetery had a mortuary chapel designed in 1843 by a Glossop architect. Nottingham Road, by contrast, had two chapels on either side of an imposing Gothic entrance assemblage designed by Edwin Thompson and the by now ubiquitous H.I.Stevens.[42]

Turning in contrast to the provision of space for the basic sustenance of life, we have already visited, and will do so once more in the last chapter, the doyen of historic Derby markets, that magnificent Market Hall of 1866. This was, however, merely the culmination of the town's endeavours to facilitate the civilised exchange of produce, animal and inanimate, and money. Before the beginning of our period, the wider western end of Friar Gate and the whole breadth of Corn Market were the result of having beast and cheese markets and a corn market respectively. In the 'Derby Mercury' for 2 January 1812 we find the following notice:

DERBY FAIR The Public are desired to take notice, that a FAIR for HORNED CATTLE, SHEEP, PIGS etc., will be held upon the NUN'S GREEN, in DERBY, on FRIDAY the 10th day of January 1812.

The markets on Friar Gate continued until 1861, long after the demise of Nun's Green, the year after H.I.Stevens (who else?) designed a new Cattle Market, with Cattle Market Hotel, on the area known as the Holmes beyond the Morledge.[43]

Animals not for sale but in the shape of horses in the permanent employ of the municipality were 'housed' in some style from 1881 when a range of buildings sprouting Gothic gables on Bold Lane provided stabling for forty-five of them in addition to blacksmith's and wheelwright's forge and workshop as well as an animal's infirmary.[44] Lastly, we have again already seen how Habershon provided a covered market behind his 1828 Guildhall which was in turn replaced by our Market Hall nearly forty years later. Just a few years after that, the picturesque stalls were to disappear from the open expanse of the newly-cobbled Market Place which became the static calling point for hansom cabs.

In the 1880s came cheap urban transport with the arrival of the tramcar, although not yet in its final electric-powered apotheosis. But the Council still had to prod the naturally-private tramway company into providing the essential service for the ordinary working man and woman of cheap and convenient transport between home and work. In the 'Derby Mercury' of 8 June 1881, Alderman Roe is reported as briefing a Council meeting on correspondence with the Tramway Company on the topic of transport for workers:

. . .the local manager had intimated that in all probability the company would run workmen's (sic) cars from the Ashbourne-road to the Midland Station for one fare, one going from the entreme end of the line on Ashbourne-road between five and six in the morning and returning five and six in the evening. If those cars were appreciated, probably similar accommodation would be provided on the other sections. The Uttoxeter-road section would shortly be commenced, and it would be completed by August, when he hoped Derby would possess as complete a system of tramways as any town in the kingdom.

So here was another step for progress, and looking back over our seventy-five years to 1812, in the space of one lifetime tremendous changes and much for the better had been accomplished. A great variety of provision had come into existence, although perhaps far too many families lacked the sort of physical framework for a home which might adequately compensate them for the loss of good country air and surroundings.

Notes

1. Quoted Maxwell Craven, op.cit.
2. Quoted in J.W.Allen, *And All's Well — But It Seldom Was*, article in *Bygone Derby* series, *Derby Evening Telegraph.*
3. Maxwell Craven, op.cit.
4. Davison, op.cit.
5. Maxwell Craven, op.cit.
6. Quoted in Davison, op.cit.
7. Ibid.
8. Maxwell Craven, op.cit.
9. Quoted Davison, op.cit.
10. Maxwell Craven, op.cit.
11. Davison, op.cit.
12. Maxwell Craven, op.cit.
13. Ibid.
14. Davison, op.cit.
15. *Report to the General Board of Health*, op.cit.
16. Ibid.
17. Ibid.
18. G.F.Chadwick, *The Park and the Town* 1966.
19. *Report to the General Board of Health*, op.cit.
20. D.Read, op.cit.
21. Quoted Ibid.
22. Ibid.
23. Quoted Maxwell Craven, op.cit.
24. Ibid.
25. Ibid.
26. Ibid.
27. William Hutton, *History of Derby.*
28. Rosemary Meynell, article in *Derbyshire Advertiser* September 1958.
29. Maxwell Craven, op.cit.
30. Ibid.
31. Ibid.
32. W.P.McCann, article of 1969, quoted D.Read, op.cit.
33. H.Butterton, op.cit.
34. *Reports to Select Committees*, op.cit.
35. Maxwell Craven, op.cit.
36. Ibid.
37. Ibid.
38. Glover, *History and Directory of Derby*, 1849.
39. Maxwell Craven, op.cit.
40. Ibid.
41. Kelly, *Directory of Derbyshire*, 1849.
42. Maxwell Craven, op.cit.
43. Ibid.
44. Ibid.

Home

*T*HE *smaller houses in Derby are generally neatly built, and many of the larger ones truly respectable. Among the private buildings most deserving of notice, may be mentioned the house of Mrs Henley in Friar Gate; of S.Evans, Esq, in St Mary's Gate; of Doctor Forester in Babington Lane; of Josh Strutt Esq. in Peter's Street; and of John Crompton, Esq. in Iron Gate; but that which far excels all others, is the house of Wm Strutt, Esq in King Street. This superb edifice formerly belonged to John Gisborne, Esq. In Full Street, Mr E.Mouseley possesses the house formerly inhabited by Lord Exeter, and which the Pretender made his residence during his short incursion upon Derby in 1745.*

This description from the 'Walk Through Derby' . . .printed and published by and for G.Wilkins and Son, Booksellers, in 1827 gives us a short glimpse and presentation of the Regency town including its most prestigious home, St Helen's House, but it was not long to remain apposite to nineteenth-century Derby.

No doubt most Victorian towns had a complete range of home environments from the opulent through the modestly pleasant to the kind of existence glimpsed in the darker pages of the public health reports. Derby was certainly no exception. The smaller terraced house with a rather dubious standard of convenience made up the biggest proportion of the stock. These terraces came by 1887 to occupy a wide swathe of territory in the shape of an arc around the central core of the town swinging west by north from London Road across Osmaston, Burton, Uttoxeter, Ashbourne and Kedleston Roads to the Duffield Road and beyond.

They were a mixture of rented and freehold owner-occupied property according to the status of the individual family which might range from the middle reaches of the working class, the family headed by the foreman or established mill-hand, through the artisan or skilled-worker group to the lower-middle, clerical, shopkeeper class. Amongst them were patches of employer-built and rented housing for the ordinary factory worker and usually of a reasonable standard, although they could sometimes be oppressively close to the place of employment as with the Foreman maltings on Babington Lane. Here the employees' cottages occupied the ground floor with all windows on one, at least the south-facing, side with the malting floor above.[1] But the 'underclass' would crowd into the sections of the older town core abandoned in the earlier part of the century by the well-to-do for their suburban villas and given over to rented accommodation and speculative 'courts'.

Few Victorians were in favour of state or local authority spending on building houses or their renovation for the benefit of those who could never come near the prospect of owning their own home, the unskilled, the unfortunate. The great Conservative leader Benjamin Disraeli declared in his novel 'Lothair', published in 1870, that poverty was . . .*not an affair so much of wages as of dwellings. If the working classes were properly lodged, at their present rate of wages, they would be richer, they would be healthier and happier at the same cost.*[2]

Neighbouring Nottingham was one of only three authorities in the country to take advantage of the 1851 Lodging Houses Act which actually gave powers to build workers' housing. Disraeli's own 1875 Artisans' Dwellings Act allowed slum-clearance but not re-housing.[3] The journal 'British Architect' castigated the Derby Corporation in 1882 for a history of dilatory inaction on housing, not taking any advantage of Disraeli's Act to clear up *tumble-down, closely confined and mostly back-to-back houses.* They rarely used their powers to shut down houses obviously unfit to be lived in. One of the few occasions on which they did so was in 1865 when they closed the notorious courts off St Helen's Street. They much preferred persuasion and if necessary prosecution to compulsory action.[4]

So the field was left wide open for speculative builders, many operating on a small-time basis. Thus in Derby there are not a great many unified terraces, whether the houses were rented or owner-occupied, but rather individually designed structures abutting each other.[5]

The working-class rented streets were under the shadow of the mills, as for example the transformed face of Nun's Green in the Regency period. In his evidence to the Factory Acts Committee of 1840, medical officer Douglas Fox took issue with his questioner's assumption that an hour would be occupied in a child-worker's day by going back-and-to between mill and home for the customary four meals:

You have taken too much for going to the mills. There is nothing like it in Derby. It does not take up five minutes to go and return; they live close to the mills generally.[6]

This was of course sound economics for the families as well as the bosses with the supreme imperative of the time of low-cost production in a state of cut-throat competition. It was imperative to live within a short walking distance of the work-place, at least before the

1880s and the tram cars, to respond to the exacting demands of long 'anti-social' hours and meagre wages, assuming that the mill owner had no hand in the siting and building of the accommodation in the first place. A good example of the resultant ties of mills and particular streets in working-class residential sectors is provided by the 1851 Census Enumerators' Returns for part of Upper Brook Street in the older silk-manufacturing area of north Derby.

Of twenty-six houses with a total population of 141, fifty people were concerned in some capacity or other with the silk industry, including many children. Many of the others were children too young to work. Again, in the returns for three courts off Lodge Lane and Bridge Street in the same part of town, of twenty-one people in three families, eleven were directly concerned with the same industry.[7]

There can have been few luxuries in many of these houses. A family in Upper Brook Street in 1851 with four wage-earners (husband, wife and, say teenage son and daughter) might have expected a combined weekly wage-packet of £2 at a time when one calculation based on the earnings of a Manchester mechanic (i.e. one-earner) of £1 13s 0d in 1859 resulted in a margin of just under ten per cent for *sundries* (anything apart from the essentials of food, light, clothing, heating and rent). However, one family in the same street, the Leakes, consisting of parents aged thirty-six and thirty-one but only the husband working as a ribbon-weaver and with five young children aged from five months to eight years, must have had a very difficult time indeed keeping a home with anything but the most rudimentary furniture and utensils in it.

Indeed, many houses in Upper Brook Street might well have illustrated the classic cycle of working-class economic life in the nineteenth century, one of poverty while the children were relatively young, prosperity after a decade when the children would be expected to begin contributing to the family economy, followed by a return to poverty with declining health and the possibility of final descent into workhouse oblivion.

Again, space would have been at a premium in many homes. The 140 people in twenty-six houses in Upper Brook Street give an average of five persons to each house. On the assumption that each rented terraced dwelling of this class might have three rooms apart from the kitchen (although this could be optimistic) we have under two people per room. This is modest compression compared to some of the northern industrial towns: Manchester was lucky to have only eight per cent of its people living more than two per room but others were twice as crowded as that.

However, back in Derby, speculators hired the larger rooms of older property to let out one or two rooms only at a time, creating tenements and consequently pockets of very high-density living.[8] In fact, a noted slum property owner was threatened with prosecution in 1850, the year after the publication of the famous Public Health Report of course, for renting out roof-space above communal privies off St Helen's Street as *sleeping rooms*.[9]

Many Derby terraces were developed by so-called 'land-societies', which had originated in Georgian times and resulted, at least earlier on, in owner-occupation on freehold terms. They were formed on a subscription basis and would purchase areas of urban land to be parcelled out in building plots. These would then be sold or leased out to members to build their own homes. It was a development that received encouragement from the 1832 Reform Act which granted the electoral voting right to the £2 freeholder, that is a male person who owned freehold property of at least that annual value: hence, for example, the naming of Franchise and Freehold streets in the Uttoxeter New Road area developed after the 1825 turnpiking. Later on in the century, many of these houses were bought up as business investments and then rented out.[10]

Derby obviously participated in the increase in house-building nationally from 1860. The national figure peaked at an annual average of 113,500 houses during the period 1875-79, dropping back to around 80,000 in the 1880s.[11] According to the 1881 and 1891 Census figures, there was an increase in the number of inhabited houses in Derby from 16,188 to 19,199 in this decade, with 115 still building in the latter year.

In the judgment of one historian, the supply of housing nationally *seems to have met effective demand*, whether or not this was true of Derby. However, their quality is another matter. The phrase 'jerry-building' began to gain currency in the 1870s as the characterisation of a development that was claimed to be unavoidable because people wanted more accommodation than they could afford and builders were expected to work miracles on the cheap.

The main corner-cutting exercise was concentrated indoors, where all classes of housing suffered to some degree. The speculative builder above all saved money and ensured at least minimum profit by not putting in 'state-of-the-art' heating, lighting and sanitation. We have already noted the gradual introduction of water-closets at least by the 1880s in Derby. But contemporary American visitors to Britain were apparently amazed at the way servants had to labour to fill jugs, basins and bathtubs with hot water.[12]

The meaner freehold terraces developed into close-knit communities with corner-shops, pubs and churches. Many of the people will have come from beyond the borders of the county let alone the town, Michael Thomas Bass MP thought that as many as 2,900 heads of families had come into Derby by the 1870s as a consequence of the railways.[13] Maxwell Craven's study of the sort of people who lived in these streets reveals occupations and proprietorships such as nailer, tailor, shopkeeper, barber, fish shop owner, shopfitter, book-dealer.[14]

A million people nationally defined as belonging to 'the middle class' still earned less than £100 per annum, although such as higher grade city clerks could earn as much as £200 and lower grades struggled to earn half that. These would be at *the extreme verge of gentility* when one contemporary authority considered it unwise to marry on £80 or even £50.[15]

A 'Spectator' article in November 1812 entitled 'The Numbers of the Comfortable' maintained that only 60,000 families in Britain out of a total of 1.5 million could be called *comfortable*, defined as being able to afford to buy 'The Times' newspaper without feeling in any way extravagant, and another 650,000 were *respectable* but *always struggling to make ends meet*.[16]. It would be people in this sort of range who would probably inhabit the sort of individualised terraces we have looked at so far.

They would not be devoid of elements of what might loosely be termed 'style', distinguishing individual features and details. The local builders had the benefit during the second half of the century of illustrated and annotated volumes of suburban-house designs published by the architectural press, and their own-in-house craft magazine 'The Illustrated Carpenter and Builder', with back-up advisory service to draw upon for easy reference and choice of designs to match customer requirements.[17] So we have the marvellous phenomenon exemplified by one terrace on the London Road where there is a sequence of eleven house doorways each of a different design composed of an assembly of varied details.

The repertoire of the speculative builder deployed so prolifically after 1850 or so was more experimentally developed in housing for the established 'middle-class' earlier in the century. The building arena would be prepared for by such advertisements as the following which appeared in the 'Derby and Chesterfield Reporter' on 16 January 1834 with precise location unspecified but with a descriptive clue to its relative height and also an allusion to *highest respectability* which might indicate the more expensive end of the market:

DERBY
The MOST ELIGIBLE SITUATION
FOR THE
Erection of Respectable Residences
IN THE VICINITY OF DERBY
TO BE SOLD BY AUCTION
By MB Brearey,
At the house of Mr Spencer, New Inn, Derby on Saturday, the 15th day of February, 1834 at six o'clock in the evening; All those THREE CLOSES of Valuable Freehold land, situated in the Parish of St Alkmund, in the Borough of Derby, on the North side of the Turnpike Road leading from DERBY to KEDLESTON, containing about
TEN ACRES,
In the possession of Messrs Wilsons, Nurserymen. One of the Fields has been used as a Nursery Garden, and the other two fields are Old Turf.
The above Property commands the most delightful views of the surrounding Country, and from the respectability of the Neighbourhood, and the contiguity to the Town of Derby, the Situation being within three minutes' walk of the Town, is highly calculated for Residences of the highest respectability.
For further particulars apply to MRS WILSON, Wardwick, or Messrs SIMPSON and FREAR, Solicitors, Derby.

Up-market elements popularised later on were the small front-garden and the bow window. Early in the century, semi-detached villas with a common front garden, possibly traversed by semi-circular driveway fronted by gate pillars, were a feature. Later, after 1860, tree-lined avenues were established as an innovation approved of by Prince Albert, as in Hartington Street and its neighbours off the Osmaston Road. This street, built in 1882 and featured in the pages of 'British Architect', had gates at either end, lime-shaded footpaths, the coat-of-arms of patron Alderman

Woodiwiss on the gables and was advertised at £50 per freehold.[18]

Such houses would probably be serviced by at least one domestic servant, the employment of whom had become a sure sign of middle-class status by the end of our period. Nationally, in 1881 one female in nine was reckoned to be an *indoor domestic,* an incredible one in three if aged fifteen to twenty! This might well not have been typical of Derby and certainly not earlier in the century with its many silk mills eager to employ girls and women, although there would always be the dales to draw upon as a reservoir of domestic labour.

The first edition of Mrs Beeton's famous 'Household Management', the manual for villa-arrangement and upwards of the time, suggested an income of £200 could support the aptly-termed *maid-of-all-work* plus an additional *girl.*[19]

The freeholders of the terraced world of the 1880s may or may not have struggled to keep a 'maid-of-all-work'. But they had become the early suburbanites, with benefit of tramcar service, with their fellow London pace-setters the subject of an article in the October 1891 issue of 'Contemporary Review' entitled *The rise of the suburbs'.* The writer describes the familiar appearance of terraced and semi-detached living, the roofs of Welsh slate often topped with ornamental ridge-tiles, the walls of dark red, grey or yellow-stock bricks, sometimes patterned, the bay windows on the ground floor, the elaborations, fancy railings, plaster mouldings, coloured tiles and glass; the privet hedges, the tiny flower gardens. A life dominated by domesticity and dullness according to the scribe, an inward-looking life of family and home, a possible ambition to move along to a more superior area, to 'keep up with the Joneses' or 'keep oneself to oneself'.[20]

For an appreciation of the contrast provided by the residences of what might be termed the 'upper middle class' we can turn to an early example encapsulated in a detailed advertisement of sale consequent on the death of the biggest silk-manufacturer in Derby, Thomas Bridgett which appeared in the 'Derby Mercury' on 9 April 1834. It will also serve to lead us into other aspects of the concepts of home and family life to round up just a little this otherwise very public survey of Victorian living in Derby.
To be sold by private Contract,
With early possession if desired,
That delightfully situated and commodious Freehold Residence, called
Grove House,
about half a mile from Derby, on the Duffield Road, with the Pleasure Grounds, Gardens and pasture land surrounding it, Porter's Lodge, Stable, Coach-house, Summer-house, and offices, the property and late residence of THOMAS BRIDGETT, Esq, deceased.
The House, which was built in the years 1824-5 of stone outside and in the most substantial manner commands a prospect unequalled in the vicinity, across the Valley of the Derwent and terminated by the Leicestershire Hills, and from its elegant interior and convenient arrangement is one of the most delightful Family Residences in the County.
The principal apartments, the Dining and Drawing Rooms, are each 25 by 20 feet, and 12 feet in height. The former of these opens on to the Pleasure Grounds.

A spacious Entrance Hall runs the whole depth of the house, and from it an elegant stone staircase leads to the lobby. The ceiling of both is richly ornamented. Besides the above, on the ground floor, are Summer and Winter Breakfast Rooms, the Library, Two Kitchens, in which are two pumps, Butler's Pantry and Housekeeper's Closet. On the first floor, Four Bed Rooms, Two Dressing Rooms, and a Water Closet, and above these six excellent Bed Rooms. The principal apartments are finished in a very elegant manner with rich cornices, fine Marble Chimney-pieces, and mahogany doors. Below, are five spacious Cellars, a hot-air stove in the passages of which regulates the temperature of the house. In a paved yard adjoining the kitchen is a Brewhouse with pump and coppers, Laundry, cold Larder, and Shoe-house.

The detached buildings consist of the Entrance Lodge on the Duffield Road, a neat Stone Summer-house in the Pleasure Grounds, Coach-house, Saddle-house, Stable, Hay Chamber, Cow-house, Cartshed. There are two pumps to these buildings.

The Ornamental Grounds have been kept in the nicest order. Several fine Timber Trees are dispersed about the premises, and two sides of the property are bounded by thriving plantations. The walls of the Kitchen Garden are lined with a variety of choice Fruit-trees, and a part of the Pleasure Ground has been planted with an orchard. Adjoining the Gardens is a Field of excellent old pasture land, tythe free. The contents, together, 7A, 2R, 1P.

There are, of course, many of the elements of substantial living that appear in this notice — evidence of the expectation of a porter, a private coach, the keeping of horses, the superior view, the spacious entrance hall, use of the term 'lobby', presence of a 'Breakfast room', a library, accommodation for a butler and housekeeper, references to 'rich cornices', marble chimney-pieces and the exploitation of the tropics in the high colonial age in 'mahogany doors'. We are here obviously in a different world to other properties briefly observed. Very few would aspire to it. As we have seen earlier, Thomas Bridgett himself rose from humble origins to live in such splendour, but the opportunities for workmen to become owners or managers of large firms probably declined during the later-Victorian years according to one modern authority. The gulf was widening, with average business profits rising nationally by an average of sixty per cent during the period 1850-80 as against a rise of forty-seven per cent in wages [21]when 'large' incomes were defined as being above £5,000 per year.[22]

Grove House could not have functioned without domestic servants. Nationally, domestic service was the biggest employer of women, as agricultural work was still for men. Obviously, the situation in Derby would not have supported these generalisations but the large houses or villas, tending to be situated in a lesser arc than the terraced housing and largely concentrated in the north-west and north of the town, would have certainly supported many servants.

In Grove House, there might not have been a place for a 'maid-of-all-work' who would have been found labouring in some of the humbler freehold dwellings, holding on to a job physically demanding in the extreme, expected to work from early morning to late evening, coping with the vertical plan of Victorian middle class houses meaning time and energy climbing stairs. Family and servants in Grove House might not have lived in the close proximity necessitated by the smaller villas, with consequent enforcement of strict rules of conduct and routine on the part of servants and therefore probable rapid turnover of staff.[23]

But there would have been the numerous fires to keep going, marble chimney-pieces or no, as the Rev Thomas Mozley, brought up in a large house in Wardwick, remembered: the servants bringing in a *big coal, three or four feet long* before going to bed at night and one of them taking *an enormous poker* in the morning and with one stroke breaking the lump in pieces *when there was at once a blazing fire.*[24]

Every house had its chimney, some like Grove House no doubt whole batteries of them. In 1825 a service was held in All Saints' for climbing boys under the patronage of a Society, founded ten years earlier *for ameliorating the condition of the infant chimney-sweepers* which funded a master sweep, Roberts by name, who refused to employ boys to sweep chimneys and whom the Society exhorted the public to employ in order to try to diminish the practice of using boy sweeps. After the service, these unfortunates *sat down to dine off roast beef and plum pudding.*

Master chimney sweeps complained that many old chimneys in Derby were crooked or unsuitable for using merely brushes, quoting as evidence a flue of a house in Friar Gate *which ran in a horizontal direction for thirty-four feet, wherein a few years previous a boy was wedged, and it was necessary to break through the wall to release him.* In 1838 a boy was reported as suffocating in the chimney of a house in Siddalls Lane, overcome by fumes from a fire not completely put out by the master sweep. It was an example of the frequent callousness of masters, regarded as an accident, no one being held to blame or prosecuted.[25]

Whatever the household, the ladies would be second-class citizens; Queen Victoria hinted to her eldest married daughter in 1859 that women were *poor creatures born for man's pleasure and amusement*[26]. One in three were unmarried at any one time and one in four never married at all. For the married, childbirth was always just around the corner at the furthest. There might be an annual addition to most families' complements. Victorian society was indeed dominated in one sense by children and young people. In 1871 nearly half the total population of Britain was aged under twenty, only less than a quarter under forty-five. This would have been noticeable on Derby streets.

But there were indicators of a more liberal future for women in line with the more promising if rather infrequent pieces of evidence this way from the past. There would have been more professions open to the daughters of Derby's villa and better-terraced families by the 1880s than the respectable but often rather ill-rewarded position of governess.[27] There were as we have seen two teacher-training institutions in the town. There were also openings as clerks, post-office workers, nurses, shop-assistants, even early typists.[28] There were now respectable 'tea-rooms' and cafes where they could meet and eat.

Public lavatories were provided and from 1885, with the publication of 'The Lady' for the top-end of the social scale, magazines catering for their distinctive tastes and concerns. Of course, women had always been heads of many households and also in charge of business concerns as well as leading lights in charities. From 1857 with the Matrimonial Causes Act and 1870 with the Married Women's Property Act their previous legal shackles were loosened and divorces in consequence increased from an annual average nationally of 150 in the 1860s to approaching 600 by the end of our period.[29]

In their own streets and about the centre of town, working class people would be easily distinguishable from their 'betters' by their very physical appearance and clothes, in Derby as in every other town. They would bear the consequences of crowded homes with perhaps a minimum water supply and unsuitable or inadequate food, leaving their pinch about the face. They bought smaller amounts of food which was therefore comparatively dearer for them and they were liable to spend up to 75 per cent of the family budget on it. In the first surveys of the physical health of the working population, not done until about twenty years after the end of our period in Edwardian times, the state of teeth was found to be particularly bad. Working people were reported as never using either toothbrush or, indeed, handkerchief.[30]

The ladies would be less colourfully dressed than their wealthier counterparts, although the benefits of mass factory production and the increase in the dyer's trade we have noticed earlier in Derby would also have trickled down by the 1880s. Beneath the surface they were now wearing drawers apparently, worn by their 'betters' since the 1830s.

The inhabitants of Grove House in Bridgett's time and later on in the century would have presented a sartorially more interesting image, although no doubt still lagging behind that current in the capital city and depicted in an article entitled 'Our Civilisation' by Eliza Liston in the June 1873 edition of 'Cornhill Magazine'. This attacked what the writer saw as its absurdities, the men wearing stiff shut collars *which rasp their necks,* showing a wide expanse of shirt-front which creased when being fastened, and coats ending in *meaningless swallow tails.* All colour was provided by the women, who after 1860 were taking advantage of new dyes able to produce vivid colour contrasts. *Our highest efforts culminate in partial nakedness in the middle of winter if we are women, in black broad-cloth in the dog days if we are men*[31].

From the mid-1860s there was a greater emphasis on curves, the bustle replacing the stiff crinoline. Whilst Derby's climatic and general social conditions will have imposed some moderating effect on the foregoing developments, we have here some indication of the best wear on formal occasions, public and private, which we shall be delving further into in the last chapters of this book, and also parade material in one of Derby's environmental success stories, the Arboretum.

Notes

1. Maxwell Craven, op.cit.
2. Quoted D.Read, op.cit.
3. Ibid.
4. Maxwell Craven, op.cit.
5. Ibid.
6. H.Butterton, op.cit.
7. Ibid.
8. Ibid.
9. Maxwell Craven, op.cit.
10. Ibid.
11. D.Read, op.cit.
12. Ibid.
13. Christian and Heath, *Yesterday's Town, Derby,* 1985, quoted M.Craven, op.cit.
14. Maxwell Craven, op.cit.
15. B.G.Orchard, *The Clerks of Liverpool,* 1871 quoted in D.Read, op.cit.
16. Quoted D.Read, op.cit.
17. Maxwell Craven, op.cit.
18. Ibid.
19. D.Read, op.cit.
20. Ibid.
21. H.Perkin, *The Origins of Modern English Society,* 1969.
22. D.Baxter, *National Income,* 1968.
23. D.Read, op.cit.
24. Quoted Maxwell Craven, op.cit.
25. Davison, op.cit.
26. Quoted D.Read, op.cit.
27. Ibid.
28. Lee Holcombe, *Victorian Ladies at Work,* 1973.
29. D.Read, op.cit.
30. Ibid.
31. Quoted Ibid.

Arboretum

THE opportunity of enjoying with their families exercise and recreation in the fresh air in public walks and grounds.

Here, in the founder's own words, we have the key concept behind Derby's Arboretum. They were Joseph Strutt's, as part of his dedicatory speech at the Guildhall on Wednesday 16 September 1840, just over a year before the disastrous fire which temporarily took that other focus for civic pride away.

The term *families* in this excerpt needs to be qualified for its full importance to become apparent: Strutt was referring especially to the dependents of the labouring classes, the workforce of the mills and, most recently, the railways which were bringing such strong fresh prosperity to the town. Strutt was seventy-five years of age at the time with four more remaining and this gift of 11 peaceful acres on the southern edge of Derby could be regarded as the final crowning of a lifetime's work dedicated to the public, as well as private, family good.

As a silk manufacturer and owner of Thorntree House in St Peter's Street in the middle of town where, as we have seen, he had for a number of years been used to sharing his 'Old Masters' collection of paintings with the general public on Sunday afternoons, he had taken to heart the urgings of Parliament, at which another member of the family served as one of the town's two representatives, that provision be made for the needs of the less fortunate in the thrusting and until recently unrestrained industrial environment of the time.[1]

According to the foremost modern authority on the origin and development of the public park, it was not until the last century that the idea of an area of land laid out mainly for the use of the public in the middle of an urban environment was conceived.[2] Granted, Hyde Park had been open to the public for just over 200 years, since the reign of Charles I, but this was in reality simply a royal park without walls.[3] In the eighteenth century a 'park' had meant an area which had been enclosed to keep it from public use rather than the opposite.

Georgian urban planning, especially in London, created the concept of 'the square' set aside solely for the use of the people in the privileged position of occupying the houses around it. But it was an original Victorian idea, faced with the triffid-like growth of the industrial town and burning with the ardour for reform, to create a useful landscape within the very confines of an urban area expressly for the use and enjoyment of the general public. There was, in fact, a sole precedent in neighbouring Leicester's New Walk, formed in 1785 with the purpose of creating a 10-yard wide promenade between what was later renamed Victoria Park and the town centre for the recreation of the inhabitants.[4]

We have already noted the dangerous multiple-pollution of the environment of the new industrial urban growths and the resultant appalling mortality rates. The Whig government at Westminster resulting from the enhanced electoral regime created by the Great Reform Act of 1832 set up a Select Committee to examine the whole idea of 'Public Walks'. The reasoning behind its recommendation to provide such public walks and also open spaces, hopefully by means of the private generosity of eminent and public-spirited individuals, must have aroused a most responsive chord in Derby's Joseph Strutt:

With a rapidly increasing Population, lodged, for the most part in narrow courts and confined streets, the means of occasional exercise and recreation in the fresh air are every day lessened, as inclosures take place and buildings spread themselves on every side.

. . .to those who consider the occupations of the Working Classes who dwell there; confined as they are during the weekdays as Mechanics and Manufacturers, and often shut up in heated Factories; it must be evident that it is of the first importance to their health on their day of rest to enjoy the fresh air, and to be able (exempt from the dust and dirt of the public thoroughfares) to walk out in decent comfort with their families . . .[5]

Five years later, the Select Committee's recommendations were backed up in a resolution passed by the whole House of Commons that in future all bills passed by request for the enclosure of specified areas of land wherever in the country they might be should include provision for open space *sufficient for the purposes of exercise and recreation for the neighbouring population.*[6] The Arboretum followed two years later.

In one way, the site of the Arboretum might be thought peculiar for its time and purpose. It may be recalled that it was then at the very edge of town and in fact the space it occupied was the Strutt family holiday sanctuary from the summer heat and odours of central Derby hardly a mile distant to the north. Even on the 1855 'Map of the Borough of Derby' drawn up for the new Local Board of Health, it is shown as still having open fields on both east (Litchurch

The Arboretum's North Lodge in Grove Street, the park's original main entrance, pictured from inside just after it was opened in 1840.

Grange) and west (with only a solitary silk-mill interrupting the empty near-horizon), and to the south a series of named streets laid out for future terracing.

But the Midland Station and Arboretum were opened within three months of each other and this southern side of Derby was to see the most rapid residential development for working families.[7] In any case, these 11 acres were what it was within Strutt's power to give away!

He decided to go outside the town for the expertise to carry out his project, choosing the foremost practitioner in the country for the purpose, John Claudius Loudon, the most knowledgeable plant-man of his time. Loudon was a Scotsman, born in 1783 at Cambuslang in Lanarkshire, and the Arboretum was to be his last major creation before his death three years afterwards at his house in Bayswater, London. He was sixty years of age and his end came as the result of catching a chill whilst laying out a cemetery in Southampton, striking at a body weakened by excessive work.[8]

Loudon had a wide range of interests, including horticulture, botany, architecture, agriculture and writing. He had a breadth of experience to draw upon for the Arboretum: he had travelled across Europe as far as Russia as a young man at the time of the Napoleonic Wars and this with his familiarity with both Italian and French meant that he brought the benefit of European perspectives. He was a prolific writer, the founder of the very first 'Gardener's Magazine' and in 1833 he had brought out his masterpiece, 'Encyclopaedia of Cottage, Farm, and Villa Architecture and Furniture'.

But he would not have achieved as much without a most harmonious marriage to a woman with like interests, and herself author of two gardening books for ladies.[9] Jane Loudon was taking dictation for yet another book for her husband when he died in 1843 and she went on to prepare posthumous publications.[10] John Loudon would surely have discussed the planning of the Arboretum at length with her in 1839-40 and perhaps she should be called to mind with her husband in the naming of Loudon Street in the neighbourhood of the park.

His publications and therefore his ideas would not have been unknown in Derby in the 1830s to others beside Strutt. On 2 January 1834 the 'Derby and Chesterfield Reporter' carried the following advertisement.

Loudon's
ENCYCLOPAEDIA OF GARDENING —
NEW EDITION
Just published, Parts 1 and II price 2s 6d each (to be completed in Twenty Monthly Parts, containing between 1200 and 1300 pages of letter-press, with upwards of 1200 Engravings on Wood), of an Encyclopaedia of Gardening: comprising the Theory and Practice of Horticulture, Floriculture, Arboriculture, Landscape Gardening & c.
By J.C.Loudon, F.L.G.H. and Z.S.
Author of the 'Encyclopaedia of Agriculture, and of

Top: *The South Lodge entrance on Osmaston Road.* Bottom:
View of the South Lodge from the interior of the park.

Cottage, Farm, and Villa Architecture and Furniture'.

The 'Encyclopaedia' already referred to is considered by one modern authority to be one of the most environmentally influential works of modern times in that we are still living *in and with Mr Loudon's England*.[11] This is because its 1,138 pages, no less, illustrated by numerous drawings by the author, laid the basis of the designs later used, as we have seen, by the house-builders and furniture-makers during the rest of the century, as retailed by successive manuals and pattern-books in the trade.

The Arboretum lodges and pavilions naturally showed Loudon's influence, the over-arching concept being the variety to be gained from the imitation of the different styles of building developed and employed in the past in Britain, Europe and other parts of the world up to that time. Just one detailed example of this influence, appearing in the original main entrance lodge for the Arboretum, was the preference for tall chimneys, useful he maintained in countries with cold weather for part of the year, and recommended to be built boldly and well above the roof-line in order to form a conspicuous silhouette against the sky.[12] This feature alone has had a considerable impact on hundreds of micro-horizons in town and country since 1833.

But it was for his contribution to the art of the design of public grounds, of which architecture was a mere embellishment, that Strutt sought out Loudon

for the Arboretum. In an 1835 number of his 'Gardener's Magazine' Loudon had written:

Public gardens are just beginning to be thought of in England; and, like most other great domestic improvements in our country, they have originated in the spirit of the people, rather than in that of the government. On the Continent, the contrary has usually been the case . . .[13]

An interesting parallel here in recent governmental attitudes to European Community ideas! Loudon's perspectives must have been impressive. Whilst the following idea was not directly applicable to the Arboretum itself though it was certainly the origin of the 'bedding out' regime in Derby parks as in those all over the country, in his 'Encyclopaedia' he commended a *Chinese* garden, *exhibiting only plants in flower, inserted in the ground, and removed to make room for others when the blossom begins to fade.*[14]

It is interesting to note that in 1831, just two years before his great book, he had visited the gardens of Alton Towers with its gracious pagoda, though he found the Towers exposition all too much. That same year he had also visited Chatsworth and designed his 'own' first garden for the Birmingham Botanical and Horticultural Society on a 16-acre site. It was this that impressed Strutt. Its main features were large glasshouses enabling the culture of plants from all over the world. Botanically, this was a crucial period for British garden design because of the new opportunities which had been opened up by, of all things, those grand victories of Trafalgar and Waterloo against Napoleon. According to the 'Journal of the Institute of Landscape Architects' for November 1954, these events gave 'England' unimpeded access to all parts of the world and made possible the introduction of all kinds of exotic trees and shrubs. Loudon, together with Paxton at Chatsworth, added at the same time the new techniques of glasshouse-based horti-culture which produced the bedding-out system to take advantage of the new possibilities.

Loudon himself was the pioneer of the so-called *Gardenesque* style with trees and shrubs *planted and managed in such a way as that each may arrive at perfection, and display its beauties to as great advantage as if it were cultivated for that purpose alone.*[15]

This was a key idea for the Arboretum. He dissuaded Strutt from going through with a copy of the Birmingham model on a smaller site, mainly because of the probable expense of upkeep, and instead go for an arboretum rather than a botanic garden, *a collection of trees and shrubs, foreign and indigenous, which would endure the open air in the climate of Derby, with the names placed to each.*[16] Strutt therefore presented him with the golden opportunity of demonstrating the principles he had evolved during the 1830s on the ideal lay-out for a public garden.

In another long article in 'Gardener's Magazine' in 1835, Loudon wrote:

It ought to be laid down as a rule . . .that there should be one main walk, by walking along which every material object on the garden may be seen in a general way . . .From this main walk there may be small episodical walks to display the particular scenes in detail.[17]

And so Joseph Strutt presented him in 1839 with

the challenge of his gift to the Corporation of an 11-acre, long, narrow and irregular site in the parish of Litchurch but with good loamy soil. Work started from July in that year in the hands of a contractor, a Mr Tomlinson.[18] Loudon's design included a broad straight walk with a focal point intended to be a statue of Strutt but replaced by *an insipid fountain* (Chadwick).

There were two pavilions at either end of this walk in 'antique' style. There was a secondary circuit walk so that, as Loudon wished, the visitor could enter the park and leave it at the same place having taken a complete view of the whole. As there was no view worth bothering with beyond the park boundaries, undulating mounds 6 to 10 feet (1.8 to 3 metres) high were raised to shut out these views and conceal visitors in the side walks from sight of the main walk. Eighty-two botanical items were planted and listed in the catalogue and 111 were added later. There were a hundred different types of roses. The total number of items in the end was 1,013.[19]

According to Loudon, the collection was *one of the most extensive ever planted.* They were grouped according to type and variety coming as they did from all parts of the country and the world. Each specimen was labelled with a number and short description which included its country of origin and its type or species. Numbering began at the entrance and continued along the right-hand side then back down the left until the entrance was reached again from the opposite direction. The gravelled walks in all measured over 6,000 feet (or nearly 1,900 metres) in length and ranged in width from 8 to 15 feet (2.5 to 4.6 metres). The gently rolling hillocks in between increased the impression of size and imparted a feeling of privacy at the same time.[20]

The numbering and cataloguing were in accord with another aspect of Strutt's intention for the Arboretum. His fellow citizens were to gain information and instruction as well as amusement and enjoyment, very earnest, Nonconformist, Victorian in one. He also had other definite ideas of his own, contained in his written instructions to Loudon:

That two lodges with gates at the two extremities should be built; and that each lodge should have a room, to be considered as a PUBLIC ROOM, into which a stranger might go and sit down taking their own refreshments with them, WITHOUT ANY CHARGE being made . . .unless some assistance such as HOT WATER, PLATES, KNIVES AND FORKS were required, in which case a small VOLUNTARY gratuity might be given. That there should be proper yards and conveniences at each lodge for the use of the public, apart from those to be exclusively used by the occupant of (each) lodge. That there should be open spaces in two or more parts of the Garden on which tents might be pitched, a band of music placed, dancing carried on. That certain vases and pedestals now in the flower garden, and also certain others in Mr Strutt's garden in Derby should be retained or introduced; and finally, that some directions should be left for the management of the garden.[21]

In other words, every possible inducement that the benefactor could think of to bring about the park's busy use was to be employed. In addition, he set up a management committee of seven (Mayor, four councillors and two others) to run the park, meeting for the first time ten days after the opening celebrations which took place betwen 16/19 September 1840, in order to formulate rules of operation duly advertised in the current week's edition of the 'Derby Mercury', Wednesday 30 September:

The Committee of Management beg to inform the public that the Arboretum is now open and that all classes of the public, conducting themselves with order and decorum, will by the Donor's express provision, be admitted FREE ON SUNDAYS AND WEDNES-DAYS in each week (except between the hours of ten o'clock am and one o'clock pm on Sundays during which time the gates will be closed and visitors excluded).

And that on all other days the public will be admitted by ticket on the following terms:

A ticket to admit all members of the same family dwelling in the same house including also Domestic Servants attending any part of each family, 10s 6d yearly.

A ticket including (in addition to the subscriber's family) visitors at his house, not residing within the distance of one mile from Derby, one guinea per annum.

A ticket to admit one person only, 7s per annum. Boarding school pupils to be admitted by ticket at 2s 6d per annum.

Single admittances to be 6d and for children under twelve, 3d each.

There are several points of interest here, including the reference to *Domestic Servants* attached to a family, provision for Boarding School pupils and the Sunday morning closure. However, more important are the facts that a charge was to be made on most days and that one of the free days was to be Sundays. The first was sad in that a working man or woman could never afford more than a single-entry ticket and possibly the majority of such people would be stretched to find the money for all the family to go in at these rates. The second was a triumph over the prevailing Sabbatarian spirit, a testimony to the essentially liberal nature of Joseph Strutt's views. Even the Great Exhibition, eleven years later, was not destined to open its mighty doors on the Sabbath!

As for some of the items in his instructions to Loudon, *certain vases and pedestals* were indeed *retained or introduced,* including one item that became a particular favourite. This was the so-called Florentine Boar, a fine marble carving of a wild pig apparently in the act of getting up to make or meet a challenge, placed on top of a substantial stone block of contrasting colour and texture and transferred from the Strutt family garden at Thorntree House.[22]

Strutt himself designed the seats which were to be placed at suitable points and to include footboards for elderly people and those with disabilities.[23] Loudon's requested maintenance instructions included attention to mowing and bedding-plants and go on to make the point that

. . .it forms no part of the design of this Arboretum to exhibit large trees, more especially of the common kinds; and whenever any one of these, or, indeed, any tree whatever in the Arboretum, reaches a greater height than 40 or 50 feet, it should be removed. That height is quite sufficient for producing shade, and

for showing the form and character of the tree, and its flowers and fruit . . .[24]

Many changes and additions were made to the park's physical appearance during the next fifty years. In 1845, the year after the death of the donor, a playing-field at the south-eastern corner of the site was bought by the Corporation and 'laid out' for the sum of £2,300, with an avenue of trees on each of the longer south-reaching sides of the new rectangle to end on Rosehill Street. It was here on Arboretum Field, in 1888, that the Derby Junction football team beat mighty Blackburn Rovers to enter the semi-finals of the FA Cup.

Further, along the frontage to that street a *Crystal Palace* for indoor activities like dancing and flower-shows was built for £3,000 after a subscription campaign headed by the Duke of Devonshire. On the inner park side it was fronted by a Flag staff Fountain, still shown on the 25 to 1 inch Ordnance Survey Map of 1883.[25]

In 1853, a new lodge and main entrance at the end of Arboretum Street were built, effectively transferring the principal entry point from Grove Street at the north end to the middle of the eastern side and thus to some degree obscuring one of Loudon's distinctive features as followed by the original catalogue. The designs for the new structure were a joint effort by John Loudon and Henry Duesbury, who was obviously in charge of carrying the project through to completion ten years after the garden designer's death, eleven years after his own Guildhall and two after his County Asylum.

It is certainly from roughly the same 'stable' as the former building, what might be described as a sculptured version of the classical style: tall central round-arched alcove for a statue of Joseph Strutt (as we have seen, originally intended as the park's centre-piece) in Victorian-senatorial pose and flanked by twin-sets of grooved flat pillars boosting pyramidal urns, all flaunted above the inscription *ARBORE-TUM GIVEN TO THE TOWN BY JOSEPH STRUTT 1840* and a screen with two heavy-headed fan-lit doors beneath triangles and lofted stone balls.[26] In 1857, the mighty Lord Palmerston very appropriately donated two cannons from Sebastopol as featuring in the Crimean War. At some time or other, the ancient medieval Headless Cross, formerly used in time of plague for clean disinfected trading by means of a hollow filled with vinegar for up-country folk to position their coin, was brought to the south-eastern corner of the park from Friar Gate.[27] Finally, in 1882, after more than forty years, all entrance charges were at long last abolished.[28]

Before looking at how the Arboretum was used during the half-century to the Queen's Golden Jubilee, it is perhaps appropriate to pause at this point to look at the park once again from a wider perspective in order to pinpoint its essential historical importance. According to G.F.Chadwick it is *the first park to be specifically designed for and owned by the public as a direct result of the movement for Public Walks*. With the Derby Arboretum was introduced *a new urban element; a garden designed from the start for public use and administered by representatives of the public themselves.*[29]

The example was soon taken up by other towns and cities across the country: in the Midlands, for instance, by Nottingham (1852), Lincoln (1868) and Walsall (1874).

However, we should note that only one additional public open space, apart from the extension to the Arboretum which we have already recorded, was provided for the people of Derby during our chosen period. This was the gift we have already covered in 1867 by Michael Thomas Bass of land at the north end of the Siddalls, on the other side of the Midland Station from the park, together with the money for its improvement. Six years later in 1873 open-air swimming baths were opened there.[30]

By this time, it could be fairly said that Derby had lost the lead position that Strutt had given it in this vital form of provision for an expanding industrial population. Apart from the fact that in that same Arboretum year of 1840, Liverpool Town Council, to Loudon's approval, had brought free public access on two days each week to their Botanic Gardens first opened in 1836 (and even this was two years after Preston Corporation had opened its undeveloped Moor Park to public access), in 1846 began an avalanche of public parking elsewhere.

In that year Philips and Victoria Parks in Manchester and Peel Park in Salford, each of 30 acres, were opened and the latter had a girl's gymnasium and swimming pool for women in the 1850s. Next year, 1847, saw Sheffield (50 acres presented by the Duke of Norfolk) and Birkenhead in the field. This latter boasted 125 acres acquired specially by Act of Parliament and designed by Joseph Paxton of Chatsworth to include two lakes, with admission entirely free. In 1853, Kelvingrove Park in Glasgow was opened and, in 1857, People's Park in Halifax with 12 acres including lake, both again by Paxton. In 1863, came what might be called the ultimate benefaction in Hull where the 20-acre People's Park was presented by a landowner who was being declared bankrupt in court at the very same time as his statue of the Queen was being unveiled as the centre-piece of the ceremonial opening!

Finally, in 1865, Alexandra Park, Oldham was supported with an increased rate by the Council there at a time when the cotton operatives of the town were suffering great distress from the trade disruption caused by the American Civil War.[31] What a progeny the Arboretum had spawned in 25 years! Derby was first, but its halo did not last long.

The combination of being first in its particular field and the almost simultaneous arrival of the railway made the Arboretum a magnet for the popular day excursion trade throughout our period and must have brought extra cash into the town. The other ingredient in a popular mix was a tradition of putting on a special programme of attractions on the annual anniversary of its spectacular opening, which was later transferred to that of Joseph Strutt's birthday earlier in the year. On that particular day it was estimated that up to 25,000 people went to the Arboretum, many of them from such places as Birmingham, Manchester and Leeds on cheap day rail excursions. As a sample of the fare offered in the park, here is a selection from the advertisement of the event in the 'Derby Mercury' for 18 June 1873:

The Arboretum fountain pictured in the 1870s.

The Renowned Band of the
GRENADIER GUARDS
*which had earned such high reputation in America
and other places*

The Excellent Band of the
SOUTH NOTTS YEOMAN CAVALRY

THE DERBY VOLUNTEER BAND

AN ORCHESTRAL BAND
From London

The Band of the
DERBY YEOMANRY CAVALRY

The celebrated Band of the
ROBIN HOOD RIFLES

THE DERBY QUADRILLE BAND

Mr EMMANUEL JACKSON, THE MIDLAND
AERONAUT,
will make an
ASCENT *from the* GROUNDS *at* FIVE O'CLOCK
In his BALLOON
PARIS POST
Holding 30,000 feet of Cubic Gas.

The REAL ROYAL & ORIGINAL
CHINESE TROUPE

ARR HEE	SING ZONG ZOU
The famous Knife-Thrower of Pekin	*Champion Chinese Sword*
ARR SAEN	TREN HEE
The Chinese Leotard	*The daring little Nankeen Wire-Walker*

THE EUROPEAN WONDERS
LES FRERES GIRARD
in Their Dashing and Rapid Trapeze Performance

PROFESSOR PETERSON'S
JOLLY DOGS
*Dancing Dogs   Acting Dogs   Leaping Dogs
Singing Dogs &* AEROBATIC DOGS

Of local north Derby interest might be an excerpt from
the equivalent advertisement for 24 June 1861, which
featured *THE DARLEY AND ALLESTREE BAND*
conducted by *Mr GLOVER*.

The reference in 1873 to the ascent of *the MIDLAND
AERONAUT* draws attention to a particular tradition
beginning with Arboretum Day One on 16 September

1840, when a balloon flight was first attempted, on
that occasion not very successfully as we shall see in
our final chapter. However, the tradition was kept
up, as other excerpts from the 1861 advertisement in
the 'Mercury' illustrate:

*The Celebrated Aeronaut, Mr H.Croxwell, will
make an Ascent from the Arboretum Grounds on that
Evening, about Five o'clock, in his New and
Magnificent BALLOON, 'MARS' and Descent of a
Parachute from an altitude of 2,000 feet.*

*Ascent of a Flying Fish which will be pursued by
an Aerial Giant and Volunteer Balloons!*

*The Young Ladies' Balloon Race! From their own
hands.*

The Boys' Own Race!

One year this particular feature of the occasion ended
in mayhem, as the following unattributed and undated
newspaper report records though the reference to *Mr
Jackson* might put it somewhere in the 1870s.

*A fete was held on Monday in the Arboretum the
most attractive feature of which was the ascent of Mr
Croxwell's balloon 'Express'. At twenty-five minutes
past six the grappling irons were loosed, but it soon
became apparent that the balloon would not clear the
trees surrounding the enclosure. Mr Croxwell, who
did not himself ascend, shouted to the occupants of
the car to throw out ballast; but in spite of every
precaution, the balloon dashed against the trees. The
persons in the car, five in number, were rescued; but
the mob, who were indignant because a local aeronaut,
Mr Jackson, had not been engaged, attempted to tear
up the balloon, and a hand-to-hand fight between
them and the police ensued. Mr Croxwell was grossly
ill-treated, and the police were pelted with stones.
Previous to this mishap one of the Indian troupe fell
from the rope on which he was performing, but his
injuries were not of a serious nature.*

Altogether, an occasion to forget in a hurry if
possible, and the crowd behaviour would have
particularly upset Loudon had he been still alive,
judging from his comments on the people in Derby
which we shall have cause to consider in the last section
of the book.

The occasion of the abolition of entrance fees
provoked an interesting editorial in the 'Derby
Mercury' of 8 November 1882 which shows that the
management of the Park had not been above criticism,
and with good reason. It might be a safe assumption
that neither Strutt or Loudon would have been pleased
with its condition forty years later, and a very adverse
comparison was made with the situation just sixteen
miles away in Nottingham. We may also detect in
the view expressed by the Editor a knock-on effect
of such occurrences as we have just witnessed by proxy
in the case of the balloon ascent that went wrong:

*The ARBORETUM, about the free opening of
which there has been so much talk, is now free to
the public for ever. We only hope that the Corporation
will take effectual means to prevent the grounds, once
so beautiful, from being destroyed; and that which
was intended by the donor for the recreation and
instruction of the public may not be turned into a
bear garden from which all decent working people
are driven by the roughs.*

*Of course, Saturday was an exceptional day; but
arrangements will have to be made very different from*

those which prevailed then if the Arboretum is to be
of any use to the town as a place of pleasant resort.

In the close days, now past for ever, it was always
a matter of surprise that, as the trees and shrubs for
which the Arboretum was originally celebrated died,
through causes over which the Committee had no
control, steps were never taken to make the place bright
with flowers. During the present year, it is true some
slight improvement has been attempted, but nothing
worthy of the place. Our neighbours in Nottingham
have long set us an example in this respect. Their
Arboretum, always free to the public, has been kept
up in a manner which has always been the envy of
Derby visitors. Brilliant flower beds form the central
attraction in well-kept grounds to which the public
resort with delight; whilst the Derby Arboretum has
never been noted of late years for anything but its
unadorned barrenness, and its barn-like glass
monstrosity, satirically named a Crystal Palace.
But under the new regime, we look for better things,
and the first improvement might well be the taking
of a leaf out of our neighbour's book in the matter
of floral adornments.

Not pretty reading, and things were ever done better,
it seems, in Nottingham. On the mystery of the decay
due to uncontrollable causes, an article in the
'Mercury' on 15 July 1881 refers to the rare trees and
shrubs giving way *before the smoke of furnaces and
the gradual hemming-in of an increasing population.*

By the 1880s, the Arboretum was truly enclosed in
a region of terraced streets in contrast to its open
borders in 1840. Its role as a refresher of jaded spirits
was more important than ever. Whilst the ever-
prowling sabbatarians successfully opposed brass band
concerts in parks, nationally, and in many instances
deprived working people, in the view of
G.F.Chadwick, of 'quite unexceptionable diversions'
on their only entirely free day, perhaps the most
touching tribute to the development to which Derby
made a unique contribution came from a Manchester
newspaper of the 1840s.

. . .*even during the rain these parks are resorted
to by the workmen.*
. . .*It is certainly something to know that mechanics,*

*Summer house pavilion, one of two at each end of the principal
walk.*

*glad of recreation, will play at ninepins, under an
ungenial sky, in preference to indulging in the more
seasonable attractions of the tap.*[32]

And before going on to consider at greater length
the variety of ways in which the people of the town
spent their leisure hours, meagre as they were in
duration for most, perhaps this is the most appropriate
point to pause for the only funeral to feature in these
pages, that of one of the two great resourcers of leisure
in this period in Derby, Joseph Strutt, giver of the
Arboretum. It took place on 20 January 1844 at eleven
o'clock in the morning. It was strictly private, as far
as the ceremony was concerned in the burial ground
of the Friar Gate Unitarian Chapel, by his expressed
wish. The funeral procession consisted of

*hearse, the late lamented gentleman's carriage, and
three mourning coaches containing relatives . . .The
banks and shops were generally closed throughout the
town, and the shutters of the majority of private houses
also, as a mark of respect to the memory of the deceased;
and along Victoria-Street, the Wardwick, and as far
as the Chapel, the streets were densely crowded with
mournful spectators . . .Hat-bands and scarfs were sent
to the members of the Corporation, and were worn
by them on Sunday morning.*[33]

The front entrance of the Arboretum in Grove Street, drawn shortly after the opening ceremony.

Artist's impression of the Crystal Palace. This illustration was included on the list of subscribers for the 'Proposed Glass and Iron Building'.

Notes

1. H.Butterton, *Derby Arboretum A Notable Public Place?* 1991.
2. G.F.Chadwick, op.cit.
3. H.Butterton, op.cit.
4. G.F.Chadwick, op.cit.
5. Quoted Ibid.
6. Ibid.
7. H.Butterton, op.cit.
8. G.F.Chadwick, op.cit.
9. H.Butterton, op.cit.
10. G.F.Chadwick, op.cit.
11. John Gloag, *Mr Loudon's England,* 1970.
12. Ibid.
13. Quoted G.F.Chadwick, op.cit.
14. Ibid.
15. Ibid.
16. Ibid.
17. Ibid.
18. H.Butterton. op.cit.
19. G.F.Chadwick, op.cit.
20. H.Butterton, op.cit.
21. Ibid.
22. Maxwell Craven, op.cit.
23. H.Butterton, op.cit.
24. Quoted G.F.Chadwick, op.cit.
25. H.Butterton, op.cit.
26. Ibid.
27. Maxwell Craven, op.cit.
28. H.Butterton, op.cit.
29. G.F.Chadwick, op.cit.
30. Maxwell Craven, op.cit.
31. G.F.Chadwick, op.cit.
32. Ibid.
33. *Derbyshire Collection No.3202.*

In Pursuit of Leisure

Exquisite Photographs
By J.A.Warwick Esq
Including views of the most interesting places in Derbyshire, such as Chatsworth; Haddon Hall; Remarkable Ruins; Ancient Crosses and other Antiquities; Peak Scenery; Residences of the Nobility and Gentry of the County. Fresh additions to this interesting series are continually being made, and from the moderate rate at which they are being published, as well as from their beauty and finish, the Publisher has commanded a large sale, and he hopes that those who have not seen these gems of photographic Art, will favour him with a call . . .

THUS in 1883[1], a Derby firm advertised a unique combination of business and pleasure. It is an extract from an attractively lettered (in the contemporary manner) notice by Richard Keene, born in 1825, the son of the manager of James Peet's silk manufactory in Bridge Street and one of a circle of photographers who, in the next year (1884), founded the Derby Photographic Society.

Together with the J.A.Warwick Esq, who features in the above section of the advertisement and was a Midland Railway superintendant and keen amateur photographer, he had ventured up the Derwent and into the Peak in 1858 with a cart specially adapted to carry all the equipment required by the contemporary photographer to record the scenes he was able to sell in reproduction for the rest of his life. His shop was in Irongate and during the following three years to 1861, he had taken a series of Derby Street scenes which, besides adding to his marketable range, provide much of the basis for our knowledge of what the town actually looked like in the middle of the last century.

Three others of the Derby photographic circle were William Abney, first president of the Society who lived at The Firs, one of those Regency villas on the Burton Road and whose father had known William Henry Fox-Talbot, Britain's pioneer photographer and through marriage a frequent visitor to Markeaton Hall back in the 1830s; W.W.Winter, who headed a photographic business on the Midland Road and which still flourishes today, also recorded street scenes in the town and took a series of portraits of Derby's Victorian mayors; and, finally, H.I.Stevens the architect.[2]

For an even more vivid record of Derby life, contemporaries, and we today, would turn to the local newspapers and journals. By the end of our period there were no less than five purveyors of news and advertisements, three weekly and two daily, to help add meaning to those leisure moments. The 'dailies', launched all but simultaneously, were a relatively late phenomenon, reflecting the nationwide consequences of the 1870 Education Act and of the trans-oceanic cable and electric telegraph. The weeklies changed during the century. *'Walk Through Derby'*, 1827 gave notice of the *'Derby Mercury'*, the first number of *which was published on Thursday, 23 March 1732, and is still continued by Messrs. Drewry and Son, and published on Wednesday evening . . .*

In 1824, Messrs W. & W.Pike began their *'Derby Reporter'*, which is published every Thursday afternoon.

There were political differences between these two. The 'Mercury' was establishment-minded and Tory, whilst the 'Reporter' reflected the views of those who wanted to see change and reform. Whilst the former indulged its readership in lengthy and detailed reports of crimes and rioting, the latter concentrated more on political issues.[3]

From 1845, the people of Derby had the benefit of greater choice for their weekly reading with the establishment of the 'Derbyshire Advertiser', proprietors the family Hobson.[4]

On Monday, 28 July 1879 the first issue of the 'Derby Daily Telegraph' came out. Just 20 minutes later appeared a rival, the 'Derby Daily Gazette', which, however, lasted but six years. Since the 'Telegraph' turned out to be a mouthpiece of the Liberal political interest, Derby Tories determined it should have a suitable rival and founded the 'Derby Daily Express' in 1884. In consequence, the 'Gazette' folded the next year, although the overlap meant that for a period of about 12 months there were actually three dailies in the town.

The 'Telegraph', of course, proved to be a permanent fixture, with a declared aim, although at first of only four pages, to provide *the finest, freshest and the most readable evening paper out of London*[5] in response to the jibe alluded to by the editor that Derby was *the largest and most influential town in the country without a daily journal of its own . . .* [6]

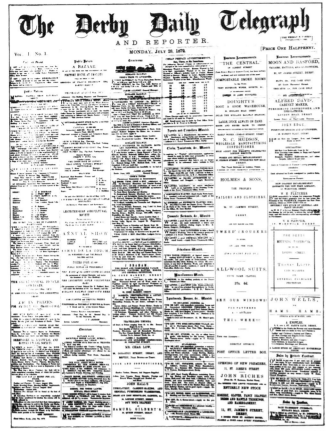

Top: *Front page of the first edition of the* Derby Daily Telegraph. Bottom (left): *Mrs Eliza Maria Pike, the newspaper's proprietor.* Bottom (right): *W.J.Piper, the paper's first editor.*

It was printed on a *single-cylinder flat-bed machine* but had the benefit of a formidable proprietor and talented journalist-editor in addition to the universal communications benefits of the 1880s mentioned above.

The proprietor was Mrs Eliza Maria Pike, who lived at The Cedars on Kedleston Road. She was the widow of John Beard Pike, whose father and uncle had been joint founders of the 'Reporter' back in 1823. Apparently she ran an all-male enterprise with a rod of iron, responding to a strike by getting in an entirely fresh complement without hesitation the next morning.

Her editor, W.J.Piper, assured readers that *nothing of importance, within the powers of the wires to transmit, will be omitted*[7] from the paper. Before the end of 1879 there were three editions daily, appearing on the streets at 1.30pm, 4.30pm and about 6pm. There was nothing but advertisements on the front page, and the only 'visual' to start with was a single line-drawing of a railway train in the notice of a Thomas Cook excursion.

But the first number also brought a nail-biting story-line dated 5 July by Archibald Forbes, famous war correspondent of the national 'Daily News' reporting the crushing of Cetewayo and the Zulus at Ulundi to reverse their earlier mauling of the British Army at Isandhlwana. The second edition, on the streets at 4pm on 28 July, posted details of the betting as at 3pm in London on the Stewards' and Goodwood Cups and the prices of produce, provisions and meat on the London markets earlier that day.[8]

Whilst in the 1880s there was growing competition for attention from the poster advertising on tramcars and the backs of sandwich-board men (the Pears' Soap 'advert' based on Millais' painting 'Bubbles' first appeared in 1886), it is the newspaper notices that still catch the local eye and, we trust, beguiled fleeting spare moments on the part of the Derby citizen.

What enticing prospects of beguilery are conjured up in this advertisement appearing in the 'Derby Mercury' on 18 December 1833:

G.RANDALL
HAIR CUTTER AND PERFUMER
Begs leave to return his sincere thanks to his Friends and the Public in general, for the very liberal support he has met with during his Residence in the Corn Market, and respectfully informs them he has removed to
NO.12, ROTTEN ROW
Where he intends keeping a large Assortment of Jewellery, Foreign and British Perfumery, Genuine Eau de Cologne; Tooth, Nail and Hair Brushes of the best quality; Tortoise-shell, Ivory, and Horn Combs of every description; Fancy Beads in general; Toys wholesale and retail.
Derby 16 December 1833

A veritable Aladdin's Cave indeed! Then this, from the same journal's edition of 20 March 1860:
TEA, COFFEE, AND GENERAL
GROCERY ESTABLISHMENT
12 1/2 MARKET PLACE,
DERBY
JOSEPH CLAYTON most respectfully informs the Nobility, Gentry, and the General Public, that his Stock is replete with a choice selection of Teas, Coffees, Spices, Raw and Refined Sugars, Fruits, and every article in the grocery trade which he is offering on reasonable terms.

If requiring genteel employment, the presently fettered eye might fall on the following, from the 'Mercury' of 15 January 1834;
WANTED
An active and Pious Mistress for a National Girls' School. Apply to Rev.W.Fisher, Derby.
Or from 19 February:
WANTED
A very Respectable Footman, he must be fully recommended for Sobriety, Steadiness, and Honesty,

and have lived two or three years Service in a
respectable Family, Enquire at the Printer's.
WANTED
*A Respectable Woman as Housekeeper, who perfectly
understands the management of a Dairy, Enquire at
the Mercury Office, Derby.*

If needing to be absorbed in the wheels of industry
at a time of extreme sensitivity, the following might
have drawn or repelled on 15 January:

WANTED
*Persons who are capable of managing Rotary Bobbin
Net Machines, Also several Youths from 14 to 16 years
of age, to learn Making Lace, Constant Employment
will be secured, Apply to Mr John Johnson, Albion
Street, Derby. No Person connected with the Trades'
Union need apply.*

If an anxious or harried parent, this might have been
balm on that very same day:

*The Misses Palmer purpose to re-open their School,
42 Friar Gate, Derby on Monday the third of February
next — 14 January 1834.*

Equally so, this if in search of a moderately gracious
lifestyle:

To Be Let
And may be entered upon at Lady-Day next
*A genteel House and Garden pleasantly situated in
the Friar Gate, Derby, in the occupation of Mr Joseph
Edge.*
*Application to be made to MR GEORGE SOWTER,
Park Nook, near Derby.*

Special Occasions

Leisure time was probably harder to come by in
the Victorian Age compared to the previous century,
although with the railway there was more choice in
how to use it. The demands of factory production
were remorseless, although Saturday half-holidays
were not unknown in many industrial towns from
about 1850 onwards (what the situation was in Derby
awaits further research as with the town's correspondence to national trends in other fields at that time),
if only to discourage artisans taking *Saint Monday*
off each week.[9]

But there were two meagre legacies from the past
in Derby which benefited the populace in this regard:
the celebration of national events and Wakes,
originating in Parish Patronal festivals. On the
Coronation of William IV in 1830, there was a civic
procession including 2,000 Sunday Schoolchildren to
the firing of cannon, and manufactories like Bridgett's
dined their workforce. At the Wakes, generally
concentrated on 1 November, there were time-
honoured sports.[10]

The situation started to loosen up in the 1870s and
1880s. In 1871 Parliament passed the Bank Holiday
Act which ordained three days' holiday for those to
whom it applied. Other salaried workers were
beginning to enjoy one or two paid holidays in the
year, one at least usually spent at the seaside. The
Great Exhibition of 1851 had provided a grand boost
nationally to the idea of taking cheap day excursions
by rail and those who could not afford these on an
individual or family basis were taken on a workforce
day outing each year.

Members of the middle class would be starting to

get to Europe: Thomas Cook began Continental tours
in the 1850s. During the following decade came
pioneer mountaineering and winter sports in the Alps
and overall the number of travellers to Europe
nationally more than doubled to a total of above
350,000 in the period 1850-70.[11]

In any case, local special events continued the
tradition of communally focussed leisure throughout
the period. Apart from the annual Arboretum Festival,
there were two visits from the Royal Agricultural Show
which were hosted in the Osmaston Park estate off
the London Road in 1843 and 1881. Their special
attraction was the presence of Royalty: for the visit
of the Prince of Wales (later Edward VII) on 15 July
1881, the Midland Railway paid for the special train
from London and provided a special siding to
Osmaston off the main line for the occasion.
Triumphal arches, paid for by Mayor Arbraham
Woodiwiss, adorned various thoroughfares in the
town: one in Midland and three in London Road on
the royal route to the show, a large double one at
the top of St Peter's Street, and one each in the Corn
Market, the bottom of Hartington Street (very
appropriately, although as we have seen not in any
sense a 'through route') and the Osmaston Road. An
estimated 50-60,000 people were in Derby that day.[12]

According to the 'Mercury' there were:
*Banners, evergreens, flowers, and plants, coloured
draperies, shields, Chinese lanterns, and words of
welcome and kindness were seen at almost every point,
and aided by the beautiful sunshine, rendered the town
gay and festive beyond description.*

*. . . .At exactly 25 minutes to one the Prince walked
quietly out of the Station, looking very well, in a white
tall hat and suit of light grey, accompanied by the
Mayor . . .*

*Throughout the entire route the streets were lined
with dense crowds, and not only every window but
every bit of balcony or elevation of any kind, temporary
or permanent, seemed alive with joyous humanity,
all cheering or handkerchief-waving according to sex.*

If the Edwardian findings about the use or non-
use of the handkerchief mentioned in Chapter Seven
were of general application, does this last section give
an indication of the social composition of the sector
of the town and/or the crowds greeting the spectacle?
Clearly, however, such special occasions were an
opportunity for communal display and expression of
loyalty for which labour was gladly suspended as a
preview in the 'Mercury' on 13 July demonstrates:

*The occasion, so long and earnestly aniticipated in
Derby, has arrived, and the town is now in full
enjoyment of all the advantages which are popularly
supposed to accrue from the presence of the Royal
Agricultural Society's Annual Exhibition. For some
time past, most of the available lodgings have been
occupied by the workers engaged in bringing this great
national undertaking to a climax; and now our streets
are crowded with strangers from every part of England
all of whom are interested in the results of those
labours, either as exhibitors, learners, or loungers. The
borough has put on a holiday aspect . . .and those
who are attracted by the Show from distant parts will
have no reason to complain that Derby treats its guests
with indifference, or mere perfunctory hospitality.
Ordinary business may be said to be suspended whilst*

the great event of the year is progressing; for, although our towns men work hard, and live economically, in general, they cannot be ranked among those who take their pleasures sadly, and everybody is prepared to seize the passing moment as it flies and make the best of it.

As regards the serious side of this leisure entertainment, the 'Mercury' preview is equally and appropriately enthuisastic:

The machinery is arranged in long rows, and there is such an extensive and varied mass of mechanism that it has required a catalogue of no fewer than 418 post-quarto pages to describe their many uses and advantages. Everything that the ingenuity of man's mind could devise and the skill of man's hand could shape is here. The eye is positively lost in wonder and admiration while gazing at the huge giants of the iron world which stand up grim and silent in the midst of so much pastoral beauty as Osmaston Park contains.

Hospitality had, of course, been traditionally dispensed in pubs and hotels, focussed particularly on the often-linked attractions of the Assembly Rooms and the races. These were occasions when the surrounding country gentry had mixed with a moderate range of their fellow humankind in the case of the former and with all and sundry at the latter. Pickford's severely gracious Assembly Rooms normally filled up once a fortnight for the assemblies, described as general meetings of *the polite persons of both sexes* when *conversation, gallantry, news and play* would be exchanged between late afternoon dinner and supper.

However, race meetings meant extra assemblies and perhaps a special informal ball known as a *Derby Rout,*[13] for the times on such occasions would have to be flexible as, according to Davison, the gentry forced a 4pm start to the races as they could not watch anything on less than a full stomach. It was their custom to dine at the King's Head on Tuesdays and the George on Wednesdays.[14] Assembly Rooms suppers might then not occur until one o'clock in the morning.

In any case, by 1812 when already for several years the races had been transferred from bleak and windswept Sinfin Moor, on the far south-western outskirts, to the Holmes down near the river, there was a far looser regimen at the Assembly Rooms where the original rules had forbidden entry to any mere *Attorney's Clerk or Shopkeeper, or any of his or her family . . .except Mr Franceys* and dancing to any *Miss in a Coat . . .without Leave of the Lady of the Assembly.*[15]

Typical house events were these, advertised in the 'Mercury' on 15 January 1834 and reported on 7 January 1846:

BALL AND SUPPER

There will be a BALL and SUPPER at the New Assembly Rooms, Derby, on Tuesday the 4 of February.

MRS WILMOT, Lady Patroness.
HUGO MEYNELL Esq.
EDWARD ANTHONY HOLDEN Esq. Stewards

The annual Christmas Ball was held in the New Assembly Room, Derby, on the evening of Tuesday, 30 December. Upwards of two hundred and thirty

---

St. Michaels' Church, Derby,

HAPPY HOME UNION

EXCURSION TO LICHFIELD,

EASTER MONDAY, 1859.

The **Train will leave Derby at half-past 10 o'clock,** but Members and Friends should be at the Station ten minutes before that time.

The party will be shown over Lichfield Cathedral at 1 o'clock.

Tea will be served in the Garden of Rev. S. Andrew, St. John's Street, at 4 o'clock.

The **Return Train will leave the South Stafford Railway Station, Lichfield, at ten minutes to 8 o'clock,** but all are requested to be at the Station, at least ten minutes before that time.

Each Member will receive a numbered ticket before leaving the carriage in going to Lichfield, and must return home in the same carriage.

The **Return Train is due at Derby Station at ten minutes past 9 o'clock.** Parents are requested to meet those children, who are too young to come safely home by themselves.

Members will find cheap and good refreshments, and will get any help they want, at Mrs. Martin's, Working Men's Association, Tamworth Street.

Members can buy for 3d, from the Secretaries, "What the Children ought to know about Lichfield." The price in the shop, is 6d.

Mr. Clarke hopes that all Members will be very careful to behave well, for he has many friends in Lichfield, and he would be sorry if they did not form a good opinion of his friends from Derby, or if they saw them setting a bad example. Mr. Clarke hopes especially that no lads will smoke, and that no one will enter any public-house.

[R. KEENE, PRINTER, DERBY.]

Handbill giving careful instructions to the young men of St Michael's Church, Derby, for a day-trip to Lichfield in 1859.

members and friends of the leading families of the town and county were present, and the proceedings passed off with great eclat. Dancing was kept up with great spirit until a seasonable hour, which gave the highest satisfaction to the company. The following were amongst the Novelties introduced: Maretzek's Walz Pas de Fleur, Koenig's Bohemian Polka, and Coote's Enchantress Quadrilles . . .

The supper was provided by Mr and Mrs Wallis, of the King's Head Hotel. Great taste and skill was displayed in the arrangements, and the viands and wines of first rate quality.

Good to detect a Continental flavour in the exercises chosen!

A permanent grandstand had been erected for the races at the Holmes, which was graced by the likes of the Duke of Devonshire, who in 1813 appeared in a *coach-and-six* with no less than ten outriders. As a focus for the country gentry the races filled all available lodging places in the town.[16]

But this particular site lasted a mere forty years until 1845, when the Midland Railway complex began to encroach unacceptably on the scene and the final venue further north towards Little Chester was decided upon. The first meeting on the Racecourse took place in May 1848 and four years later a grandstand was finished designed yet again by Henry Duesbury between his assignments at the Guildhall and County Asylum, with an elegant round-headed arcade on the second of three tiers flanked by cone-roofed towers and with a balustered high observation point breaking the pitch of the roof in the centre.[17]

Hostelries

The hotel trade was altered by the coming of the railway. Mr Wallis, whom we have met with his lady wife providing refreshment at the Assembly Rooms, had been at the King's Head at the time of the opening of the Birmingham and Derby Junction Railway in 1839 and had invited the directors and shareholders to eat their celebratory cold meal at his establishment, arranging their conveyance between platform and hostelry in a fleet of carriages.

The railway had to be co-operated with, not fought against.[18] It added two new venues in the town for business and pleasure with the Midland Hotel and nearby Brunswick Railway and Commercial Inn. Both opened for custom in 1843. With the former charging double for most items compared with the latter (for example, *Bed 4s 0d (20p)* compared to *2s 0d* per night) and specifically advertising *Servant's Bed* and such other items as *Sitting Room* and *Wax Lights*, they obviously had different classes of customer in mind. Indeed, Queen Victoria herself graced a night at the Midland Hotel in 1849 and it went on to be twice extended with new wings in 1874 and '84.[19]

During the earlier part of the century, town-core inns were centres of 'leisure' business too, as the following typical notice from the 'Derby and Chesterfield Reporter' on 7 November 1833 illustrates:
CANAL SHARES
To be sold by Auction
BY MR ROWLAND BREAREY
At the King's Head Inn, on Tuesday next the 12 November 1833, at 6 o'clock in the Evening;
Two shares in the Derby Canal. Further particulars may be known by applying at the office of Mr Brearley, 14 Corn Market.

This, however, tended to decrease as traditional ways of doing things gave way to the 'shock of the new' from the 1840s on.

Naturally, it was the pub which was the hospitality-dispenser for the vast majority of Derby folk if only because of the very number in existence. Drunkenness in fact was a major Victorian social problem.

Consumption of alcohol nationally reached an all-time peak in the mid-1870s with 1.30 gallons of spirits going down per head. 1876 was the peak-year for beer with 34.4 gallons per head! The government of course benefited from taxes and licensing dues, giving rise to Robert Lowe's quip of 1873 that the habitual drunkard was *the sheet anchor of the British Constitution.*[20]

We have already speculated on the average hostelry's charms for bleakly accommodated and sometimes brutally exploited working men. To illustrate the extent of what was on offer in Derby and hence the corresponding concern of the strong Temperance movement in the town, it is an interesting exercise to go through the relevant section of the Trade Directories of the time.

For example, Pigot's 1835 'Directory of Derbyshire' lists 127 hotels, taverns and pubs and 42 retailers of beer in Derby for a population of about 30,000 or one dispenser of alcohol for every 200 people. We have already seen that there were well over 200 dispensers in the 1880s. To put real substance to the situation, it is worth recording the names of the hostelries in and around the central core in 1835 for any sentimental comparison with the 1990s.

Sadler Gate: *Bell Inn Hotel (post), Coach & Horses, Half Moon, Horse & Jockey, Three Tuns.*
St Mary's Gate: *King's Arms & County Tavern*

Morledge: *Bird-in-Hand, Bishop Blaize, Boat, Crown, Noah's Ark, Telegraph.*
Full Street: *Horse & Trumpet*
Corn Market: *King's Head Hotel, Red Lion, White Lion Hotel, Tiger Hotel, Angel*
St Helen's Street: *Old Spot*
St Peter's Street: *Nag's Head Hotel, Barley Mow, Crown & Anchor, Durham Ox, Green Dragon, Green Man, Thorn Tree, White Swan, Marquis of Anglesey*
King Street: *New Inn, New Flower Pot, Old Flower Pot, Seven Stars & 2 Retailers of Beer.*
Lodge Lane: *Brown Bear*
Bridge Street: *Holly Bush, Old Three Crowns, Pheasant, Ram and 2 Ret.*
Market Place: *Cross Keys, Rose & Crown, Royal Oak*
Brook side: *Queen's Head*
Bold Lane: *Flying Horse, Shakespeare, Star and Garter & 1 Ret.*
Bridge Gate: *Fox & Owl, Roe Buck, Shakespeare and 2 Ret.*
Iron Gate: *Robin Hood, Talbot*
Agard Street: *Golden Eagle & 1 Ret.*
Friar Gate: *Greyhound, Old White Horse, Old White Lion, Rising Sun, Wheel and 2 Ret.*
Walker Lane: *George & Dragon, Wheat Sheaf, Hare & Greyhounds.*[21]

Sport

An occasion of mass leisure activity which came to an end in Derby during our period was Shrovetide Football. On 1 February 1834, during the Silk-Mill Lock-Out, the editorial column of the 'Pioneer' magazine for Trades Unionists urged members not to take part in what it described as a stupid game. It went on:

It has been an ancient custom in Derby, for the inhabitants to assemble in the Market Place, on Shrove Tuesday, and commence a savage struggle, to decide which parish shall be able to carry or push a huge ball stuffed with cork-shavings, to a goal in either parish, one of which cannot by any means be reached without the combatants wading up to their necks in the river. Regardless of every thing but success in this silly exploit, the different parties undergo the most astonishing inflictions; half drowned, crushed, kicked, bruised, and, in some instances, downright killed, still the combat rages; no quarter-no-mercy-nothing but barbarous recklessness and supreme folly. Magistrates cannot put a stop to it, nor military put it down. Unionists must do it!

According to Davison, the practice originated in an old apprentice-holiday. The rival teams were supposed to be drawn from the parishes of All Saints' defending a goal at Nuns' Mill to the North and St Peter's defending Gallows Baulk to the south. The 'toss up' took place in the Market Place at noon.[22] By the beginning of our period the 'Derby Mercury' carried repeated protests from the town's intelligentsia about the mayhem caused by the vastly augmented parish teams and the loutish behaviour so encouraged in the streets. In 1845 the game was denounced as *dirty, unmanly and absurd play.* The previous year a letter to the 'Mercury' suggests a variation on the time-honoured filling to the ball, the writer complaining with other peaceable people of being *assaulted in the Wardwick by a band of men carrying small bags of*

BOROUGH OF DERBY.

CAUTION.

The Mayor and Magistrates of this Borough, having been requested by the Secretary of State to take efficient measures to prevent Persons assembling on Shrove-Tuesday, or Ash-Wednesday, for the purpose of

PLAYING AT

FOOT-BALL,

Notice is therefore hereby given,

that if any Persons shall be found in the Public Streets, Passages or other Public Places within this Borough, for the purpose of Playing at Foot-Ball, or for any other riotous or unlawful object, such Persons will be Prosecuted and dealt with according to law.

HENRY MOZLEY, Mayor.

Town-Hall, Derby,
March 3rd, 1845.

Printed by Wm. Bemrose, Derby.

soot, with which they begrimed the clothes and faces of the passers-by.[23]

Another letter from a gardener complained of fences and crops on the outskirts of town being damaged. However, it all came to end the very next year in 1846, when the crowds 'participating' were such that the

1832 forces of Nottingham Dragoons and special constables had to be called in. Several balls were in use by this time, the Mayor was hit on the shoulder with a brickbat, the Riot Act was read again and the troops went into action against the 'players'. At the subsequent trial, the counsel for prosecution argued that the vast increase in the size of the town since the beginning of the century rendered such a game unsuitable in the modern age. The prisoners were dismissed since the charges were not serious. But when the Dragoons were brought in the year after, the trouble had disappeared and the game in Derby at least was a thing of the past.[24]

The Trades Unionists had had an answer to it a dozen years previously. The 'Pioneer' on 22 February 1834 had carried a letter from *A PLANE DRIVER* dated *Derby, 14 February* and signed *Yours in Union*, reporting on how all the Unionists in Derby had boycotted that year's Shrovetide Football after the appeal noted earlier:

And although this bear-like custom has been renewed this year, yet it was very obvious it was merely a miniature of what it has been and that the abettors were no friends to the union of the working classes; while all those who joined in the savage strife were either agricultural labourers, or men of weak minds . . .

Instead, says the writer, the Union organised two days of processions, on the Tuesday to Duffield, *a delightful little village, four miles on the Buxton Road*, when some 5-6,000 women and over 1,300 men (the proportions of the sexes is interesting here!) marched from the Infirmary, London Road, about one o'clock, in order of march: women, lace-makers, joiners and carpenters, shoemakes, plasterers, wood sawyers, tailors, broad-silk weavers, labourers, framework knitters, smallware weavers, twisters, silk throwsters, bricklayers and stonemasons.

They were joined at Duffield by union members from the villages and all went on to a field opposite the White Lion Inn. A large fire was lit in the centre, a marquee was set up with seats for the ladies and the surrounding hills were crowded with onlookers. Mrs Vicars of Belper, *a strong advocate for the interest of the working classes*, gave an address from the top of a wagon. The return to Derby passed through the town centre with the singing of hymns and popular songs. On the following day, there was another procession to Spondon, *a pleasant little village three or four miles on the Nottingham Road*. There was the same order of march as on the previous day and the same recourse to a field, but this time by the women only, the men going on to Ockbrook. Then back to Derby at 6pm with band playing and hymns being sung.

There were obviously better ways of playing football! The 'Derby Mercury' for 7 May 1884, admittedly forty years after the demise of Shrovetide Football in the town and also coming from the genteel haven of the Cricket Club be it noted, carried the following notice:

Derbyshire County Football
We understand that the Derbyshire County Cricket Club has decided upon the formation of a football-club, under Association rules, in connection with county cricket, and already considerable progress has been made in the matter. The club have acquired the ground under a lease, and purpose making such alteration thereon as will meet the requirements of the game. Ample arrangements will also be made for the convenience of the public. It is desired to render football worthy of the patronage generously bestowed upon it by the public, and the committee will endeavour, therefore, to arrange matches with eminent clubs, thereby enabling the public to witness matches of a higher order than have hitherto been played in Derby. The subscription is fixed at 5s, which, we think, will be thought to be sufficiently moderate. The secretary, Mr William Parker of Amen Alley, will be glad to enroll members.

This was rather late in the day in terms of the national scene. From as early as 1850, football — the game had yet to develop into 'soccer' as we know it today — had come into its own as the mass entertainer, with the Saturday half-holiday beginning to spread and the ever-present railway factor well-rooted even then. In mid-Victorian times, clubs focussed around schools, Sunday schools, other church and chapel groups, boys' clubs, cricket clubs (in need of winter occupation), pubs, institutes or firms.

In 1870, the Football Association was formed, the split coming between the soccer clubs and those that eventually formed the Rugby Union, not over whether handling should be allowed but whether it was acceptable to 'hack' an opponent.

In 1871, the FA Cup competiton began and during that decade 'gentlemen's clubs' in the Home Counties down south and soccer-playing public school old boys between them shared what eventually became the world's most prestigious trophy. However, in the 1880s, challenging northern competition came to the fore. Just the year before the formation of the club in Derby, an era change happened on the national scene when the Old Etonians lost to the professional Blackburn Olympic. Then Blackburn Rovers won the FA Cup three times in a row — once in a replay at the County Ground, Derby, in the first FA Cup Final to be played outside London — and the amateurs' grasp was loosened.

Some of the elements of the modern game were now in place: professionalism was legalised in 1885; and the Football League was formed in 1888. There were admission charges and in addition to the regular 'fans', who were mainly of the 'artisan' and 'lower middle white-collar' classes, the toughs and vandals following the local precedent we have witnessed with Shrovetide Football.[25]

To illustrate this development, the 'Derby Mercury' for 14 April 1886 carried a report of the FA Cup Final replay, played at Derby on 10 April between the holders Blackburn Rovers and West Bromwich Albion. The initial match had been played at The Oval in Surrey, another ground famous for its summer game. The reporter continued:

The Rovers' team includes half a dozen players who have in the past been awarded International honours, while the Albionites have yet such distinction to win.

After an hour's heavy snowfall in the morning, which seemed to render the contest problematic, the sun came out at one o'clock and all snow had disappeared by the scheduled kick-off time:

When the whistle blew for half-time the game stood one goal (kicked by Sowerbutts) to none in favour

Derby photographers W.W.Winter were called to the County Ground one day in 1884 to take this photograph of Derby County FC, who began life as an offshoot of the hard-up county cricket club.

of the Rovers. *The Albion failed to score in the second half, but Brown scored for the Rovers, who won by two to none.*

. . .After the completion of the above match, the cup — an insignificant article as cups go, but it would be all the same if it were but a bit of blue ribbon, was placed on a table in the verandah of the pavilion, and on its being noised abroad that it was to be presented to the winners a large crowd gathered in the field in front. 'Jimmy Brown', the captain of the Rovers, was greeted with loud cheers when he appeared on the verandah. (After speeches) the cup was then carried off triumphantly, and Major Marindin presented the medals.

The crowd then dispersed. It seems all so delightfully innocent now! The ceremony was obviously much more like a cricket competition finale than the Wembley circus. The sports reporting was also on the ultra-laconic side compared to the Nordic sagas we have come to expect in the present century!

But to try to put our finger on the precise position of Derby County by the very end of our period, obviously just before the dawn of modern fame and glory, the 'Mercury' for 2 February 1887 carried, beneath a report of the second round of the FA Challenge Cup, in which Derby did not feature, the following:

Amongst matches of interest on Saturday were the

following: Derby County and St Luke's played a draw, one goal each; Derby Midland beat Long Eaton Rangers by four to three. Both the semi-finals in the Derbyshire Minor Cup were decided, Long Eaton Rangers 2nd beating Duffield by two to none, and Primitives beating Midland 2nd by two to one.

In fact Derby County had been knocked out of the FA Cup in the qualifying competition, by the Birmingham club Mitchell St George's, but until they became founder-members of the Football League in 1888, outside of the cup games they were still playing friendly matches against other local sides and their results largely recorded in the summary paragraphs devoted to such exploits.

We have seen cricket in Derby begetting association football whatever the separate enthusiasms no doubt witnessed in scores of unenclosed venues about the town. Right at the beginning of our period there were two predominant cricket teams in the area, the South Derbyshire Cricket Club playing on Chaddesden Park with the patronage of the Wilmot family of Osmaston Hall and the Derby Town Cricket Club playing on The Holmes. The latter moved to the Racecourse in 1863, when H.I.Steven's Cattle Market near The Holmes affected the water-table and led to the drying out of the pitch there. Five years after that, the South Derbyshire team are recorded playing opponents called the Australian Aborigines (September 1868).[26]

Derbyshire cricket team of late 1880s vintage, posing in front of the scoreboard after they had declared for the first time, against Essex at Leyton.

Afterwards, the Aborigines, who were on a tour of England, entertained spectators with a display of boomerang-throwing.

However, the situation was not acceptable to some, judging by a letter published in the 'Mercury' in June 1861 from a Derbyshire cricketer, who remarked on its backwardness compared with Nottingham. He urged the Town Club to organise regular fixtures and encourage the game by adapting the rules (premonitions of one-day stuff?):

Let each bowler have so many overs, and if anyone have a long stand when he is handling the willow, let him give up that his fellow players may have the chance of an innings. And should others less experienced in the science, lose their wickets the first or second over, give them a few extra balls, and not grudgingly say of one, 'He is out, and make him go out!

He prefaces this appeal with this eulogy of the game:

Amongst the most popular pastimes, none has made such rapid progress . . .than the athletic and scientific game of cricket. Were the French to call us a nation of cricketers, they would be as near the mark as when they term us a nation of shopkeepers, as it is quite exceptional to meet with an Englishman who has not enjoyed the recreation I am speaking of.

Do we rejoice or weep at what has happened since

then? The writer's last sentence still has its resonances, however, when our TV news bulletins still regularly include the fortunes of the England cricket squad! His initial challenge was possibly answered almost ten years later when the 'Mercury' published the following report in its issue of 4 November 1870:

On Friday afternoon a public meeting was held in the Grand Jury Room, Town Hall, Derby, to consider the best mode of establishing a cricket club in Derbyshire which should represent the strength of the whole county.

The motion was proposed by Mr Walter Boden who believed it was in 1867 that the strength of the county was tried by a match between the cricketers of the north and those of the south portions of the county. Financially the match was not a success, but it brought together many cricketers who would not otherwise have met. This year, as they would be aware, had been played, one between the strength of the county and Marylebone Club, and the other between the gentlemen of Derbyshire and the gentle men of Kent, in both of which Derbyshire was victorious. He now proposed 'That a cricket club for Derbyshire be formed which shall represent the strength of the whole county, and that it be called the Derbyshire County Club (Hear, hear).*

Elsewhere by this time, a Gloucestershire doctor,

the impressively large and bearded figure of W.G.Grace, had become in the no doubt uniquely male public awareness of the age an equal personality with W.E.G. (Gladstone) himself. In 1873, the regular County Cricket Championship was under way — albeit the early champions being decided by the sporting Press rather than by an official competition structure — and in 1880 the first Test Match was played.[27]

By 1880, in fact, there were three-day county fixtures in Derby with a following which might be envied in 1993 to judge from the 'Mercury' report that same year, 8 June 1881:

A strong Derbyshire team was brought together on Monday to meet Kent, who fixed the match of their northern tour for Whit Monday at Derby. A rather cold wind blew across the ground, but rain held off until just before the conclusion of play. Sharratt had prepared a capital wicket, which was surrounded by a 'gate' of several thousand people.

Scores: Derbyshire 179 and 165; Kent 173 and 172 for 3. There were, however, reporters sympathetic to the interests of the ladies as in the same issue there was mention of the Arboretum Festival that day and also what was described as the usual Temperance demonstration, apart that is from the match between Derbyshire and Kent, *which drew a large number of visitors but ladies require a great effort to enable them to become enthusiastic over cricket.* Immensely patronising or genuinely sensitive?

There were other sports, too, with a more restricted following but beginning to be worthy of note. Bowling was carried on at various green venues, such as Friar Gate, Nottingham Road and upper St Peter's Street as well as those [28] attached to public houses.

In 1857 was founded the Derwent Rowing Club and from the next year it organised regattas for twenty years. On the same side of the river, Derby School started a rowing club the same year, 1863, in which they moved site to St Helens House nearby, though it survived for just twenty-five years. In 1879 was founded the Derby Town Rowing Club with a boathouse on the opposite Chester Green side of the river. It attempted to revive the regatta the following year after a lapse of two years but unhappily it endured a wash-out which discouraged a continuation for another twenty years.[29]

Finally, sixty years after James Wantling, an employee of the china works, gained distinction for long-distance running for purses of up to 200 guineas in the 1820s, the St John's Harriers Athletics Club was founded in the school next to the church of that name in the West End of the town.[30]

Theatre and Music

Coming indoors once more for a strictly spectator activity, there were occasional circus performances which, according to the 'Derby Mercury', attracted *numerous and fashionable audiences.* In the issue of 7 January 1846, the paper reported:

. . .On Thursday evening Mr W.O'Dale, the star rider of America, made his appearance in a surprising equestrian act, in which he performed some of the most extraordinary feats ever witnessed, whilst the horse was at full speed . . .The two Esslers, considering

they are children, are most excellent tight-rope dancers, and were applauded by the audience . . .

On Monday was presented the grand equestrian spectacle of Timour the Tartar. The piece was produced on a scale of grandeur that was never before attempted in this town, and reflects great credit on the management of Mr Hughes. In the procession to the tournament, four Egyptian camels were introduced; two of them harnessed to a splendid car, drawing Timour and the Princess Zorilda, with all the pomp and circumstances of the time . . .

This possibly took place in a building on the north side of Bag Lane where the Co-operative Society later established their emporium, although there was, indeed, another resident company whose premises were burnt down in March 1879.[31]

By this time the Corn Exchange, the official opening of which had been graced by a performance from Jenny Lind *'The Swedish Nightingale',* had become the home of drama and music-hall in Derby before the appearance of the Grand Theatre in 1886. The heyday of the music-hall in the town would not arrive until the early years of the present century, and performances at the Corn Exchange would probably not have qualified for the denunciation of the genre in the Trades Union 'Beehive' journal in 1868 as *glaring temples of dissipation . . .debased by the low songs and vulgar exhibitions.* But it is to be hoped that they will have included the light, the glitter, the songs that commented on working-class experience of courtship, marriage, family, old age.[32]

However, the role of the old Bold Lane Theatre in the earlier years of the century should not be forgotten in the story of the drama and of theatre in Derby. It hosted one to three nights stands by the famous stars of the day, such as Kean, *the greatest tragedian since Garrick,* playing Richard III, Othello, and Shylock in 1817 and again in 1824. It was noted on the other hand, at that time, that Derby audiences were most enthralled by melodramas featuring *ghosts, horrors and thunderstorms.*[33]

Words arranged in more serious format were the speciality of the Philosophical Society which had started in the eighteenth century and had continued to thrive in the early part of our period, first in St Helen's Street where it had a library of 1,500 books and also a small museum, then from 1839 in the Atheneum Club. It was some of its leading lights, such as Edward and Joseph Strutt and Douglas Fox, who were responsible for beginning the Mechanics' Institute which we have seen organising series of general interest lectures in the 1830s.[34]

Finally, there was much music in Derby, both passive and participatory. In the former vogue, a three-day Music Festival held every three years ran until 1831, when it went every year for another twenty years before disappearing, all held in support of the Derbyshire General Infirmary.[35] There were also celebrity concerts at the Theatre, the Mechanics' Institute and the Assembly Rooms. Three musicians of world renown are known to have performed at these concerts. The first was Paganini, as advertised in the 'Derby Mercury' for 16 October 1833:

Positively for THIS NIGHT ONLY
THEATRE ROYAL, DERBY
PAGANINI

Andrew Melville, founder of Derby's Grand Theatre. It was whilst waiting for a connecting train at Derby Station in October 1885 that Melville took a stroll in the town and saw the need for a new theatre.

SIGNOR PAGANINI respectfully announces to the Nobility, Gentry, and Public resident in DERBY and in the Vicinity, that he will give a

GRAND CONCERT
AT THE THEATRE
On THURSDAY, 17 OCTOBER 1833.

Being positively the LAST TIME he can possibly have the honour of appearing before them, previous to his departure for the Continent, on which occasion he has engaged those highly celebrated Vocalists,

MISS WELLS and MISS WATSON
THE Concert will be arranged by
MR WATSON

Composer to the Theatre Royal, English Opera House, and Covent

Garden, and Member of the Royal Academy of Music. In 1838 Johannn Strauss brought his band to the Mechanics' Institute, which must have added an early ambience to the new classical lecture hall there.[36] Of lesser, if national import was the performer whose notice appeared in the 'Derby and Chesterfield Reporter' for 28 November 1853:

MR HOLMES,

Professor of the Pianoforte in the Royal Academy of Music, London

Has the honour to announce to the Nobility, Gentry, his Friends, and the Public generally, that his CONCERT will take place

At the Theatre Royal, Derby
THIS DAY, THURSDAY Evening, 28 November 1833

But perhaps the musical celebrity honours for this eventful three-quarters of a century in the town must go to the concert advertised in the 'Derby Mercury' for 2 September 1840 and therefore just a few days before the grand opening of the Arboretum. Curiously, no venue is recorded and it is noticeable that the target audience did not include the 'ordinary' citizens of the town, perhaps because of the price of tickets. However that might have been, the appearance in Derby of one of the musical 'giants' of all time in the form of the contemporary wizard of the pianoforte, Franz Liszt, was announced in the following terms:

GRAND MORNING CONCERT
THURSDAY, 10 September, 1840,
TO COMMENCE AT ONE O'CLOCK PRECISELY.

M.LISZT.

MR LAVENU has the honour to inform the Nobility and Gentry of Derby and its neighbourhood, that he has succeeded in engaging M.LISZT, the extraordinary Pianist, who will, on this occasion, perform his Marche Hongroise, his Grand Galop Chromatique, Morceaux Choisis from his celebrated Recitals, and a Grand Duet with Mr Mori . . .
. . .Family Tickets, to admit four, 21s; Single Tickets, 6s; to be had of Mr STENSON, Music Seller.
At the request of many Families wishing to reserve Seats, a few Stalls will be set apart close to the Orchestra at 10s 6d each, to be had of Mr STENSON
**THE GRAND PIANO FORTE on which M.Liszt will perform is one of Erard's new Patent, and is brought
expressly from London for the occasion.

This piano, in fact, was a new model made in Paris and draws attention to the fact that there was a commercial aspect to Franz Liszt's recital: he was demonstrating the product of the prestigious firm of Erard of Paris.[37] The Derby showing was a part of a grand six-month tour through Europe on the part of the great maestro which had started a month or so earlier and would go on till the following January. Apart from the purpose already alluded to, Liszt was contributing to a plan to put up a statue to Beethoven at Bonn 13 years after his death.[38] He had another recital on his schedule for 10 September: after the Derby performance ended in mid-afternoon he and his party left by coach-and-horse for Nottingham.[39] The report of the recital in the hall of the Mechanic's Institute in the 'Derby Mercury' for 16 September praised
. . .a delightful performance, executed with much elegance and vast expression which seemed to draw all his immense powers into action. The great rapidity and unerring truth of the different passages, every note telling, as it were, gave it the semblance of a magnificent orchestra, rather than a piano-forte display.[40]
Derby was obviously suitably impressed!

In more participatory vein, the Derby Choral Society was formed in 1817 by William Gover who also helped to found the short-lived Derby Philharmonic Society (1835-40). From 1828 the Choral Society gave four annual concerts in the new Guildhall and had 60 members by 1830. They established a particular tradition of Christmas concerts at the new Victoria Street Congregational Church from 1860 on.[37] From their previous era comes an interesting 'Derby Mercury' report dated Wednesday 24 December 1845 about the Christmas offering that year. It reflects the dominance of Handel's 'Messiah' in English musical taste throughout the century, particularly at that season of the year with its echoes to this day, and also the special approach of music criticism at that time:

DERBY CHORAL SOCIETY

The numerous and respectable attendance at the second concert of this society, which took place at the New Assembly Rooms on Friday evening last, afforded an unequivocal proof of the interest which is felt in the prosperity of the society, and of the growth in musical taste in our town, as well as a desire to become acquainted with some of the beautiful compositions of our great composers . . .
After the overture to 'The Messiah' had been performed by the band, Mr Drew gave the opening recitative and air very finely. Mr Lowe's deep mellow bass voice told well in the recitative 'Thus saith the Lord', which he gave with good effect. We cannot speak too highly of the singing of Miss Radford . . .more especially in the beautiful air 'He was despised', which we think was the best vocal piece of the evening. We must not omit to mention the Pastoral Symphony. The solemnity of the movements appeared fully to produce their intended effect upon the auditory, and the whole band seemed to enter into the spirit and design of the immortal composer. The choruses, particularly 'For unto us', and the 'Hallelujah' were exceedingly well given, the latter especially.
The above sublime oratorio was no small test of the musical strength of the town; but the result proved that both band and choir were equal to the task, and gave with great effect the solemn grandeur and impressive sentiments of this masterpiece of sacred musical composition.

We get the feeling from this that the performance of even such ultra popular works as *Messiah* had been a rarity up to this time.

From the 1840s, brass bands came into great prominence with national competitions at Bell Vue, Manchester, and, slightly later, London's Crystal Palace. We have seen how their music featured at the Arboretum Festivals. However, their popularity provided a focus for the ever-present living shadow over weekend leisure hours in the form of the sabbatarian principle. The ban on Sunday band-concerts in parks enforced from the 1860s did not go unchallenged, at least in the Press. The London journal 'City Press' thundered out in June 1870:
Shall we permit bands to play in the parks on Sundays? Shall we compel people, who roam about the parks, and throng the suburban highways, to go to Church, and make an exhibition of sham piety?[41]
However, it was not till after our period that London's galleries and museums were opened to the public on Sundays.[42] This conflict situation also applied to local transport in Derby in the 1880s to support, or not to support, greater choice in how to spend Sunday leisure. The issue came to a head in the town over the Sunday running of the tramcars on 3 June 1881 when a meeting was called to debate

the principle, as reported in the 'Mercury' on Wednesday 8 June:

The Derby Tramways Company having commenced on the 29th ult. to run their cars on the Normanton-road route on the Sunday, in spite of the petition, influentially and numerously signed, which was presented to them in December last urging them to carry on the traffic only on weekdays, a meeting to protest against the innovation was held in the Christ Church Schoolroom on Friday evening last. Meantime it had been announced that on the following Sunday the cars would run on the Ashbourne Road and Osmaston Road sections.

The Chairman gave it as his belief that . . .*everyone in the room believed that the running of tramcars on Sunday was desecrating the Lord's Day, and breaking one of the commandments just as much as stealing or committing a murder . . .the people in the Normanton Road and the Streets adjacent were very anxious that they should not be again subjected to the indescribable annoyance which they had to endure on the previous Sunday . . .*

He added that the company chairman's response had so far been that . . .*as cars were run on Sundays in other towns he did not see why the people of Derby should not have the same privilege.*

This he rejected because:

Derby being a comparatively small town the trams were not needed as they might be in some larger places. Where the lines ran for three or four miles there might be something said for it, but the distance from one end to the other of the longest section in Derby could be walked in a quarter of an hour, so it could not be a very great convenience to anybody.

The Rev A.Olivier maintained that when he canvassed many of the poorer classes for signatures to the previous petition

. . .*he rejoiced to find there was not a single person who did not say that the running of tram-cars on the Sunday was utterly unnecessary and unjustifiable.*

A gentleman interjected from 'the floor' that . . .*he now rode in the cars on an average two or three times a day, but if the company ran them on Sunday he would not use them at all. He did not say that would be very general, but he thought a large number of those whose opinions were most worth having would do so.*

Mr W.R.Roe said that the December petition had received over 6,000 signatures. He had also talked to the staff involved who worked 15-16 hours per day. One of them hoped to get one Sunday off in three. None expected to get an addition to their weekly pay of 12s to 16s.

This report clearly shows the heat engendered by the issue and the division in the town which those passionately concerned about it detected in the populace at large. There were raised the effect of the journeys of some on the environment of others in the cause of leisure use, the welfare of those operating a system for the benefit of others, the assumption of corresponding thought from a sampling of fellow-citizens and so on.

How extensive was the support for the indirect restriction of leisure in this way is obviously difficult to judge, dependent on such factors as the extent and unfractured nature of the influence of the churches in this regard and the proportion of folk for whom tramcar travel was a realistic option in their personal or economic circumstances. But it also brings us back to the consideration that any account of the leisure activities during our period in Derby, as in any other town, inevitably involves most if not all of the other aspects of life we have encountered in our survey, including employment, education, parks, transport and religious belief — a seamless web indeed!

Notes

1. Maxwell Craven, op.cit.
2. Ibid.
3. Ibid.
4. *Derby Evening Telegraph Centenary*, op.cit.
5. Ibid.
6. Ibid.
7. Ibid.
8. Ibid.
9. D.Read, op.cit.
10. W.A.Richardson, *Citizen's Derby*, 1949.
11. D.Read, op.cit.
12. *Derby Mercury*, 20 July 1881.
13. Maxwell Craven, op.cit.
14. Davison, op.cit.
15. Maxwell Craven, op.cit.
16. Davison, op.cit.
17. Maxwell Craven, op.cit.
18. Roy Christian, *Railway Derby*
19. Ibid.
20. D.Read, op.cit.
21. Pigot, *Directory of Derbyshire* 1835
22. Maxwell Craven, op.cit.
23. Davison, op.cit.
24. Ibid.
25. Geoffrey Best, *Mid Victorian Britain 1851-75*, 1971
26. Maxwell Craven, op.cit.
27. D.Read, op.cit.
28. Maxwell Craven, op.cit.
29. Ibid.
30. Ibid.
31. Ibid.
32. D.Read, op.cit.
33. Davison, op.cit.
34. Maxwell Craven, op.cit.
35. Ibid.
36. Ibid.
37. Jeffery Tillett in Derby Civic Society 'Newsletter' Summer 1990.
38. Ibid.
39. Ibid.
40. I am grateful to Mr.Tillett for drawing my attention to this episode.
41. Maxwell Craven op.cit.
42. D.Read op.cit.

Celebration

THE seventy-five-year sequence from Regency to Golden Jubilee was clearly an extraordinarily active and decisive one. How much so in the consciousness of an ordinary working man or woman in this full lifetime's span is obviously difficult to estimate in comparison with the experience of someone living through the previous century, which is probably a more appropriate comparison to make than with someone born in 1912 and living till 1987, when so much 'noise' and bustle has come in from the outside world into the consciousness of the individual through twentieth century means of communication such as radio and television.

These must have fundamentally altered human perception from that based on living experience, however humdrum for most people, plus the printed word alone. But there were certainly some incredible changes to Derby in the course of the nineteeenth century: an almost total transformation of the physical fabric of the town, the foundations laid for what was to happen during the present century for good or ill. In fact, the 'Derby Mercury' at one point when yet another street upheaval was proposed for the town's core complement pleaded for a halt to the process of seemingly perpetual change which was being inflicted on its good citizens!

But there was also much to celebrate in an age when this particular feeling was entered into communally to a much greater extent than it has been since, in this the first period of history when the temptation to celebrate or mourn the achievements and calamities by proxy and courtesy of the media, especially on the other side of the globe, is very strong.

It would seem fitting to end a review of seventy-five years given over largely to expansion and construction by revisiting this, our Victorian town, for three occasions of popular rejoicing, two local and one national, to sample its nature and the form the expression took; and by so doing possibly add something more to the impressions we may have built up through the contemporary reporting of and reactions to what was happening in this sector of time.

But first, a brief glimpse of the earliest occasion for communal celebration during our chosen period to match the one that ended it in a national rather than local mood. Davison, writing long afterwards in 1906, describes the reaction of Derby when news came through on Thursday 15 June 1814 that Napoleon Bonaparte, with whom the country had been at war since the previous century, had been banished on to the isle of Elba:

. . .the general rejoicings began with the usual bell-ringing, the streets being profusely decorated with garlands and arches of flowers, and the churches and principle buildings gaily decked with flags and banners.

Joseph Strutt's house at the bottom of St Peter's Street attracted particular attention,

the rooms being lighted with candles and lustres, the windows filled with orange trees and other greenhosue plants, the word 'Peace' in large letters being emblazoned across the front of the house.[1]

The mention of *greenhouse plants* provides a link with the occasion for the first real outburst of universal rejoicing during the Victorian period proper which took place in 1840 for the opening of the Arboretum. Three days were given over to the celebrations, interestingly with each having a different focus. The first day, Wednesday 16 September, was given over to those of town and county with some political influence through vote or property; the second, Thursday 17th to the workpeople; the third, Saturday 19th, had the children as the focus of a specifically family day.

The first was advertised in the following terms in the 'Derby Mercury':

These beautiful gardens will be opened to the public. The following are the arrangements agreed by the Committee to celebrate the occasion:

At twelve o'clock the shops will be closed and business suspended for the day. At the same time the Town Council will assemble in the Guildhall where J.Strutt Esq., the munificent donor of the Arboretum, will deliver to the Mayor, Aldermen and Councillor the DEED OF GIFT conveying these delightful grounds to the use of the public for ever!

At the close of the proceedings the Mayor, Aldermen and Councillors will form in a procession accompanied by the stewards, their fellow townmen and gentlemen from the country who may honour them by their attendance, and proceed to the Arboretum. When the procession is admitted to the grounds, which will be announced by a flourish of trumpets, the whole assembled multitude will give three times three enthusiastic cheers for the benevolent donor! After which the National Anthem will be sung in chorus accompanied by the bands and trumpets. Dancing will then commence in the places prepared for the purpose at two o'clock. There will be an ascent of the magnificent Montgolfie Balloon. Tea making will take place in the grand Arboretum pavillion! At four o'clock the ascent of the great Arboretum balloon will

*take place announced by the discharge of cannon!!
Dancing, promenades and other recreation will
continue until dusk when the bands accompanied by
the Corporation and visitors will leave the gardens
and proceed to the Market Place where the National
Anthem will again be sung before the Company
separate.*

Joseph Strutt, in handing over the beautifully
illuminated Deed of Gift at the Guildhall, delivered
a speech for the occasion in which he described his
action in presenting the Arboretum to the town as
a fitting response to the very significant changes that
had recently taken place in Derby and also to the
personal good fortune life had bestowed on him. He
referred to the recent *increase in the trade and
population of Derby,* to the new buildings being
constructed, to *the completion of three new railways*
with their focus upon the town which would mean
its becoming a most important communications
centre, to the success of the New Mechanics' Institute.

What his fellow citizens needed now was *the
opportunity of enjoying with their families exercise
and recreation in the fresh air in public walks and
grounds.* He mentioned that Parliament had itself
pointed out this need and encouraged an appropriate
response to it. He went on to praise Mr Loudon's
work and to say that he wished to ensure the future
of his gardener, Mr Charles Brown, and his family
by being allowed to live in one of the Arboretum
cottages at his customary rent of 2s per week.

In conclusion, he made the very important point
that he believed it was only by making available such
beautiful places as the Arboretum to the public that
they would learn to respect and conserve them. It
depended on such as himself to do so: *as the sun has
shone brightly on me through life, it would be
ungrateful in me not to employ a portion of the fortune
which I possess for that purpose.*[2]

As the procession went down the Cornmarket, brass
bands to the fore, a glance to the left at the junction
with Victoria Street would reveal a portrait placed
on the front of the brand new Royal Hotel with the
inscription beside it, *look here, we shall never see his
like again.* It was apparently a reasonably fine day,
although not a perfect one for it proved too windy
to achieve a successful balloon launch that afternoon.
Inside the Arboretum there was the huge refreshments
marquee graced with portraits of Queen Victoria,
Prince Albert and Joseph Strutt; at the gates, guests
could exit holding a copy of the Deed of Gift
accompanied by the donor's speech, all hot from a
special printing press placed just inside. The official
day ended with the planned retreat procession behind
bands at seven in the evening. They paused outside
Thorntree House for a rendering of 'The Old English
Gentleman' before going on to the Market Place for
'God Save the Queen' and a resounding final cheer.[3]

In retrospect, John Loudon's descriptive catalogue
summarised the proceedings thus:
*On Wednesday the numbers attended (About 1,500)
of the class which will take both pride and pleasure
in supporting these splendid gardens in their present
perfect state . . .*

Hierarchy was far from dead!

Thursday the 17th started grey and wet but the sound
of the church bells was nevertheless universal above

an expectant buzz. In mid-morning, Joseph Strutt was
presented at Thorntree House with a souvenir writing
case by the printers and bookbinders of the town. It
was lined in rich maroon velvet on the inside and
decorated with the Strutt arms on the outside and also
the inscription:
*The Poor Man's Friend, In Opening Those
Beautiful Grounds On The Day Of Rest From
Laborious Employment To Facilitate The Wholesome
And Rational Enjoyment Of The Working Classes
(1840).*[4]

At 12.30pm, the second-day procession of trade and
working people moved off in drizzle from their Friar
Gate assembly point, participants sporting colourful
scarves, rosettes, ribands or sashes and waving flags.
There were again bands at the front and two display
carts pulled by horses. The sun soon broke through
round the corner in Bridge Street, the forty-five-minute
procession thereafter reaching the Arboretum gates via
Lodge Lane, King Street, Queen Street, Irongate,
around the Market Place, Corn Market, St Peter's
Street, Osmaston Street and Grove Street.[5] All were
crowded with onlookers.

The list of participating groups was as follows: *The
United Ancient Order of Druids, The Rechabites, The
Oddfellows, The China Manufactory, The Printers
and Bookbinders, The Brushmakers, The Riband
Weavers, The Pheasant Friendly Scoiety, The Chequer
Friendly Society, The St Mary's Catholic Benefit
Society, The United Sisters' Society, The Mechanics'
Institution.*[6]

This is a fascinating selection of town industry,
clubs and self-help groups, although hardly
representative of Derby's multifarious trades and
industries. Some of the participating groups had
apparently expended up to 17s per member on the
preparations for this event which in some cases could
have meant the equivalent of a week's wage!

Once again within the Park things did not entirely
go according to plan. Not only did the obligatory
balloon flight fail once more, first catching fire and
then getting tangled in a tree in the continuing windy
conditions, but there was also miscalculation in the
refreshments department, something we shall see
happening again twenty-five years or so later.
Loudon's descriptvie catalogue put it all most
diplomatically:
*The most ample provision was made of the best
quality, for regaling upwards of 6,000 persons; but
owing to the immense numbers in the gardens, it was
found impossible to supply their wants fast enough.
The spacious tent erected for the occasion accommodated 600 persons at a time. This, on the Wednesday,
had been found sufficient for the convenience and
enjoyment of the whole party. But on this day, when
there were between five and six times as many persons
to be entertained, it was impossible to attend to the
wants of the multitudes as the Stewards wished; and
in consequence, some disappointment ensued. It
should not be forgotten, however, that this was the
first time that it was ever attempted, in Derby, to
entertain 600 persons in one place; but it appears nearly
3,000 persons more were present than were anticipated.*

The town was indeed growing up with a vengeance!
However, there was dancing on the adjacent field, soon
to be incorporated in the Arboretum fold itself, as

we have seen. Regardless of any disappointments, and despite the crowds of working folk and even a group of lively teenagers careering about the place, not one tree or shrub was recorded as suffering the least damage. This prompted the great John Loudon to pronounce: *Such a population is worthy of the noble gift that has been made to them.* [7]A moment in its history for Derby to savour, surely!

Again there was evening activity, this time a successful launch of the giant balloon at last from in front of the Royal Hotel down in the centre and also fireworks at the foot of those newly gleaming giant ionic columns. Apparently, the Derbyshire General Infirmary's normal Wednesday and Thursday's input of out-patients was down to one in six![8]

Saturday the 19th dawned resplendently, brilliant sun and peerless blue sky as the children of the town lined up behind Mr Joddrell's band and streamed in through the Park gates in Pied Piper style to 'God Save the Queen' at 2 o'clock. There were traditional games such as leap-frog, thread-the-long-needle and drop-the-glove, dancing to Mr Glover's band and the luscious possiblities of Mr Hunt's cake-stall. Yet another lustily rendered 'God Save the Queen' at 7pm ended the day for yet another estimated 6,000 folk, a Saturday judged by many *the pleasantest day of their lives,* unblemished by a single oath and graced by an exit *orderly and quietly as if we were retiring from a place of worship.*[9]

Nearly twenty-five years later, in mid-February 1864, a curious visitor to Derby would have experienced:

A couple of hours of sunshine in the afternoon of a changeable and stormy day, and a procession consisting of volunteers, Policeman, Town Councillors, Aldermen, The Mayor, supported by two clergymen, followed by the architect bearing the plans of the Market, the Clerk of the Works carrying a polished mallet, and a Chamberlain with the presentation silver trowel on a crimson silk cushion, guarded by sundry members of the police force disguised in long cloaks and three-cornered hats, armed with ancient halberds, with a hundred workmen in their everyday dress, a few more policemen and another company of volunteers, with a good humoured crowd of lookers-on.[10]

The Market Hall was conceived, but it was to be over two long years before the official grand opening could take place on Tuesday, 29 May 1866. In the morning there was the cermonial procession: *The Mayor and Corporation, nobility and gentry, 1st Battalion of the Derbyshire Rifle Volunteers.* The chief guest was the Duke of Devonshire.[11] Members of the nobility present were the Duke of Rutland and Newcastle, Lords Scarsdale, Bagot, Belper with three Cavendishes and two Manners, the Marquis of Hartington (Secretary of State for War) and members of prominent families including those providing names for many of the streets of the town: Chandos-Poles, Cokes, Curzons, Basses, Strutts, Vernons, Wilmots.[12] Special trains were put on from places near and far, including Birmingham, from where places on *covered carriages* could be reserved for 2s 6d return, [13]Tamworth, Burton, Leicester, Loughborough and Kegworth.

In the programme for the afternoon's musical celebration appeared the following plea: *It is the earnest request of the committee that the company attending the oratorio will not indicate their approbation by any audible expression of applause,* Victorian sensibilities to the fore, and seats ranged in price from 2s 6d to one guinea. [14]According to the report in the 'Derby Mercury' of 6 June, the afternoon,

Irongate decorated for the visit of the Prince and Princess of Wales in December 1872.

More street decorations, this time in the Cornmarket, for a visit by the royal couple. This time the Prince and Princess of Wales attended the Royal Agricultural Show at Derby in July 1881.

though obviously a splendid success overall, was not all roses for everyone:

At the conclusion of the oratorio (600 performers including 70 violins, conductor Mr Alfred Mellon) the band and chorus, who had so ably acquitted themselves in the orchestra, were to have been entertained at dinner in the Corn Exchange which was too crowded.

The indefatigable committee and the waiters did their very best to obviate as far as possible any inconvenience to the ladies and gentlemen from Birmingham, Nottingham, and Leicester, who had so kindly come to assist in the efficient rendering of the great work of the immortal Handel, but notwithstanding the attentions paid, many were not accommodated.

One of the choir, writing for a district paper, says: '*The arrangements for supplying the performers with refreshment though very liberal on paper, were simply execrable. Both food and room were utterly insufficient, so that in many cases it was a free and easy scramble to get anything to eat or drink without any attempt at order. Several of the singers preferred to get refreshments at other places in the town.*

In the evening, there was a Mayor's banquet for seventy 'friends' at the Royal Hotel, the company including the Mayors of Nottingham, Leicester, Lincoln and Lichfield. In his speech to the company, Alderman Roe declared: *They called it a Market Hall, but it had turned out a music hall, and he had been informed that it was quite equal to Birmingham Town Hall. The Mayor of Nottingham responded that it quite surpassed all ideas which he had formed respecting it and was much pleased with the building, which was noble in its proportions and beautiful in its colouring.*

On Friday evening 1 June there was another concert, this time by 1,000 Sunday School scholars of the town

accompanied by an organ. Again there were faulty arrangements to report: more tickets were sold than the new hall could accommodate! However, *with one or two exceptions the female singers were attired in white, and when the choir rose to sing the opening hymn a burst of applause testified the admiration of the audience at the pleasing sight.*

At last came Jubilee Year 1887. How to celebrate such an event, a half-century as a symbol of a nation's endeavours as 'workshop of the world', of which Derby represented a not insignificant corner? On 9 February, the 'Derby Mercury' announced a five-guinea prize competition for an idea on the subject and at a meeting at the Guildhall on 25 February, the Mayor appointed a committee to organise the town's response. It must be said that judging by the objective evidence regarding what actually happened imagination was not one of the qualities the committee possessed in abundance!

However, the greater day arrived, Tuesday, 21 June and on the Wednesday of the following week the 'Mercury' duly carried its report, the introduction to which is worth quoting at length for its mode of reflection upon the Derby story and also upon occasional Derby weather:

Never in the history of Derby has there been a day more worthy to be remembered than the 21 June 1887. There have been days when great functionaries have been amongst us, and the town has put itself in holiday attire, and done due honour to its visitors; there have been occasions when great public enterprises have been inaugurated or brought to a head or when private philanthropy has conferred great benefits upon the town, which the citizens have recognised in a public manner; yet we believe that none of those days will live so long in the memories of those who were privileged to see them as the days when Derby celebrated the reign of good Queen Victoria, the 'monarch without reproach'. We say days, because, though Tuesday witnessed the official celebration and thanksgiving, there were rejoicings on Wednesday which would move the hearts and influence the minds of over 20,000 little ones, the majority of whom will, we hope, in the course of years, succeed to their fathers and mothers in the responsibilities of citizenship of the good old borough . . .

All things combined to make the Tuesday's proceedings a great and memorable success. The public officials had done their part, private individuals had done theirs, and the weather, the one thing about which everybody was a bit anxious, could not have been better. Day by day the people have been wondering whether the lovely weather which we have been enjoying since Whitsun week would break before the Jubilee arrived, but on Tuesday morning all doubts were set at rest. A warm sun was tempered by a fresh breeze from the north-east, and only a few fleecy clouds flitted across the sky during the day to break the monotony of the vast expanse of blue. It was in fact what has come . . .to be regarded as 'Queen's weather'. The streets in the centre of the town were ablaze with colours, and whilst the bright beams of the sun lent brilliancy to the decorations, the gentle breeze served to show them off to the best advantage.

Early in the morning the bells of the churches were clanging out their message of joy, and also in many cases an invitation to the celebration of the Eucharist, the true thanksgiving service of the Church. Following the example set by their pious but 'unreformed' predecessors on the occasion of the Jubilee of George III, on 25 October 1809, the Mayor and Corporation marked the day by attending in state a special service in All Saints' Church. It would also have been according to the precendent then set had a guard of honour from the barracks accompanied them, but unfortunately the martinets of the War Office placed their veto upon the proposal. The civic procession was, however, representative of all that is best in the citizenship of Derby, and of all those various classes and public bodies which go to make up its happiness and prosperity. The procession was timed to leave the Town Hall at half-past ten, and soon after ten o'clock those invited by the Mayor to take part in it began to arrive, being marshalled into their place by the Chief Constable and other officials of the police force.[15]

It included representatives of the police, armed forces, *Friendly and Other Societies*, Midland Railway and various official bodies such as the School Board and Board of Guardians (Poor Law).

In the evening there was an official banquet *on a scale of unusual splendour*. A selection from the menu reads:

SOUPS
Turtle Clear

FISH
Whitebait
Salmon, Fennel Sauce
Turbot, Lobster Sauce

ENTREES
Sweetbreads
Larded Veal Cutlets and Mushrooms
Quails

Queen Victoria, whose Golden Jubilee was celebrated by Derbeians on 21 June 1887.

REMOVES
Haunches of Venison
Quarters of Lamb
Asparagus
Ox Tongues
Spring Peas and Potatoes

RELIEVES
Leverets
Ducklings
Spring Chickens

SWEETS
Cabinet and Bakewell Puddings
Fruit Tarts, Jellies, Creams
Ice Puddings
Cheese Straws   Loving Cup

DESSERT
Pines, Grapes
Apples, Cerries
Strawberries, Oranges
Kent Cobs, Dried Fruits

WINES

Milk Punch	*Maderia*
Hock	*Sherry*
Claret	*Champagne*
Sherry	*Claret*
Loving Cup	*Port*

COFFEE[16]

Those were the days! There were, of course, loyal toasts to Royal Family and Armed Forces. Establish-

Jubilee celebrations at the Royal Corner. Troops come to attention as the bunting flies.

Derby's Guildhall, decorated to mark 50 years of Queen Victoria's reign.

ment expects! On the following Sunday, the Mayor, Sam Whitaker, led the Corporation in solemn procession once again, this time to Victoria Street Congregational where he was a member for an act of worship.

For ordinary citizens there were traditional sports on Cockpit Hill and of course the decorations:

The decoration of the town on the whole did Derby credit. There were a few gaps here and there, but the town generally bore a very gay and festive appearance, and compared, so far as we have heard, very favourably with many other towns.[17]

Their describing took well over one full column of one of the voluminous pages of the 'Mercury' of those days. Here are two contrasting episodes referring to three different parts of the town:

Nottingham Road was very showily adorned with garlands, streamers and festoons. One of the best arranged erections in that part of the town was the large archway of shrubs at Mr G. Wheldon's malthouse, the premises were also ornamentally decked with banners and streamers. Mr Booth's decorations were tastefully got up, a line of small flags and shrubs extending from his shop across the street. The Bride Inn, Mansfield Road, appeared to great advantage. A large number of garlands were erected across City-road, and Mansfield Road had also its floral and other emblems . . .The other streets in the same direction likewise contributed their quota towards making the celebration a brilliant success. In the Wardwick the first decorations to be noticed was the Mechanics' Hall, which had a display of drapery and flags, and for illumination an imposing cross, circled, and the initials V.R. on either side. The Free Library does not easily lend itself to decoration. It was festooned with coloured strings from masts to the tower; there was a large illuminated inscription, 'Victoria's Jubilee, 1887' over the principal entrance, and lines of coloured lamps were displayed along the

rows of windows. A profusion of flags helped to make the Library frontage very pretty indeed . . .

. . .It was pleasing to see how warmly the work of decoration was taken up by the inhabitants of the poorer quarters of the town. In many of the small streets of Castle Ward this was especially noticeable, and Eagle Street and Castle Place may be taken as examples of the enthusiastic spirit in which the poor paid honour to the 'poor men's Queen'. In the Morledge the decorations were very elaborate, and on Tuesday afternoon there were 'Old English sports' on Cockpit-Hill for prizes subscribed by the inhabitants of the neighbourhood. Similar sports were also held on the piece of land by Christ Church. In King's Mead Ward, also, the poor, so far as they could, gave a festive appearance to their unlovely streets.[18]

There must have been assurance in the tried and tested forms adopted. And the 'Mercury's' Editorial for that memorable edition gave, perhaps, as substantial a basis for thought as the previous week's official chef had for his no-doubt robust clientele:

It is difficult to suppose that the next fifty years can have any thing like so much progress in store for England. There is no fear of stagnation; but there can be no great expectation of a new age of discovery in which the present age will be revolutionised as completely and as quietly as the old order of fifty years ago was replaced by that we know today. But it will not do for England to spend the next half century in ease and contentment . . .The condition of England question is still with us. The poor are still poorer, and less well fed, well-housed, well-clothed, and well-taught than they should be.

Surely we can say 'Amen' to that over a hundred years later! On this showing, Derby thinking was anything but complacent, even more appropriately had the editor possessed a crystal ball of more than common clarity. How innocent a pastime is looking into the future, how well-worn the art of hindsight!

Notes

1. Davison op.cit.
2. John Loudon, *The Derby Arboretum Containing a Catalogue of the Trees and Shrubs,* 1840
3. Ibid.
4. Ibid.
5. Ibid.
6. Ibid.
7. Ibid.
8. Ibid.
9. Ibid.
10. *Derbyshire Advertiser, 19 February 1864.*
11. *Derby Evening Telegraph,* article 26 March 1986.
12. Ibid, article 1 August 1984.
13. Ibid, 26 March 1986.

Index

advertisements 21, 80, 89, 92-3, 96
aeronauts 88
Agard Street 26, 67, 72, 75, 96
Albert Street 13, 24, 51, 58, 60, 71, 75
alderman 48, 61-2, 72, 78, 81, 105, 107-8
All Saints' 9, 11-12, 14-16, 23-4, 32, 37-8, 46, 54, 63, 66-7, 74, 82, 96, 109
Allenton 20
Allestree 44, 89
Allport, James 40
Alton Towers 38, 54, 86
Anglican 14, 53, 56-7
Arboretum 10, 19, 28-9, 34, 83, 84-90, 94, 101, 103, 105
Ashbourne Road 18, 29, 38, 72, 77-9, 104
Assembly Rooms 13-15, 62, 95, 101, 103
Assize courts 15, 42, 64-6
Atheneum 10, 49-51, 77, 101
athletics 101

Babington House 18
Bakewell, Robert 16
bands 89-90, 103
banquet 109
Bass, Michael Thomas 10, 51-2, 60, 62, 80, 88
Becket Street 44, 52
Birmingham 21, 25, 28-9, 42, 46, 71, 86, 88, 107-08
Birmingham and Derby Junction Railway 10, 25, 96
Bishop Lonsdale College 10, 77
Board of Guardians 44, 52, 63-4, 109
Board of Health-Report/ Public Health 10, 18-19, 33-5, 72-4, 80, 84
Bold Lane Theatre 16, 43, 71, 101
Borough 10, 16, 18-19, 26, 41, 48-9, 61-2, 66-8, 72, 74-5, 81, 97
bowling 101
Brandreth, Jeremiah 66
Bridge Gate 22, 24, 38, 54, 56, 75, 96
Bridge Street 10, 34, 38, 43, 56-7, 80, 92, 106
bridges 9-10, 12-14, 26-8, 38, 49, 51, 54, 58, 74-5
Bridgett, Thomas 34, 37, 43-4, 63, 81-3
Brittania Foundry 9, 38, 56
Brook-Street Chapel 14, 42
Brook Street (Upper) 14, 37-8, 72, 75, 80
Brookside 49, 52, 58, 96

Burton Road 12, 20, 37, 79

carriage 28-9, 37, 40, 53, 107
carriers 20, 22
Castlefields 10, 16, 18, 56
celebration 12, 28, 51, 58, 87, 105-9
cemetery 10-11, 20, 77-8
census 18, 36, 80
Chaddesden 11-12, 20, 67, 99
Chapel 13-15, 42, 52, 57-8, 77-8, 90, 98
Chellaston 13, 38
Chester Green 38, 56, 60, 62, 74, 98
child labour 34-7, 42, 76, 79
Children's Hospital 10, 76
chimney sweeps 8, 82
churches 10, 14, 25, 52-8, 60, 74, 98, 101, 103-04, 106, 109-10
circus 101
City Road 13, 26, 38, 41, 110
clothes 83
coaches 10, 12-13, 20-23, 25, 28-9, 66-78, 90, 95, 103
Cockpit Hill 20, 35, 110
Convent of St Vincent 10, 56, 77
Cook, Thomas 12, 28, 93-4
Cooperative Society 10, 24, 101
Corn Exchange 10, 50, 71, 101, 108
Corn market 13, 21-2, 25, 28, 41, 49-50, 58-9, 62, 75, 78, 94, 96, 106
corporation 61-2, 67, 74, 79, 87-9, 90, 106, 109-10
County Gaol 10, 19, 66-7
County Hall 64
County Lunatic Asylum 10, 75-6, 88, 95
courts 66, 73, 80
cricket 10, 98-101
crime 64, 66-7
Crisis newspaper 41-2
Cross Lane 11, 18, 58
Crown Derby China Factory 13, 37, 56, 63, 106

Darley Grove 18, 26-7
death rate 72
Derby and Chesterfield Reporter 9, 40-1, 43, 62-4, 67, 81, 85, 92-3, 96, 102
Derby Canal 14, 16, 20-21, 32-3, 53, 96
Derby Choral Society 8, 103
Derby (College) School of Art 10, 52, 77
Derby County Football Club 10, 98-9
Derby (Daily) Evening Telegraph 10, 12, 92-3

Derby Daily Express 10, 93
Derby Mercury 10, 12, 20-1, 24-30, 41, 43-4, 48-9, 52-4, 62-4, 66-8, 71, 75, 77-8, 87, 89-90, 92-6, 98-101, 103-05, 107, 110
Derby Photographic Society 10, 92
Derby racecourse 10, 95, 98
Derby School 77, 101
Derby School Board 10, 52, 77, 109
Derby Tramway Company 29-30, 78, 104
Derbyshire Advertiser 10, 48, 92
Derbyshire County Cricket Club 10, 98
Derbyshire General Infirmary 16, 18, 72, 75, 98, 101, 107
Derwent 13-14, 16, 26, 28, 32, 34, 38, 43, 49, 58, 60-62, 74, 77, 80, 92
Devonshire, Duke of 21, 51, 62, 70, 88, 95, 107
Disraeli, Benjamin 19, 79
Duesbury, Henry 10, 46-7, 76-7, 88, 95
Duffield 22, 26, 98-9
Duffield Road 12, 19-20, 49, 76, 79-80, 82

excursions 12, 21, 28, 67, 88, 93, 95
executions 9-10, 66-7
Exeter House 10, 15, 51, 58, 79

Factory Act 10, 34-5
Factory Act Committee 34-5, 42-3, 53, 76, 79
Factory Act Inspector 35, 76
family 12, 16, 30, 33, 37, 41, 54, 57, 61, 63-4, 77, 80-82, 84, 87, 94
Farington, Joseph 11-13, 19
Fiennes, Celia 13, 38
fire/fire brigade 9, 19, 46, 75, 84
flooding 10, 49, 74-5
foundry 10, 38-9, 62
Fox, Douglas 34-6, 42, 61, 69, 73, 76, 79, 101
Free Library and Museum 10, 51-2, 62, 77, 110
Friar Gate 14-16, 18, 26-8, 39, 61-3, 66-8, 71, 76-9, 82, 88, 90, 94, 96, 101, 106
Friendly Societies 42, 63, 106, 109
Friends' Meeting House 14
Frost, Mr, millowner 41

gaol/prison 9-10, 68
gas lighting 9-10, 36, 39, 71-2, 75

gentry 15, 21, 92-3, 95, 102
Georgian 14-15, 37, 52, 54, 57, 77, 80, 84
Gladstone, William Ewart 12, 19, 29, 76, 101
Gothic style 11-12, 38, 52, 56-8, 60, 78
Grand Theatre 10, 12, 52, 75, 101-02
Great Northern Railway 10, 19-20, 26, 28-9, 37-8, 58, 60
Green Lane 19, 72, 75-7
Guildhall 10-11, 19, 46-7, 49-52, 54, 56, 60, 66, 68, 71, 75-6, 78, 84, 88, 95, 103, 105-06, 110

Habershon, Matthew 10, 46-7, 52, 56, 78
hairdresser 22, 24, 93
Handel, George Frederick 48-9, 103, 108
Handyside, Andrew 10, 26, 28, 38-9, 62
Harrison, J., engineering 24, 38
Hartington Street 81, 94
Haslam's Foundry 10, 26, 38-9, 62
Holy Trinity Church 10, 56
horse traffic 10, 14, 22, 24, 29, 37, 53, 60, 78, 103, 106
houses 14, 18, 27, 38, 51, 64, 79-84, 86
Hutton, William 16, 63, 74

industries, various 37-8, 41, 46, 62, 106
iron 14, 16, 34, 36, 38-9, 46, 48-9, 51, 56-7, 60, 95
Irongate 12-13, 22, 24, 58, 60, 73, 77, 79, 96, 106

Jacobean House 15, 18
Jubilee 10, 12, 24, 29, 32, 37, 60, 74, 88, 105, 108-10

Kedleston Road 18, 29, 44, 56, 58, 79, 81, 93
Keene, Richard 29, 92
King Street 12, 14, 21, 37, 39, 51, 57, 77, 79, 95-6, 106
King's Head Hotel 21-2, 25, 41, 70, 96
Kirtly, Matthew 40

Leeds 25, 37, 40, 46, 57, 88
Leicester 12, 18, 20, 26, 28, 30, 84, 107-8
leisure 92-104
lighting 18, 72
Liszt, Franz 10, 103
Litchurch 10, 18-20, 26, 39, 57, 62-3, 72, 74-5, 84, 87

Little Chester 10, 14, 19, 26-7, 60, 95
Littleover 11, 16, 20, 49, 58
Liverpool 12, 28-9, 38, 40, 46, 56
Lock-Out 10, 40-3, 58, 62, 64, 96
lodge 85-7
lodging houses 72, 79
Lombes 16, 32-3
London 12-14, 20, 25-6, 29, 41-3, 46, 49, 52-3, 63, 67, 71-2, 81, 84-5, 88, 92-4, 98, 103
Loudon, John 19, 85-9, 106-07

Macklin Street 11, 58
Manchester 20-21, 38, 40, 46, 72, 80, 88, 90, 103
Markeaton Brook 13, 18, 26, 34, 37, 39, 49, 51, 58, 59, 71-4
Market Hall 10, 47-9, 78, 107-08
Market Place 9, 15, 24, 29, 37, 46-7, 58-60, 62, 67, 71, 73, 93, 96, 106
Mayor 10, 15, 43-4, 48, 51-2, 61-2, 67, 72, 87, 92, 94, 98, 105, 107, 108-10
Mechanics' Institute 9-10, 28, 49, 51, 60, 77, 101-03, 106, 110
Melville, Andrew 52, 102
Mickleover 18, 20, 29, 63, 75
Midland Counties Railway 10, 21, 25-6, 28
Midland Hotel 10, 51, 96
Midland Railway Company 10, 26, 29, 38-9, 92, 94-5, 109
mills 9, 13, 18, 33-6, 40, 42-4, 76, 79, 80, 84
Moore, Ambrose 34-6
Morledge 13, 20, 37-8, 44, 72, 78, 96, 110
Municipal Corporation Act 61, 68

Napoleon (Bonaparte) 8, 12, 21, 86, 105
Nonconformists 14, 53, 57, 87
Normanton/Road 11, 13, 19, 29, 34, 56, 58, 70, 104
North Midland Railway 10, 25-6
Nottingham 12, 16, 18, 21, 25-6, 28, 51, 66-7, 71, 77, 79, 88-90, 98, 100, 103, 108
Nun's Green 18, 34, 56, 61, 70, 78-79

O'Connor, Feargus 10, 43
Oddfellows, Society of 34, 40, 106
Old Silk Mills 9, 13, 16, 24, 32-4, 38, 40-1, 43, 58, 75

Osmaston Road 18, 29, 57, 63-4, 79, 81, 86, 94, 104, 106
Owen, Robert 10, 40-42

Paganini 10, 101-02
Palmerston, Lord 19, 88
Park(s) 84-6, 88-90, 94-5, 103, 106-07
Parliament, Acts, members of 10, 12, 26, 40, 51, 53-4, 61, 63, 68, 70, 72-4, 76, 79, 80, 84, 88, 92, 106
Paxton, Joseph 86, 88
Piazzas, the 15, 51, 60, 62
Peel, Sir Robert 67
perambulators 49
Phoenix Foundry 10, 38-9
photography 92
Pickford, Joseph 15-16, 26, 95
Pike, Mrs Eliza 92-3
Pioneer Newspaper 41-2, 96, 98
Police 25, 46, 48, 64, 67-8, 70, 75, 89, 107
pollution 40, 72-4, 84
Poor Law 10, 36, 44, 52, 62-3, 109
population/inhabitants 14, 18, 41, 51, 54, 63, 72, 77, 82, 84, 86, 106-07
Post Office 12, 29, 49-50, 58, 60
Prince of Wales 10, 68, 94, 108
Prince Regent/George IV 12
printers 40, 106
prison/gaol 9-10, 68
public houses 15, 21-4, 26-7, 42, 54, 63-4, 80, 96, 98
Pugin, A.W. 54, 56

Queen Street 13, 22, 37, 58, 77, 106

races 20, 95
railway 18, 20-22, 24, 26-7, 29, 34, 38-40, 81, 84, 88, 93, 96
Reform Bill 10, 64, 67, 70, 80, 84
Regency 11-12, 14-15, 18, 20, 34, 37-8, 58, 60, 64, 79, 92, 105
riot 67-8, 70, 98
roads 20-21, 81
Roe, Thomas 78, 108
Rykneld Mills 9, 34
Roman Catholics 15, 24, 53-4
rowing 10, 101
Royal Agricultural Show 10, 68, 94, 108
Royal Hotel 10, 28-9, 49-50, 57, 106-08

sabbatarianism 10, 30, 52-3
Sadler Gate 13, 20-2, 24, 58, 72, 75, 96

St Alkmund's 9-10, 13-14, 54-7, 63, 67, 74, 81
St Helen's House 10, 13, 18, 26, 68, 77, 101
St James' Street 10, 58-60
St John's 10, 38, 56-7
St Luke's 10-11, 19, 56, 99
St Mary's 10-11, 15, 24, 38, 54-6, 74, 106
St Mary's Gate 57, 79, 96
St Michael's 10, 13, 58, 63, 95
St Paul's 10, 56
St Peter's Street/church 10, 14, 18, 21-2, 54, 58, 60, 63, 67, 72-3, 76, 79, 84, 94, 96, 101, 105-06
St Werburgh's 10, 13, 54, 63, 66
Salisbury, Lord 10, 12
schools 8, 10, 56, 63, 73, 76-7, 87, 93-4
servants 81-2, 87, 93, 96
Sheffield 21, 26, 28, 39, 51
shops 22, 24, 30, 48, 70, 75
Shot Tower 8, 11, 13, 20, 32-3, 70
Shrewsbury, Earl of 38, 54, 56
Shrovetide Football 10, 96-8
Siddals 82, 88
silk industry 10, 19, 32-6, 38-9, 41, 58, 76, 80-81, 84-5
Spondon 16, 20, 66, 98
Station 10, 16, 18, 22, 25-9, 38-40, 49, 51, 57, 62, 78, 85, 94, 102
steam 21, 32-3, 53, 69
Stevens, H.I. 54, 57-8, 60, 76-8, 92, 99
Strand 10, 58, 60, 74
Strauss, Johann 10, 102
streets 18, 36, 46, 50, 58, 70-1, 73, 79-80, 85, 88, 90, 92, 96, 103-04, 107-08, 110
Strutt, Edward 55, 62, 67, 101
Strutt, Jedediah & Joseph 10, 18-19, 34, 49-51, 60-61, 77, 79, 84-90, 101, 105-07
Strutt, William 13, 16, 76
Sunday Schools 53, 76-7, 94, 98, 108

telegraph 12, 29, 92
terraced housing 11-12, 29, 71, 79-81, 90
Thorburn, T.C. 48
Thorntree House 60, 84, 87, 106
Trades Union 24, 40-44, 64, 94, 96, 98, 101
trams 10, 20, 22, 29-30, 53, 80-81, 103
transportation 42, 64, 66

Unemployment 36, 44, 63
Unitarian 14, 76, 90
Uttoxeter New/Old Road 9-10, 18, 20, 29, 37, 58, 63, 77-80

Vernon Street 9, 19, 30, 67-9
Victoria, Queen 10, 12, 49, 88, 96, 106, 109-10
Victoria Street 10, 14, 22, 29, 49-50, 52, 57-8, 60, 75, 90, 106, 110
Victorian 11-12, 17, 22, 27, 33, 36-9, 44, 46-9, 52-5, 57-8, 62, 64, 67, 72-4, 76-7, 79-80, 82, 84, 87-8, 92, 94, 96, 98, 105

Wardwick 15, 38, 49, 51-2, 58, 60, 72, 81-2, 90, 96, 110
water (works) closet, power 10, 34, 72, 80
Wellington, Duke of 12
Wesleyan Methodist Chapel 10, 14, 57
women, position of 35-7, 63, 67, 82-3, 85
Woodiwiss, Abraham 26-7, 58, 62, 81, 94
workhouse 10, 63-4, 66, 69, 80
Wright, Joseph 15, 37, 70, 77